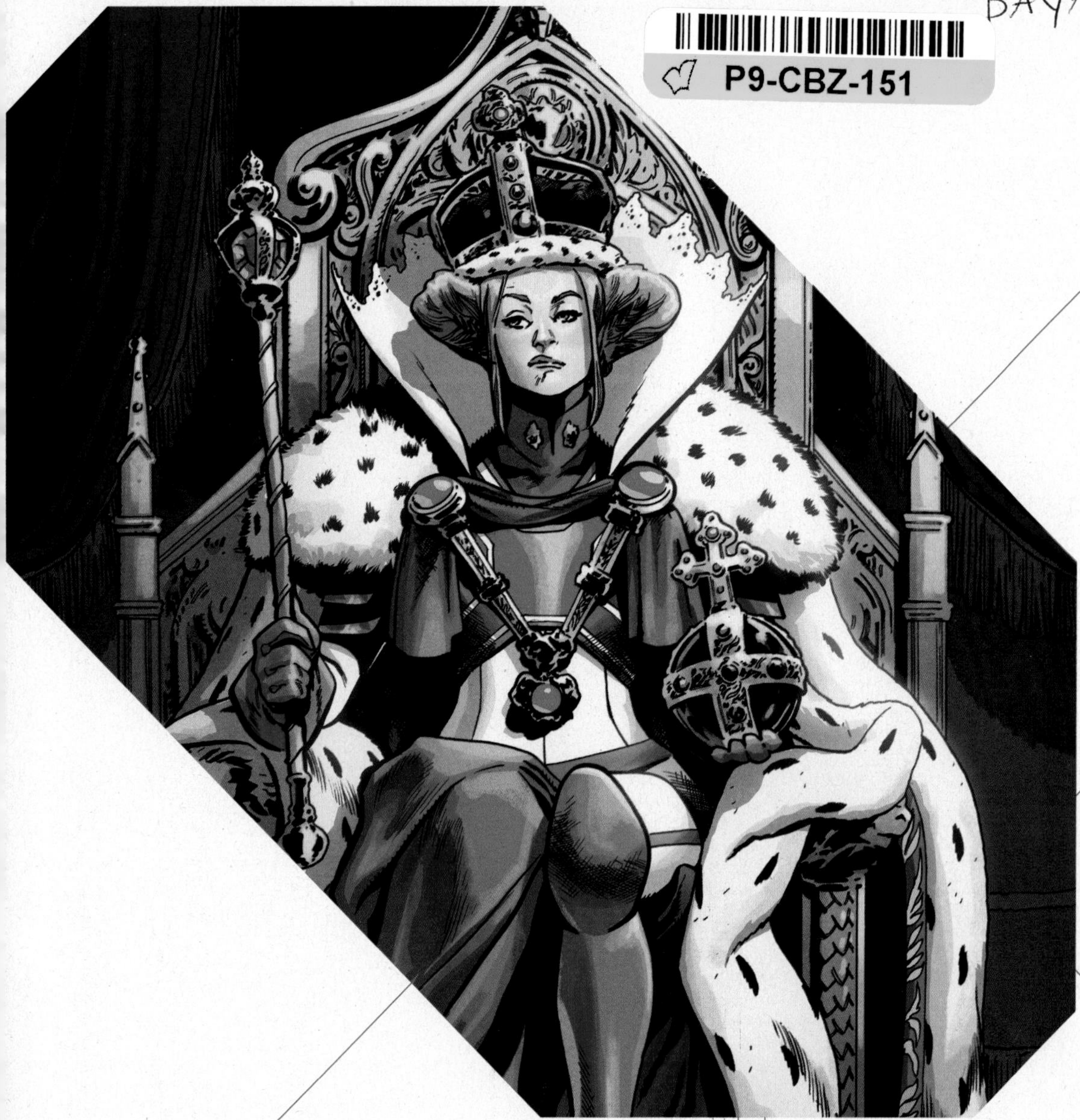

REIGN OF X VOL. 4. Contains material originally published in magazine form as WOLVERINE (2020) #10, EXCALIBUR (2019) #17, X-FACTOR (2020) #6, CABLE (2020) #8 and CHILDREN OF THE ATOM (2021) #1. First printing 2021. ISBN 978-1-302-93166-7. Published by MARVEL WORLDWIDE, INC., a subsidiary of MARVEL ENTERTAINMENT, LLC. OFFICE OF PUBLICATION: 1290 Avenue of the Americas, New York, NY 10104. © 2021 MARVEL No similarity between any of the names, characters, persons, and/or institutions in this magazine with those of any living or dead person or institution is intended, and any such similarity which may exist is purely coincidental. **Printed in the Canada.** KEVIN FEIGE, Chief Creative Officer; DAN BUCKLEY, President, Marvel Entertainment; JOE QUESADA, EVP & Creative Director; DAVID BOGART, Associate Publisher & SVP of Talent Affairs; TOM BREVOORT, VP, Executive Editor; NICK LOWE, Executive Editor, VP of Content, Digital Publishing; DAVID GABRIEL, VP of Print & Digital Publishing; JEFF YOUNGQUIST, VP of Production & Special Projects; ALEX MORALES, Director of Publishing Operations; DAN EDINGTON, Managing Editor; RICKEY PURDIN, Director of Talent Relations; JENNIFER GRÜNWALD, Senior Editor, Special Projects; SUSAN CRESPI, Production Manager; STAN LEE, Chairman Emeritus. For information regarding advertising in Marvel Comics or on Marvel.com, please contact Vit DeBellis, Custom Solutions & Integrated Advertising Manager, at vdebellis@marvel.com. For Marvel subscription inquiries, please call 888-511-5480. **Manufactured between 8/6/2021 and 9/7/2021 by SOLISCO PRINTERS, SCOTT, QC, CANADA.**

10 9 8 7 6 5 4 3 2 1

REIGN OF X

Volume
4

X-Men created by Stan Lee & Jack Kirby

Writers:	Benjamin Percy, Tini Howard, Leah Williams, Gerry Duggan & Vita Ayala
Artists:	Adam Kubert, Marcus To, David Baldeón, Phil Noto & Bernard Chang
Color Artists:	Frank Martin, Erick Arciniega, Israel Silva, Phile Noto & Marcelo Maiolo
Letterers:	VC's Cory Petit, Ariana Maher, Joe Caramagna, Joe Sabino & Travis Lanham
Cover Art:	Adam Kubert & Frank Martin; Mahmud Asrar & Matthew Wilson; Ivan Shavrin; Phil Noto; and R.B. Silva & Jesus Aburtov

Head of X:	Jonathan Hickman
Design:	Tom Muller
Assistant Editors:	Lauren Amaro & Shannon Andrews Ballesteros
Associate Editor:	Annalise Bissa
Editors:	Mark Basso & Jake Thomas
Senior Editor:	Jordan D. White

Collection Cover Art:	Mahmud Asrar & Matthew Wilson

Collection Editor:	Jennifer Grünwald
Assistant Editor:	Daniel Kirchhoffer
Assistant Managing Editor:	Maia Loy
Assistant Managing Editor:	Lisa Montalbano
VP Production & Special Projects:	Jeff Youngquist
SVP Print, Sales & Marketing:	David Gabriel
Editor in Chief:	C.B. Cebulski

[reign_of_x]

[kra_]
[koa_]

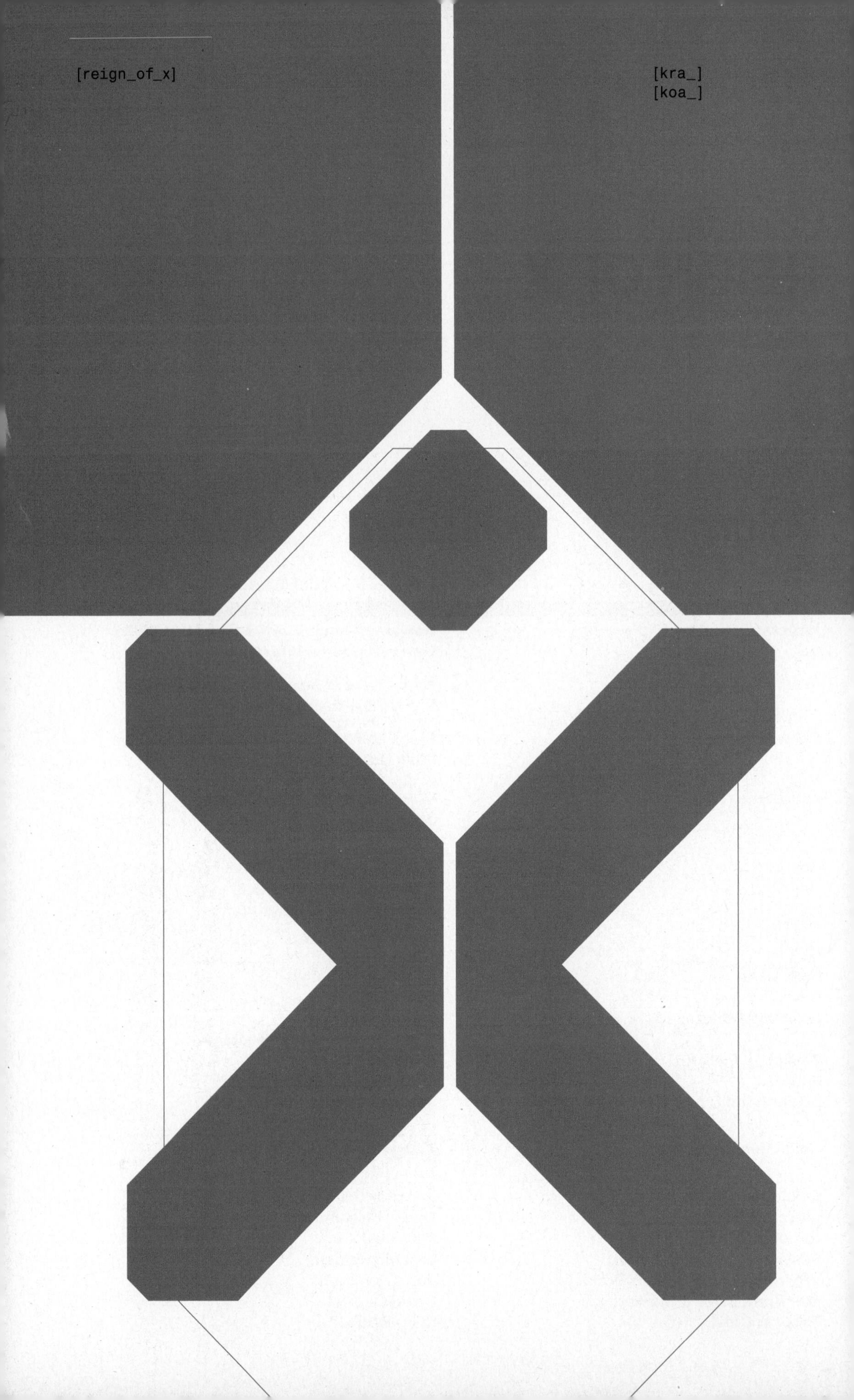

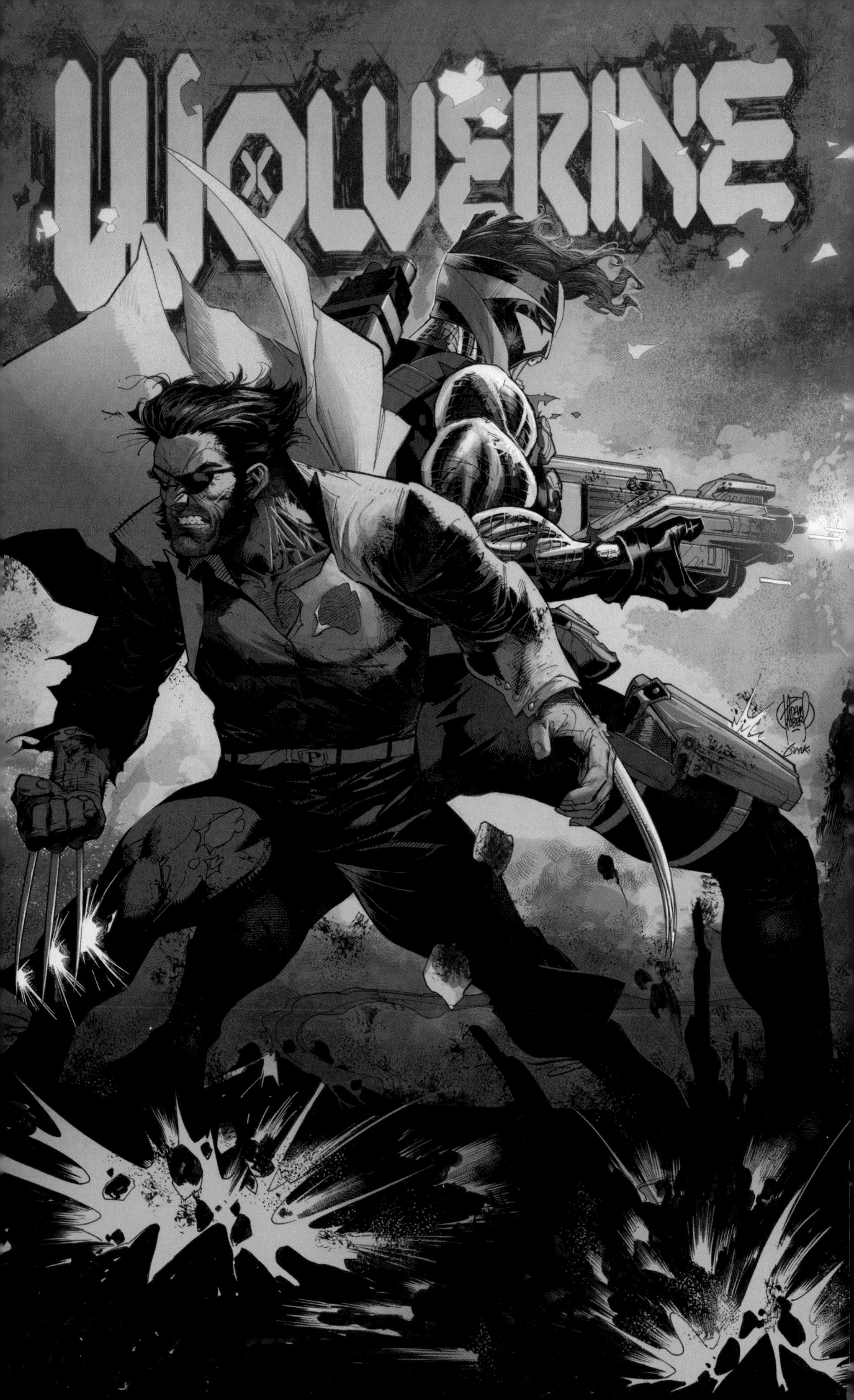
WOLVERINE

[00_best_]
[00_there]

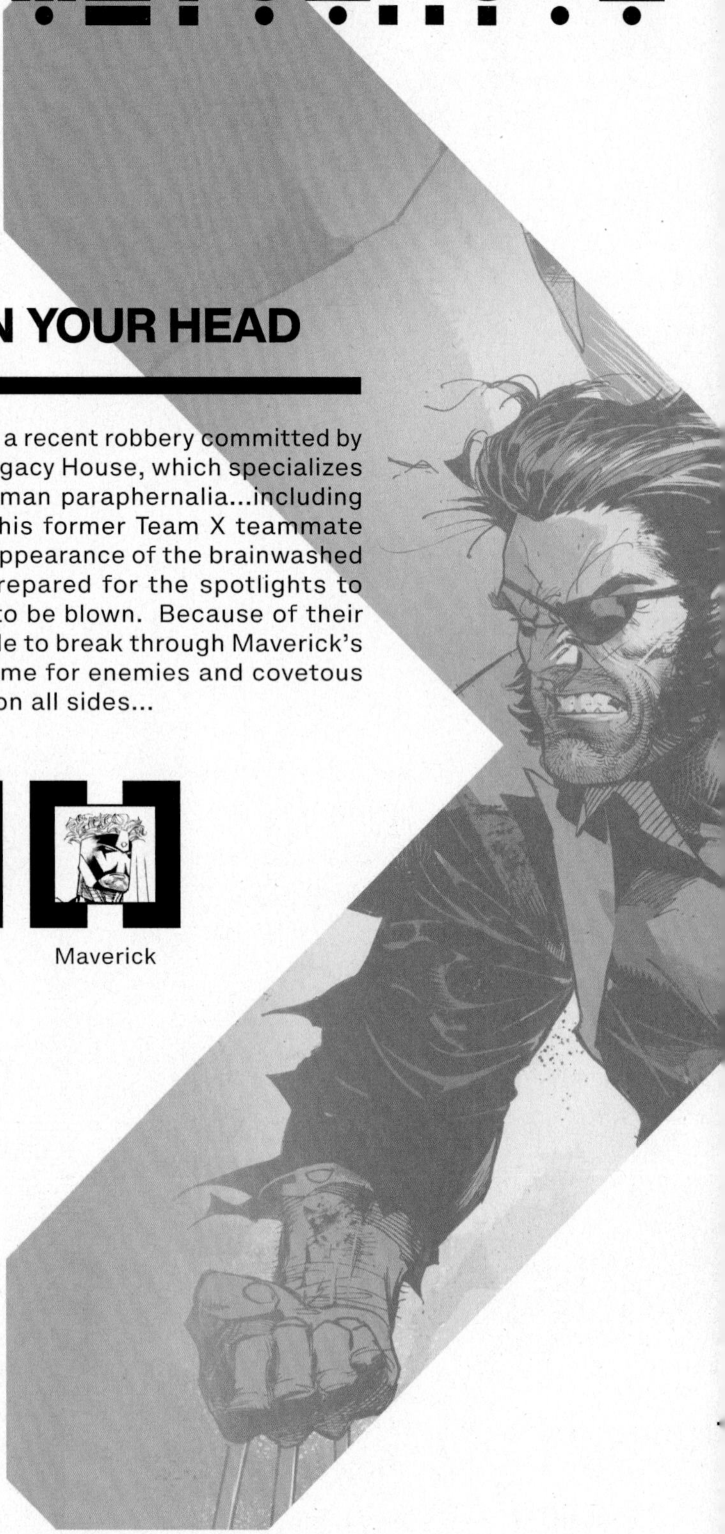

BOUNTY ON YOUR HEAD

Wolverine's investigation of a recent robbery committed by the Mercs led him to the Legacy House, which specializes in auctioning rare superhuman paraphernalia...including Logan's severed arm and his former Team X teammate Maverick! Stunned by the appearance of the brainwashed Maverick, Logan was unprepared for the spotlights to turn on him and his cover to be blown. Because of their shared past, Logan was able to break through Maverick's reprogramming -- just in time for enemies and covetous bidders to surround them on all sides...

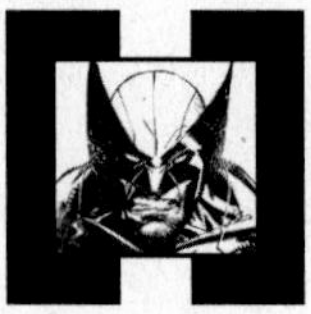

Wolverine

Maverick

[00_Reign]
[00___ofX]

WOLVERINE

[X_10]

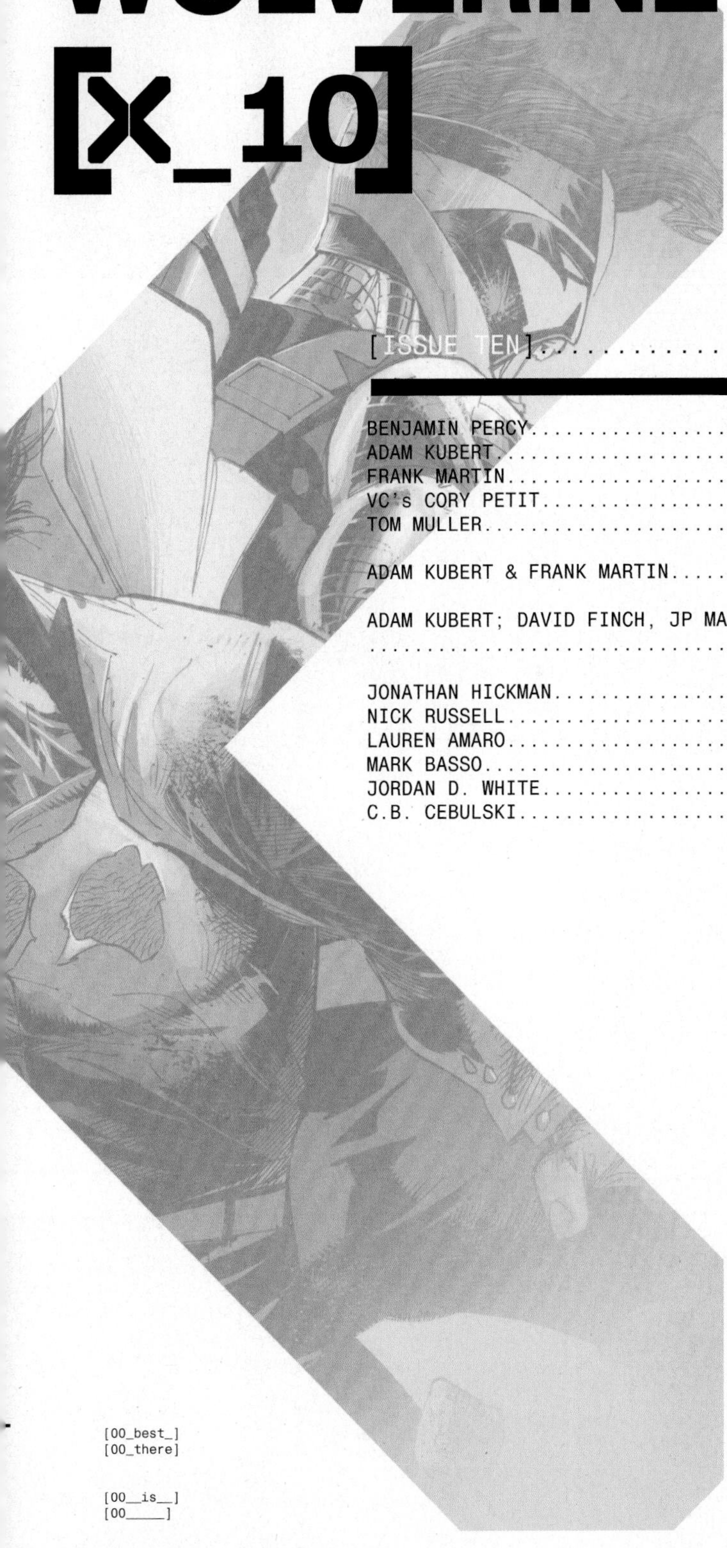

[ISSUE TEN]........................MERCENARIES

BENJAMIN PERCY..................................[WRITER]
ADAM KUBERT.....................................[ARTIST]
FRANK MARTIN..............................[COLOR ARTIST]
VC's CORY PETIT.................................[LETTERER]
TOM MULLER......................................[DESIGN]

ADAM KUBERT & FRANK MARTIN.................[COVER ARTISTS]

ADAM KUBERT; DAVID FINCH, JP MAYER & FRANK D'ARMATA........
.................................[VARIANT COVER ARTISTS]

JONATHAN HICKMAN...............................[HEAD OF X]
NICK RUSSELL..................................[PRODUCTION]
LAUREN AMARO............................[ASSISTANT EDITOR]
MARK BASSO.......................................[EDITOR]
JORDAN D. WHITE...........................[SENIOR EDITOR]
C.B. CEBULSKI............................[EDITOR IN CHIEF]

[00_best_]
[00_there]

[00__is__]
[00______]

[00_bub_]

[00____X]

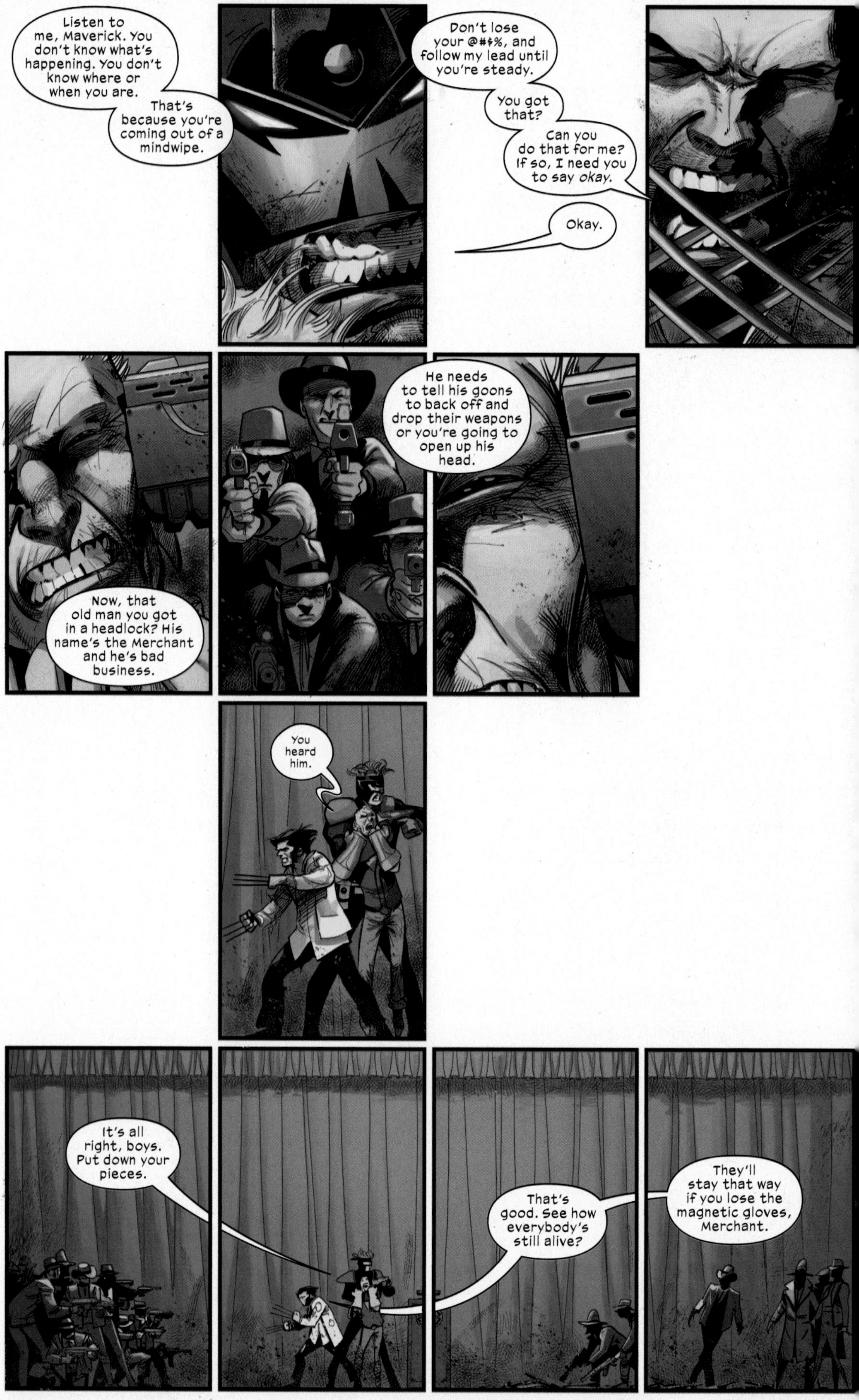
Listen to me, Maverick. You don't know what's happening. You don't know where or when you are.
That's because you're coming out of a mindwipe.
Don't lose your @#$%, and follow my lead until you're steady.
You got that?
Can you do that for me? If so, I need you to say *okay*.
Okay.
Now, that old man you got in a headlock? His name's the Merchant and he's bad business.
He needs to tell his goons to back off and drop their weapons or you're going to open up his head.
You heard him.
It's all right, boys. Put down your pieces.
That's good. See how everybody's still alive?
They'll stay that way if you lose the magnetic gloves, Merchant.

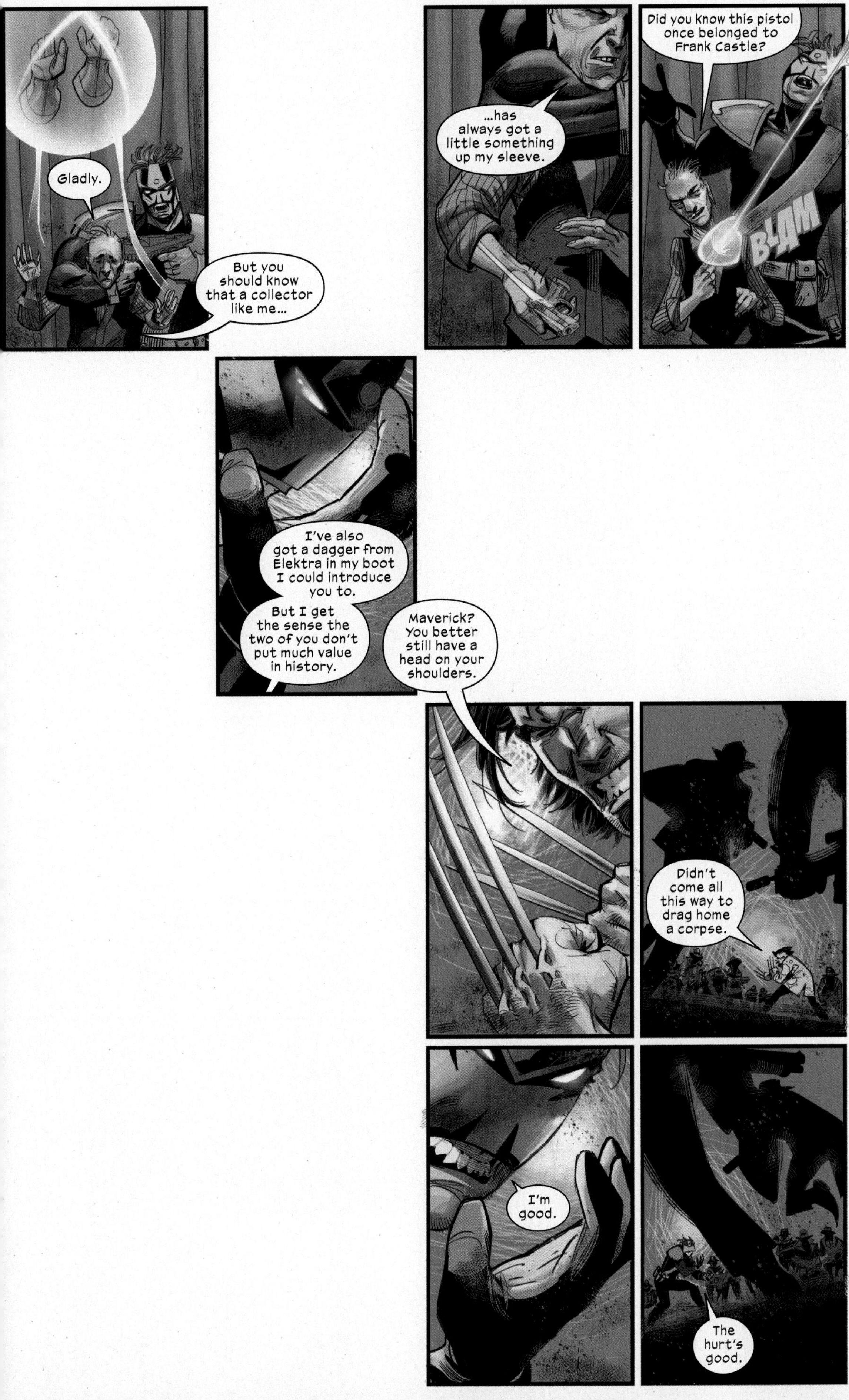
Gladly.
But you should know that a collector like me...
...has always got a little something up my sleeve.
Did you know this pistol once belonged to Frank Castle?
BLAM
I've also got a dagger from Elektra in my boot I could introduce you to.
But I get the sense the two of you don't put much value in history.
Maverick? You better still have a head on your shoulders.
Didn't come all this way to drag home a corpse.
I'm good.
The hurt's good.

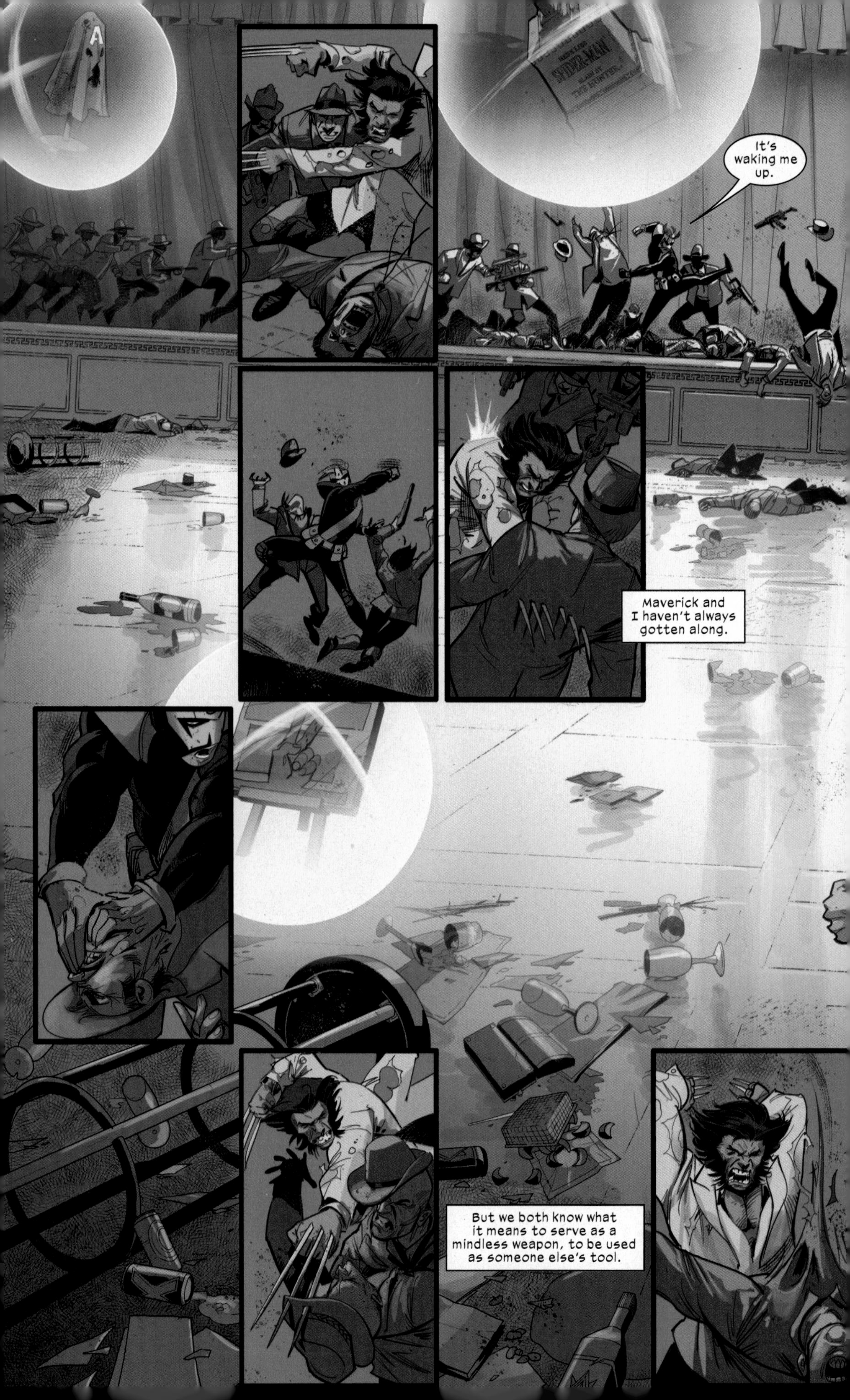

It's waking me up.
Maverick and I haven't always gotten along.
But we both know what it means to serve as a mindless weapon, to be used as someone else's tool.

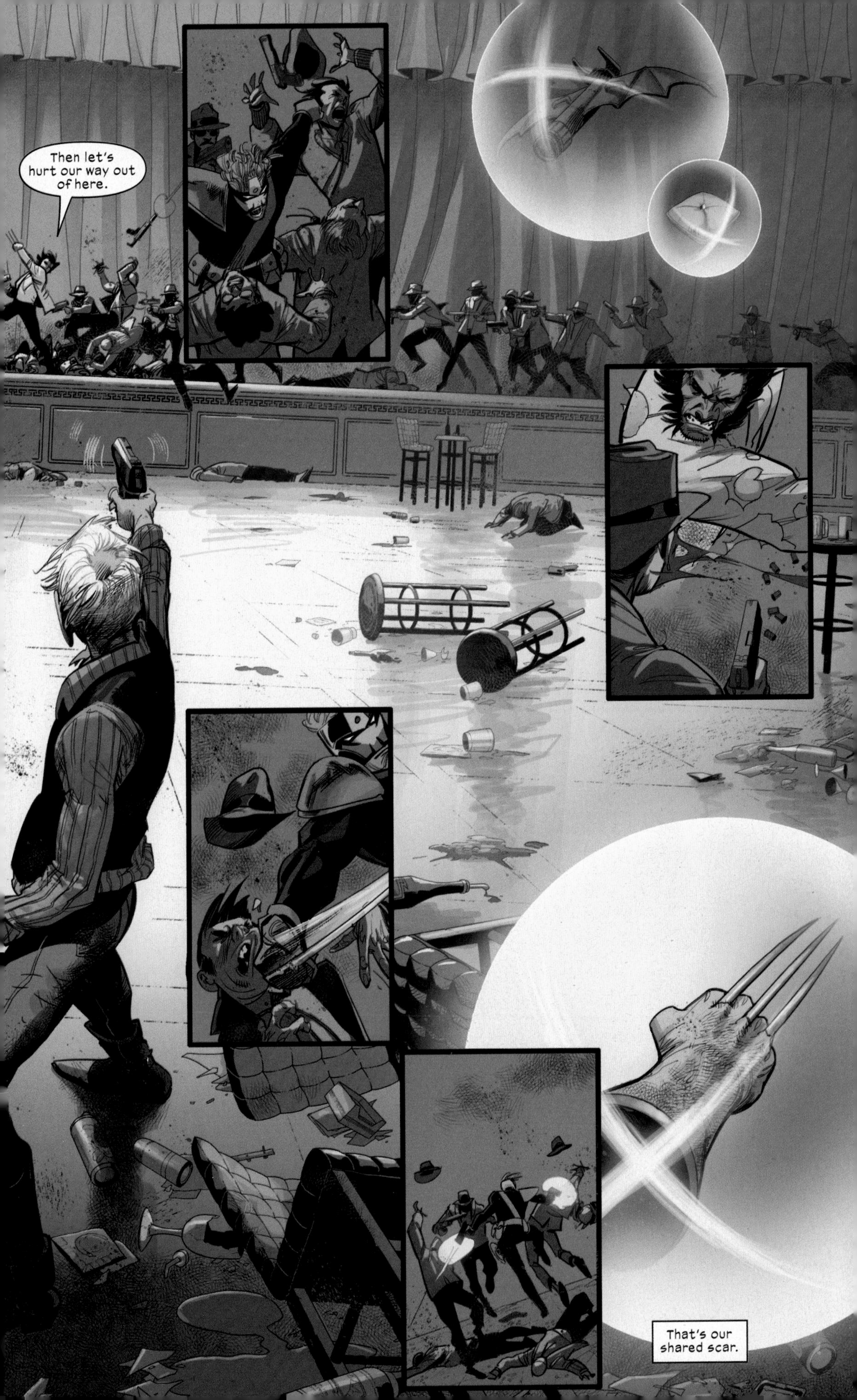
Then let's hurt our way out of here.
That's our shared scar.

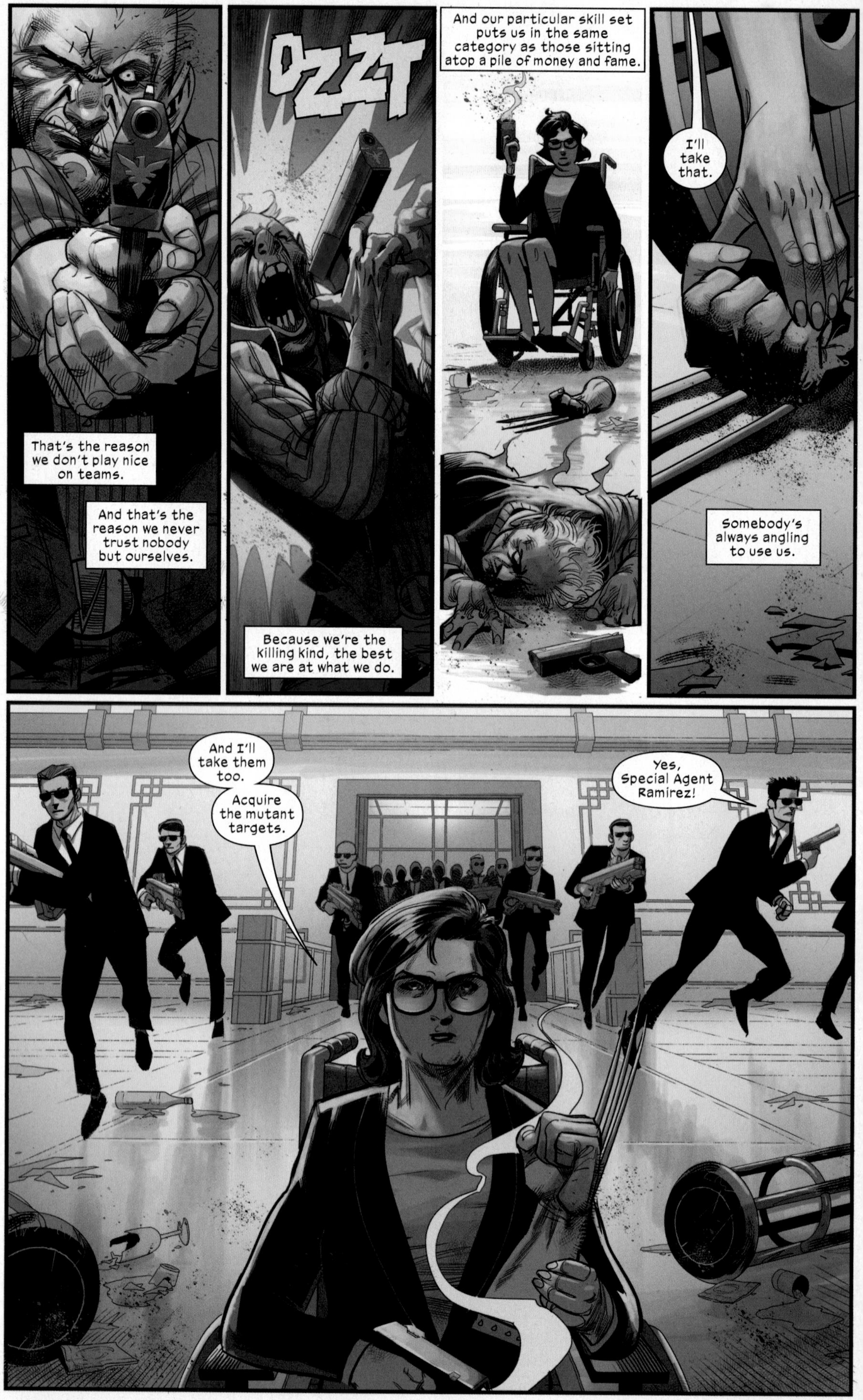
That's the reason we don't play nice on teams.
And that's the reason we never trust nobody but ourselves.
DZZT
Because we're the killing kind, the best we are at what we do.
And our particular skill set puts us in the same category as those sitting atop a pile of money and fame.
I'll take that.
Somebody's always angling to use us.
And I'll take them too.
Acquire the mutant targets.
Yes, Special Agent Ramirez!

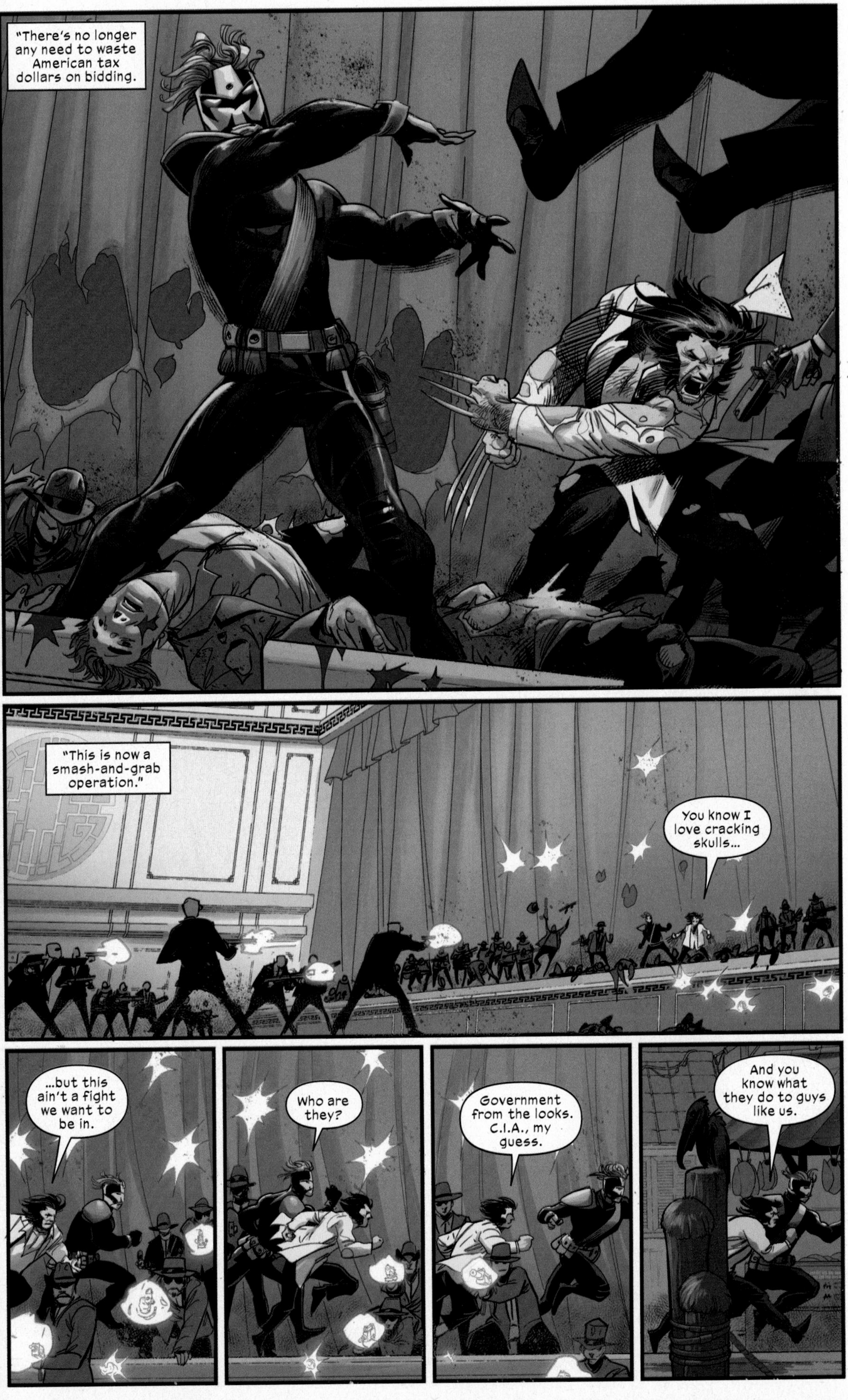
"There's no longer any need to waste American tax dollars on bidding.
"This is now a smash-and-grab operation."
You know I love cracking skulls...
...but this ain't a fight we want to be in.
Who are they?
Government from the looks. C.I.A., my guess.
And you know what they do to guys like us.

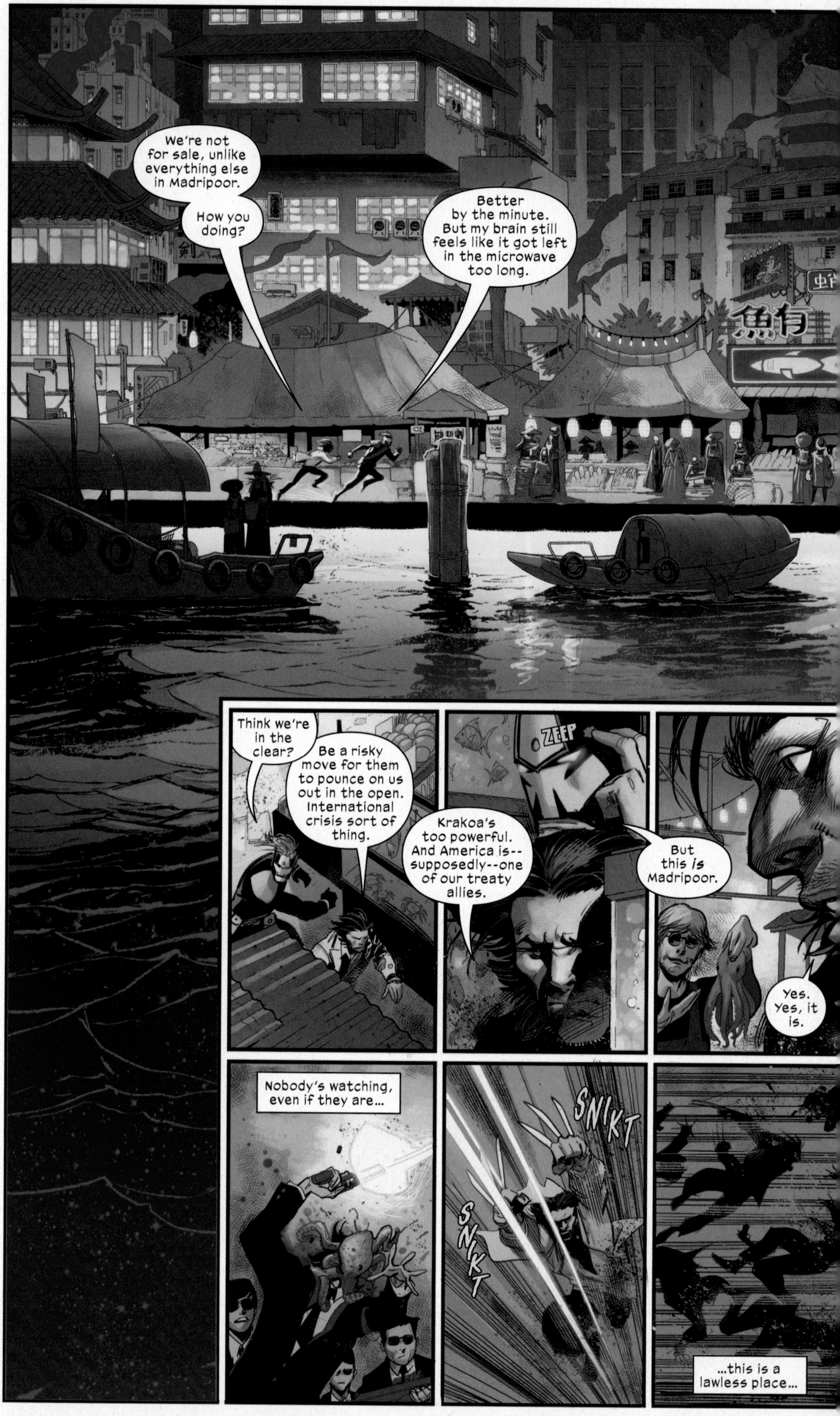
We're not for sale, unlike everything else in Madripoor.
How you doing?
Better by the minute. But my brain still feels like it got left in the microwave too long.
Think we're in the clear?
Be a risky move for them to pounce on us out in the open. International crisis sort of thing.
ZEEP
Krakoa's too powerful. And America is--supposedly--one of our treaty allies.
But this *is* Madripoor.
Yes. Yes, it is.
Nobody's watching, even if they are...
SNIKT
SNIKT
...this is a lawless place...

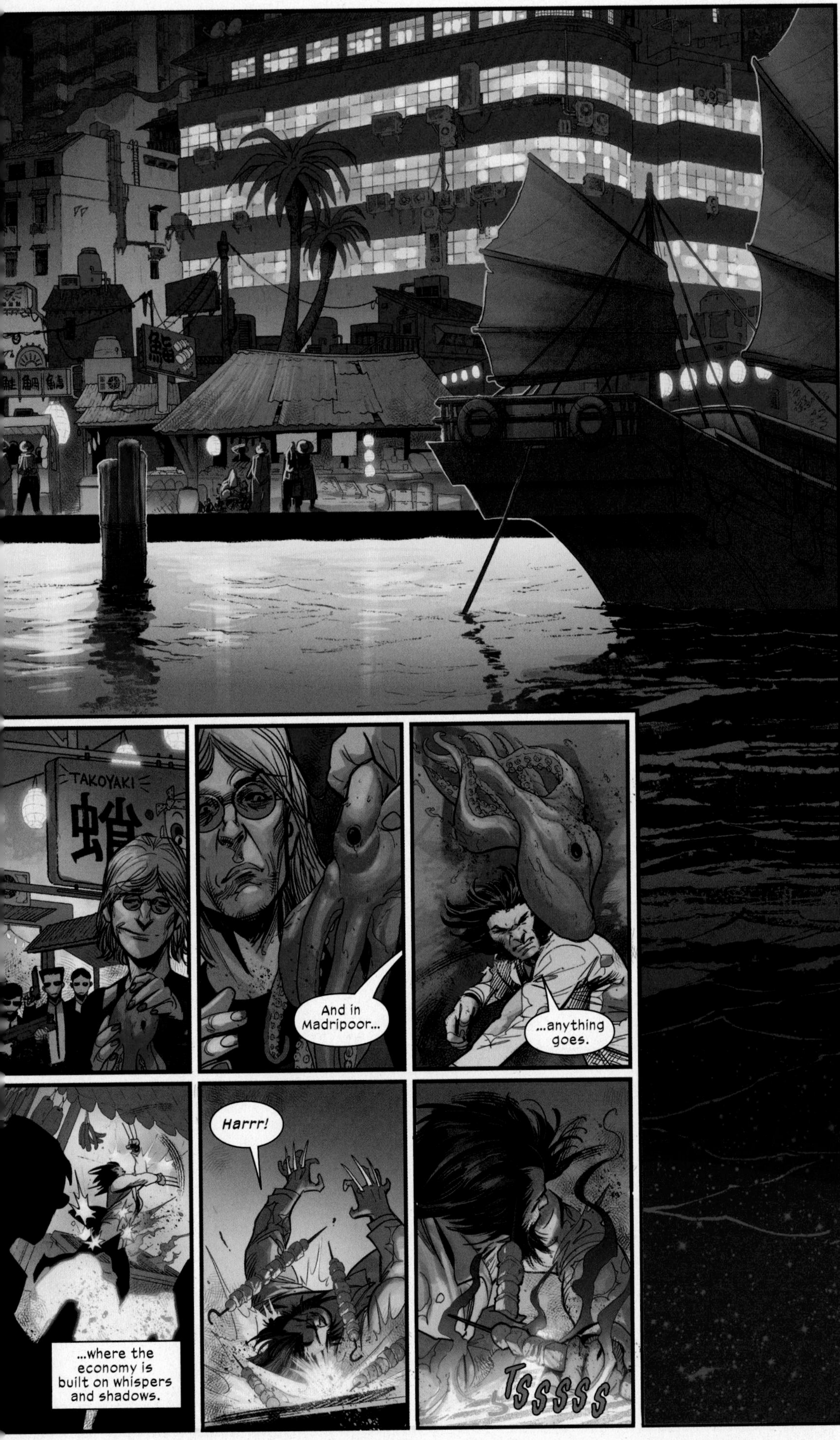
TAKOYAKI
And in Madripoor...
...anything goes.
...where the economy is built on whispers and shadows.
Harrr!
TSSSSS

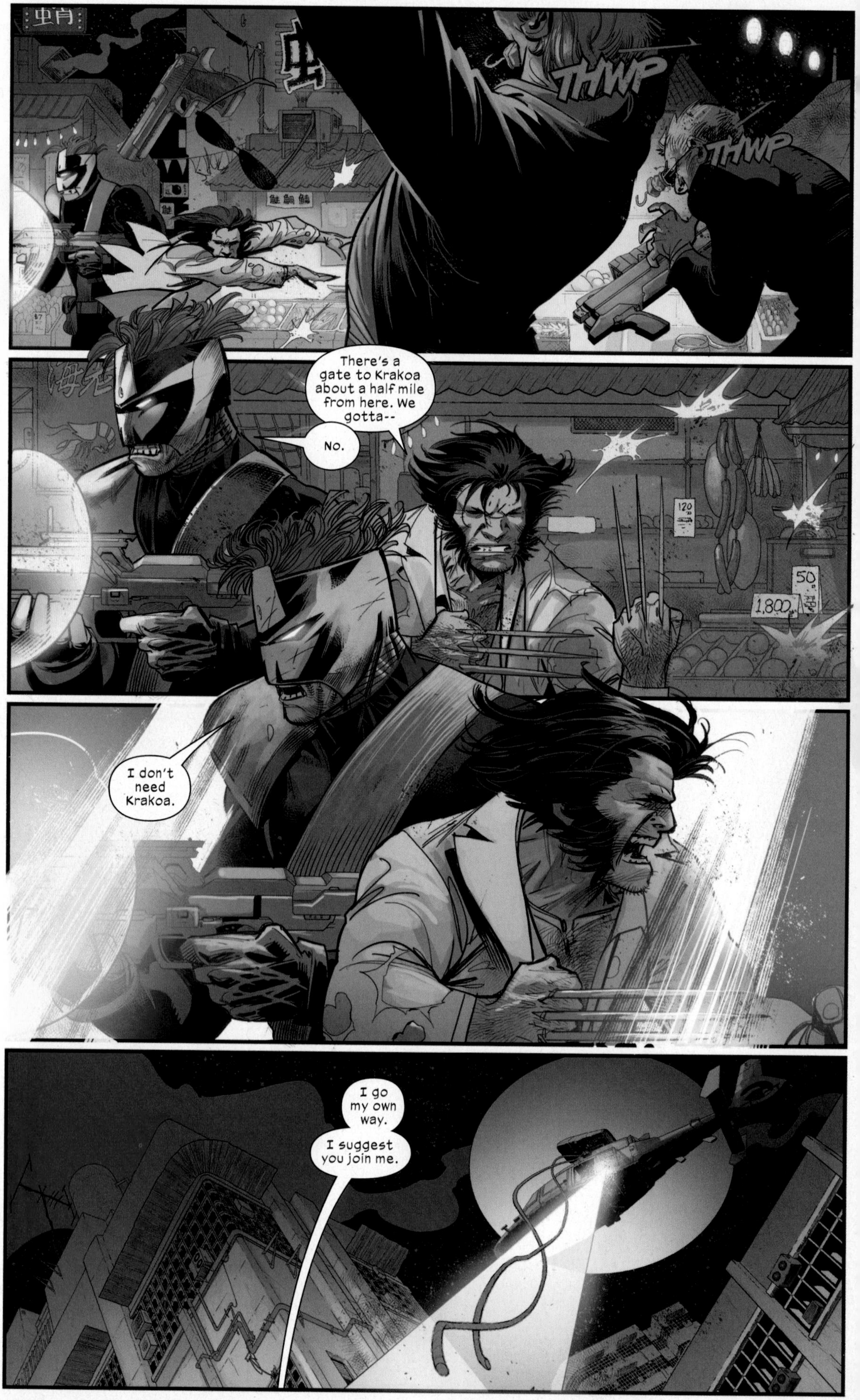
THWP
THWP
There's a gate to Krakoa about a half mile from here. We gotta--
No.
120
50
1,800
I don't need Krakoa.
I go my own way.
I suggest you join me.

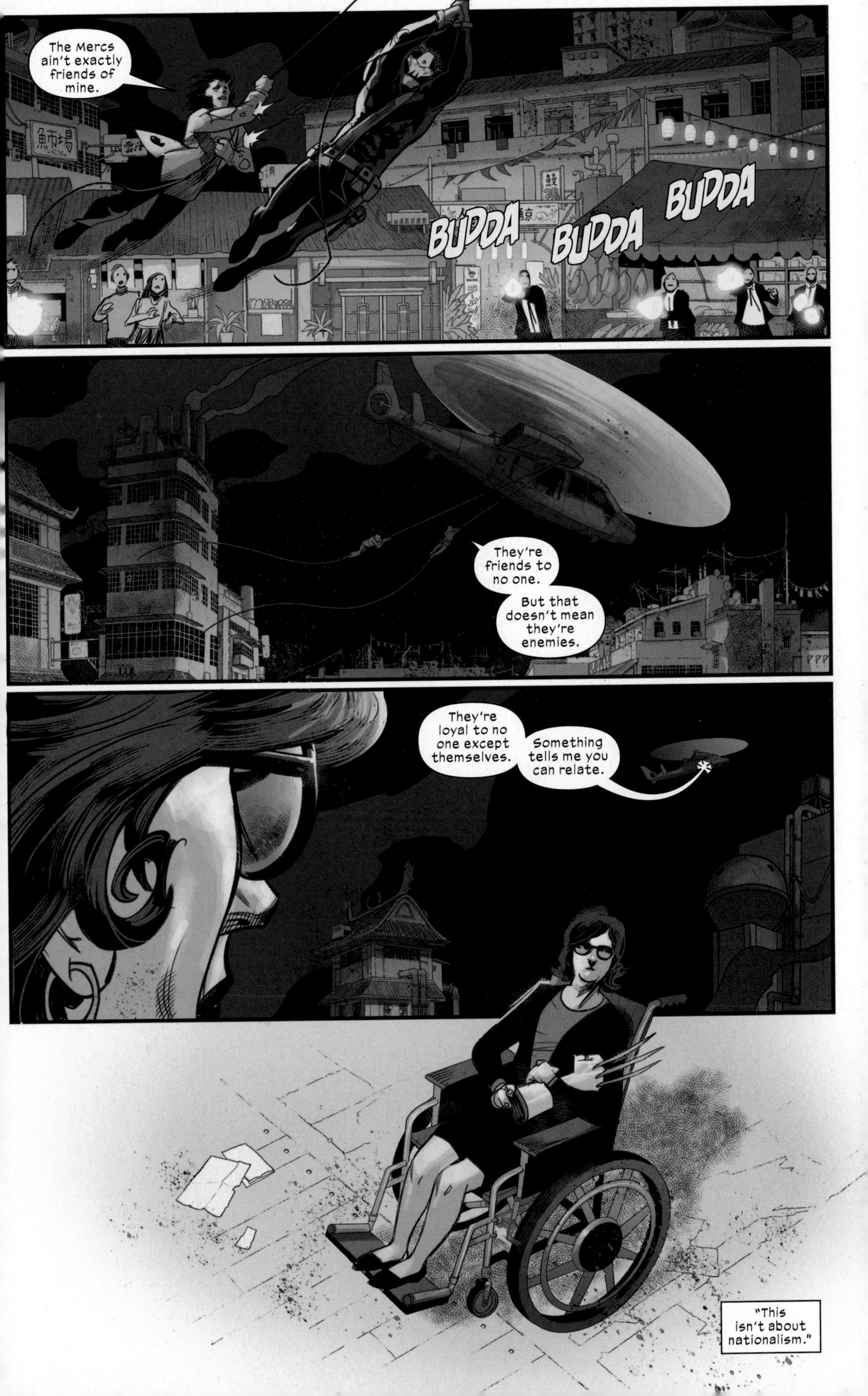
The Mercs ain't exactly friends of mine.
BUDDA
BUDDA
BUDDA
They're friends to no one.
But that doesn't mean they're enemies.
They're loyal to no one except themselves.
Something tells me you can relate.
"This isn't about nationalism."

[reign_of_x]

[kra_]
[koa_]

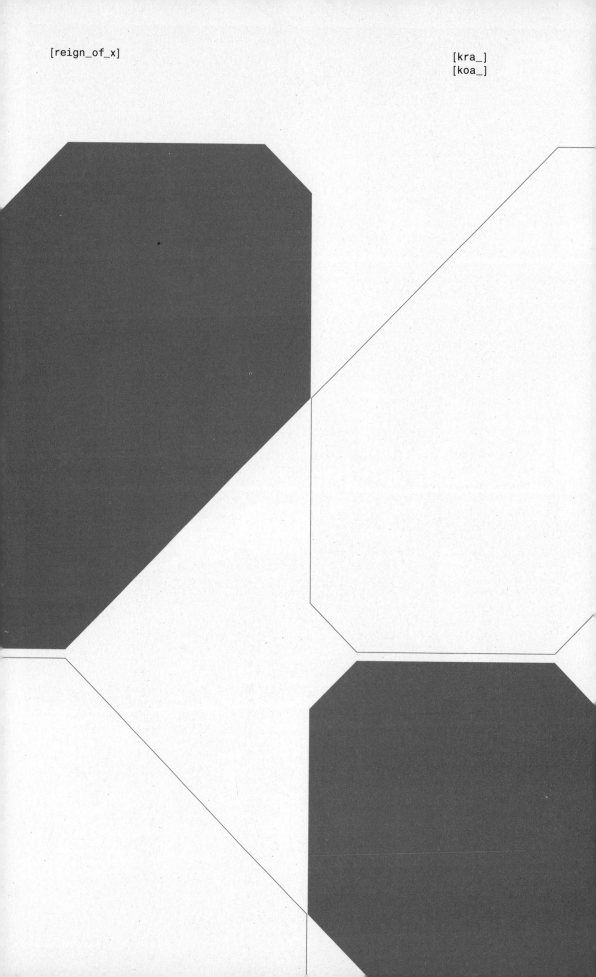

C.I.A. PHONE LOG

Decrypted /// Analog Scramble///

Caller Identification: Special Agent Delores Ramirez /// X-Desk

Ramirez: We failed to acquire the target.

> **Director:** You were outbid?

Ramirez: Outgunned.

> *<Silence lasting ten seconds>*

> **Director:** You assured me this would be a quiet operation.

Ramirez: I didn't anticipate Wolverine's presence. He's an agent of chaos.

> **Director:** Please tell me you haven't jeopardized the treaty?

Ramirez: Not exactly.

> **Director:** Not exactly? That's a half-assed answer to what could be a politically and economically calamitous reality. You assured me --

Ramirez: I assured you that anything goes in Madripoor. What happens there stays there. We're fine.

> **Director:** We are far from fine.

Ramirez: Yes, the mutants will know we made a move, but they're not going to do anything about it. Because they're back-alleying on their promises as much as we are. That's why the X-Desk is so necessary.

> **Director:** I'm honestly starting to question whether that's true. The last thing I need is --

Ramirez: I know how to rectify the situation.

> **Director:** Oh?

Ramirez: Our goal was to buy Maverick, yes?

> **Director:** Your goal.

Ramirez: I believe a more transactional approach is still possible. If the auction funds are still available to me?

> **Director:** Keep talking.

> *<Signal lost>*

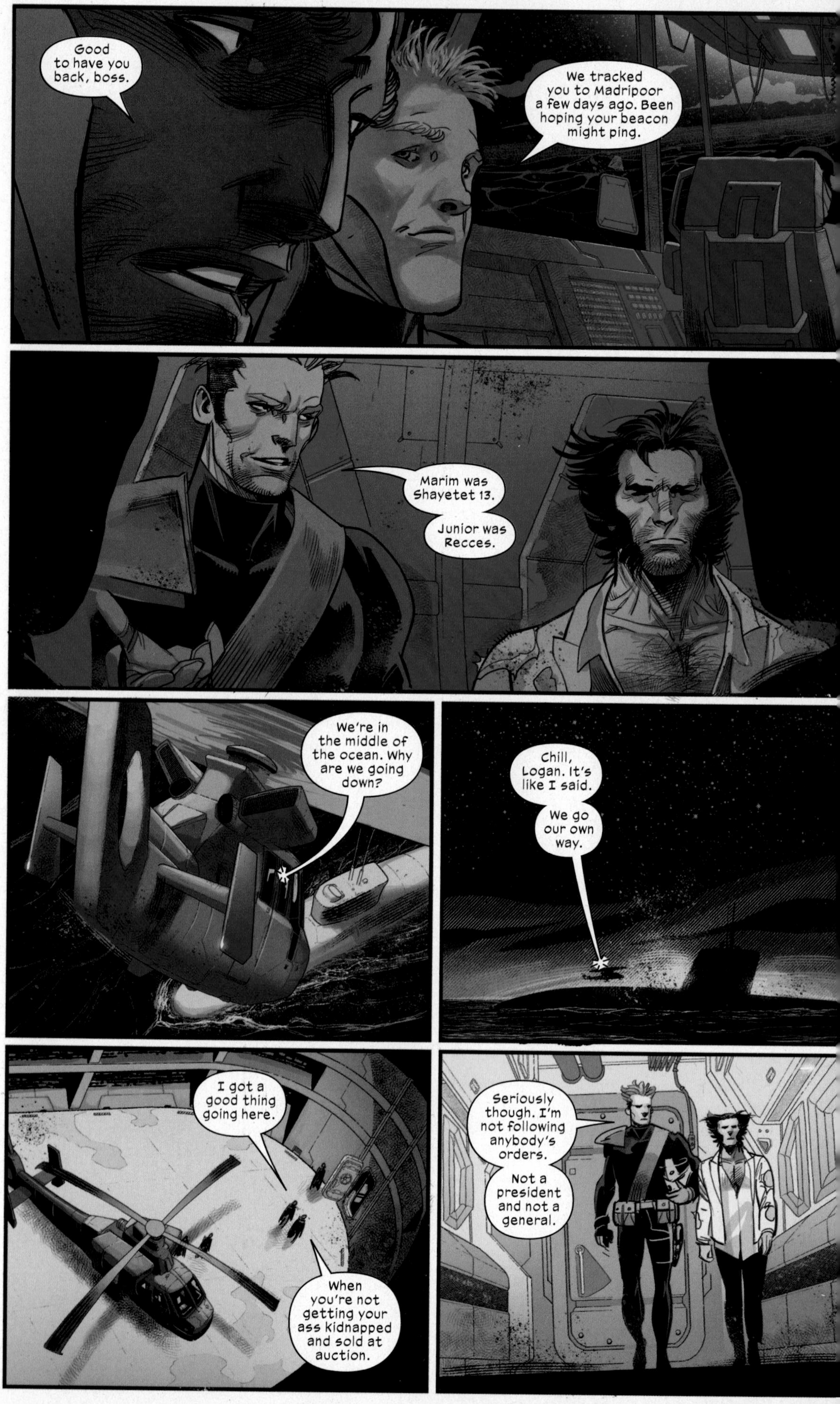
Good to have you back, boss.
We tracked you to Madripoor a few days ago. Been hoping your beacon might ping.
Marim was Shayetet 13.
Junior was Recces.
We're in the middle of the ocean. Why are we going down?
Chill, Logan. It's like I said.
We go our own way.
I got a good thing going here.
When you're not getting your ass kidnapped and sold at auction.
Seriously though. I'm not following anybody's orders.
Not a president and not a general.

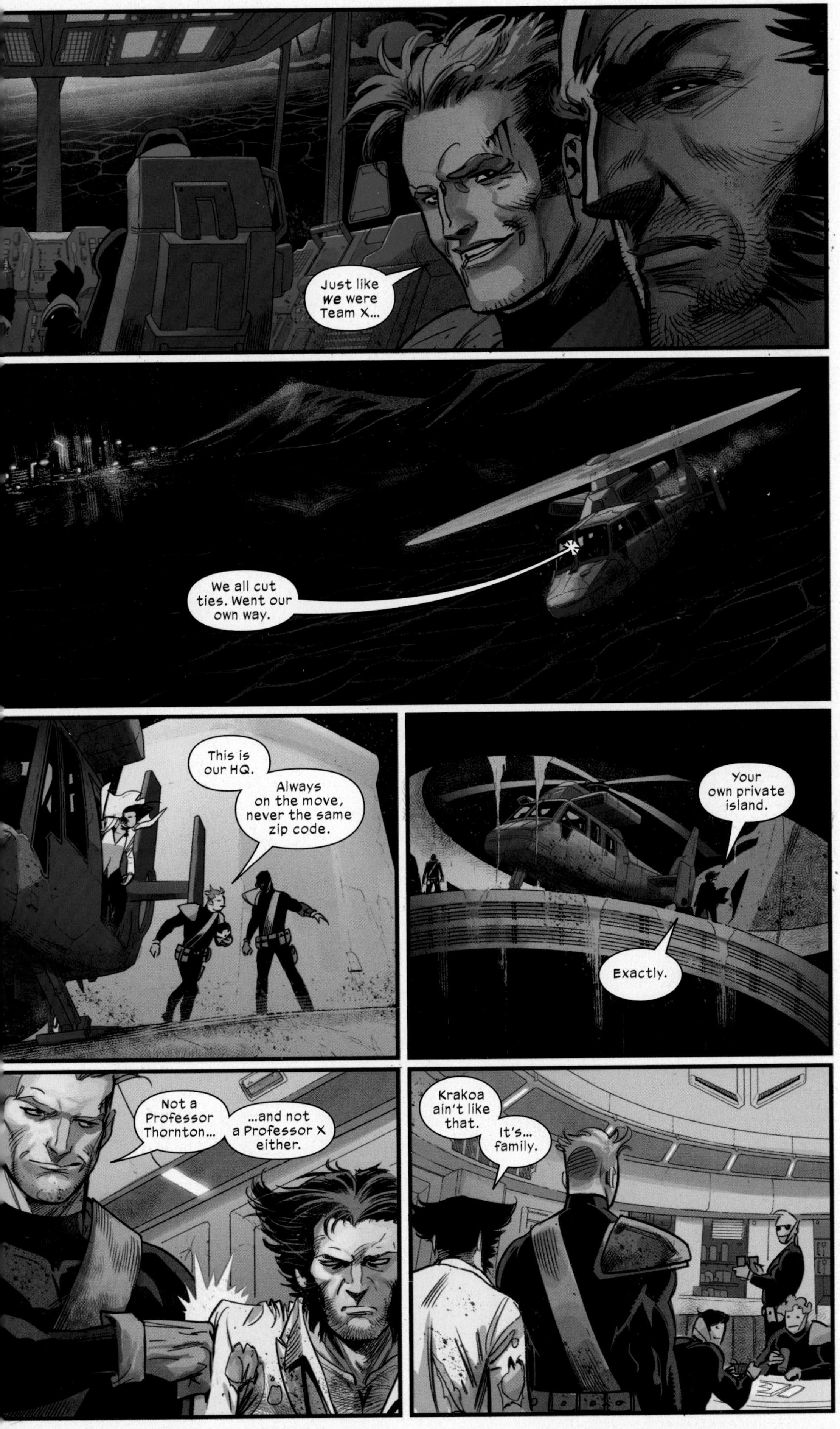
Just like we were Team X...
We all cut ties. Went our own way.
This is our HQ.
Always on the move, never the same zip code.
Your own private island.
Exactly.
Not a Professor Thornton...
...and not a Professor X either.
Krakoa ain't like that.
It's... family.

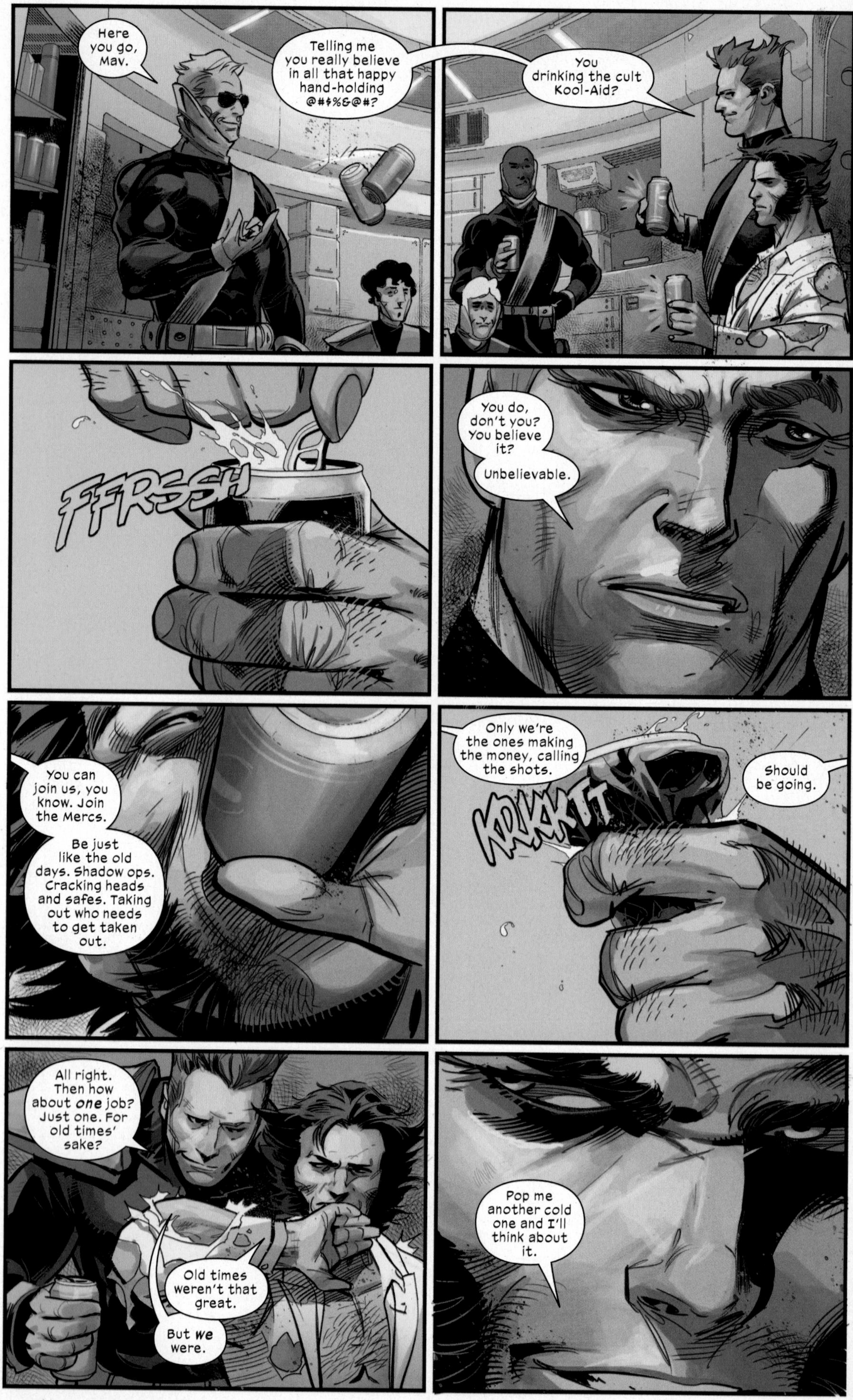
Here you go, Mav.
Telling me you really believe in all that happy hand-holding @#$%&@#?
You drinking the cult Kool-Aid?
FFRSSH
You do, don't you? You believe it?
Unbelievable.
You can join us, you know. Join the Mercs.
Be just like the old days. Shadow ops. Cracking heads and safes. Taking out who needs to get taken out.
Only we're the ones making the money, calling the shots.
KRUKTT
Should be going.
All right. Then how about *one* job? Just one. For old times' sake?
Old times weren't that great.
But *we* were.
Pop me another cold one and I'll think about it.

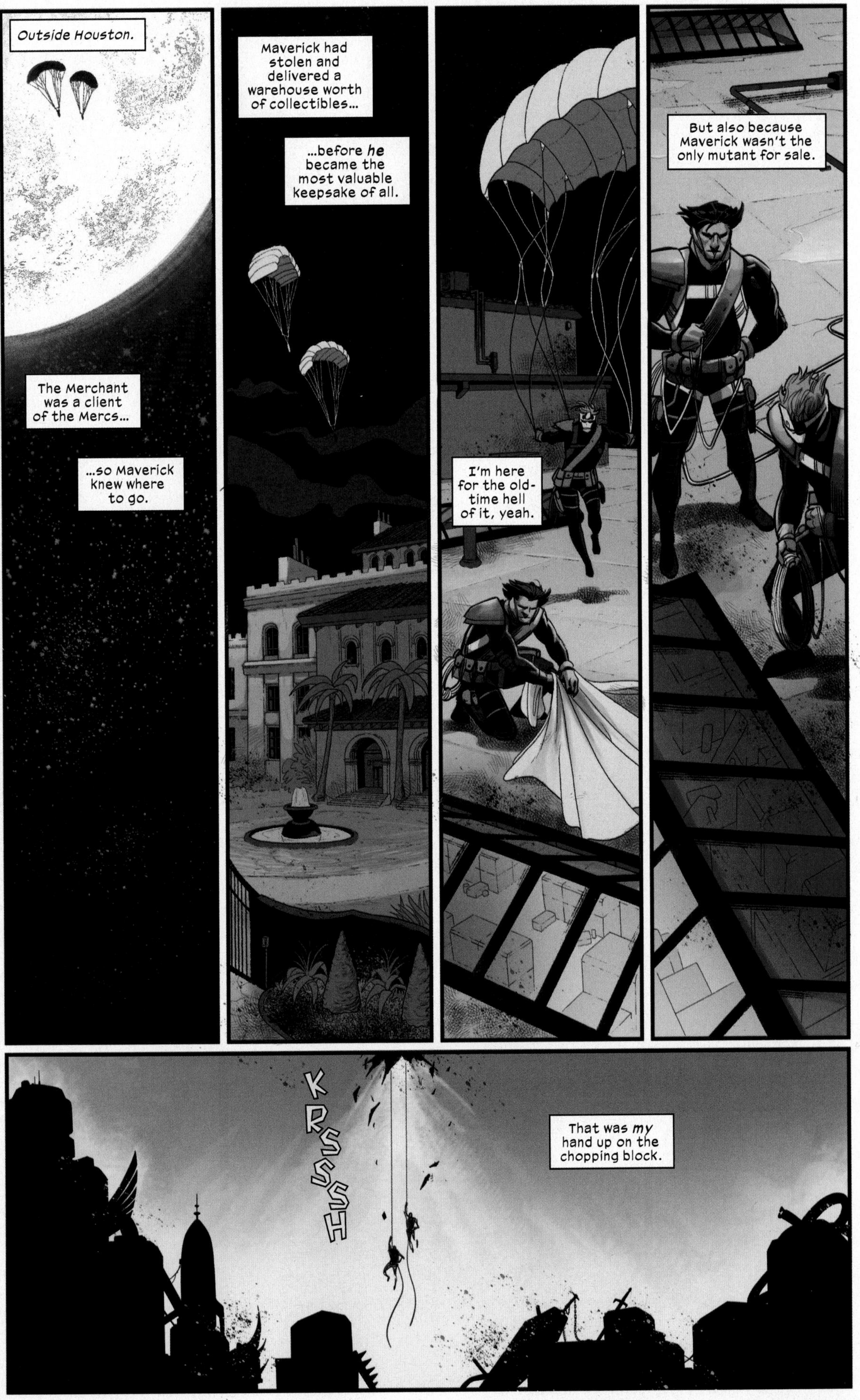
Outside Houston.
The Merchant was a client of the Mercs...
...so Maverick knew where to go.
Maverick had stolen and delivered a warehouse worth of collectibles...
...before *he* became the most valuable keepsake of all.
I'm here for the old-time hell of it, yeah.
But also because Maverick wasn't the only mutant for sale.
KRSSSH
That was *my* hand up on the chopping block.

[reign_of_x]

[kra_]
[koa_]

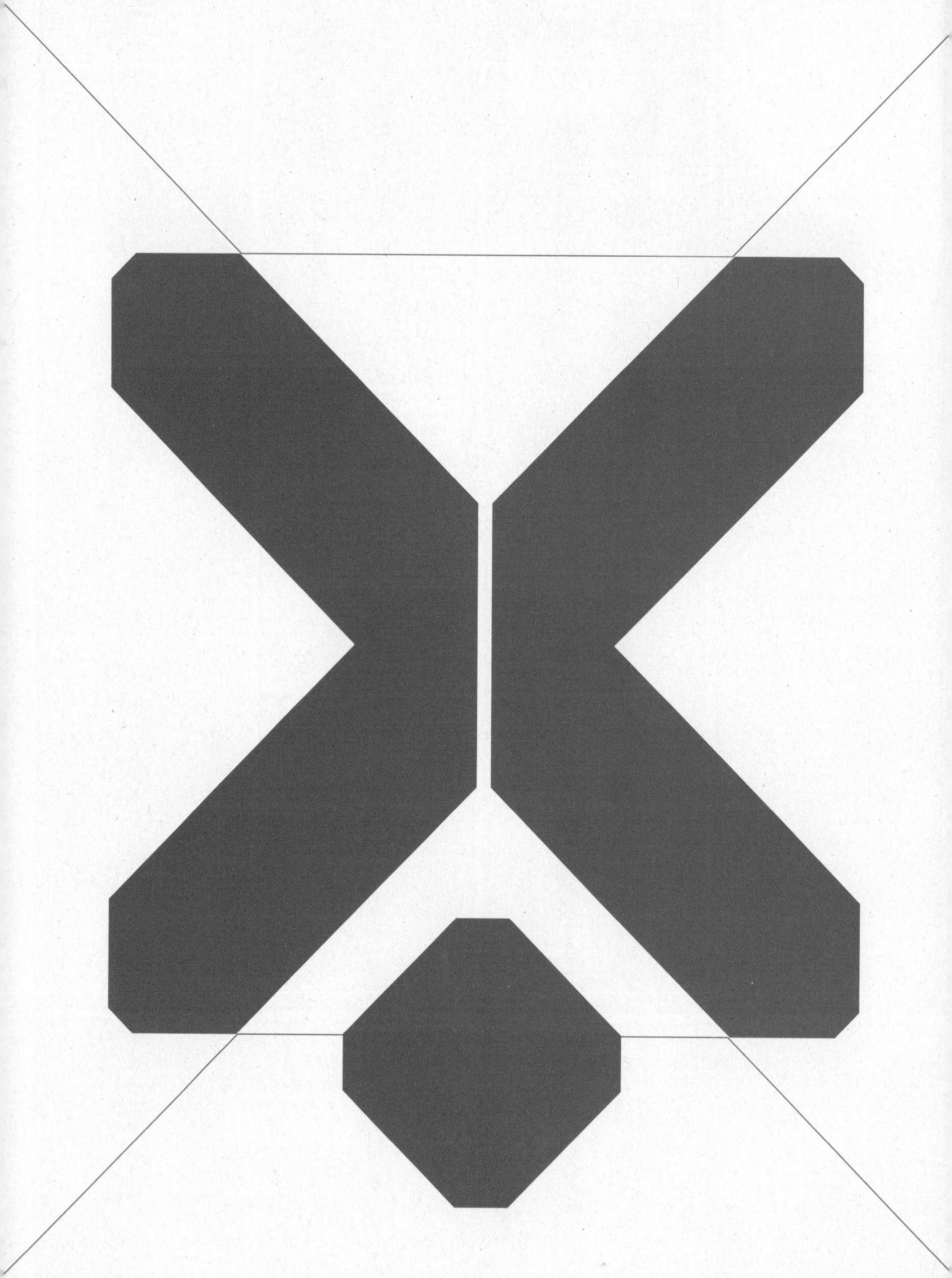

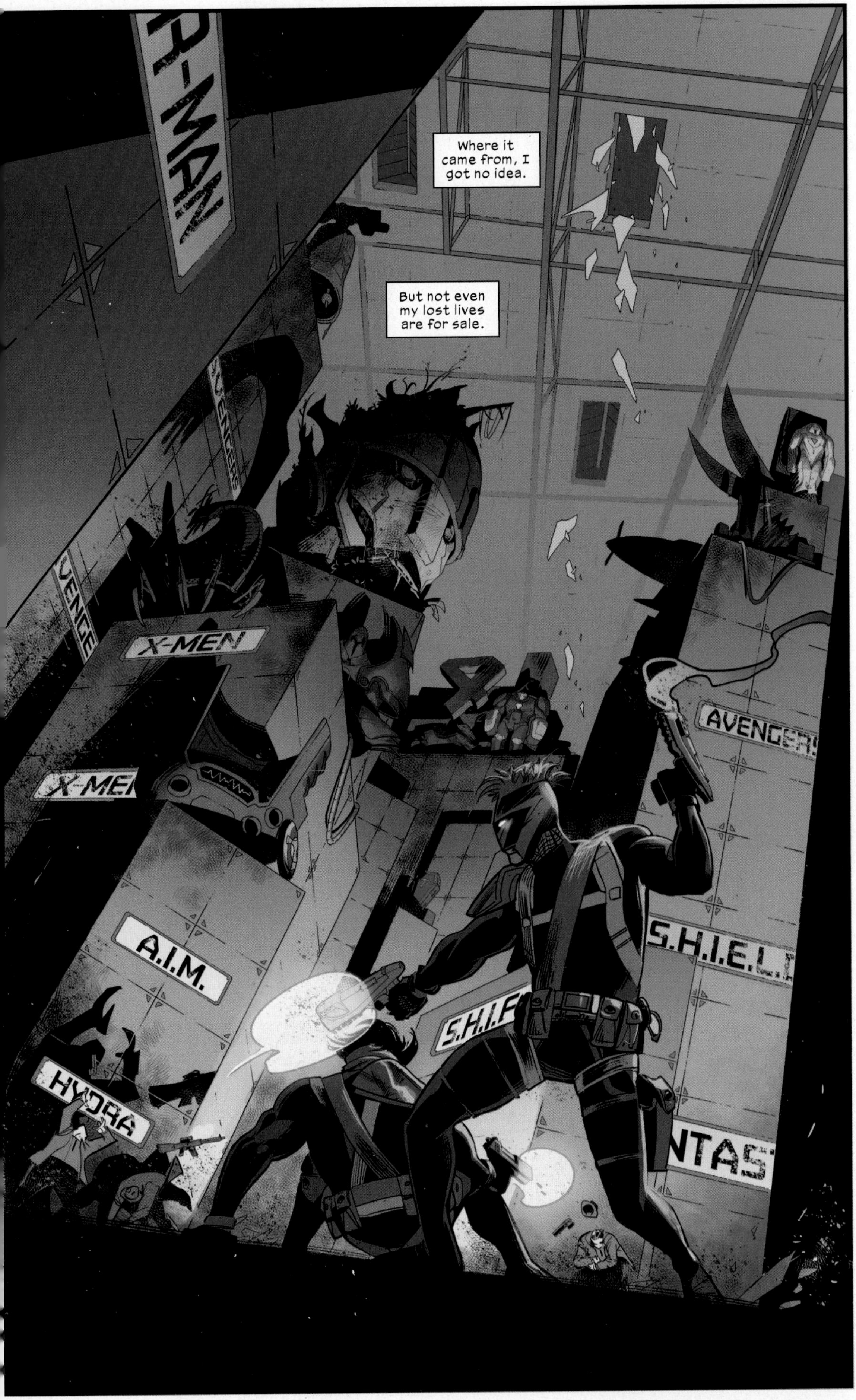
Where it came from, I got no idea.
But not even my lost lives are for sale.
X-MEN
AVENGERS
X-MEN
A.I.M.
HYDRA
S.H.I.E.L.
AVENGERS
S.H.I.E.L.

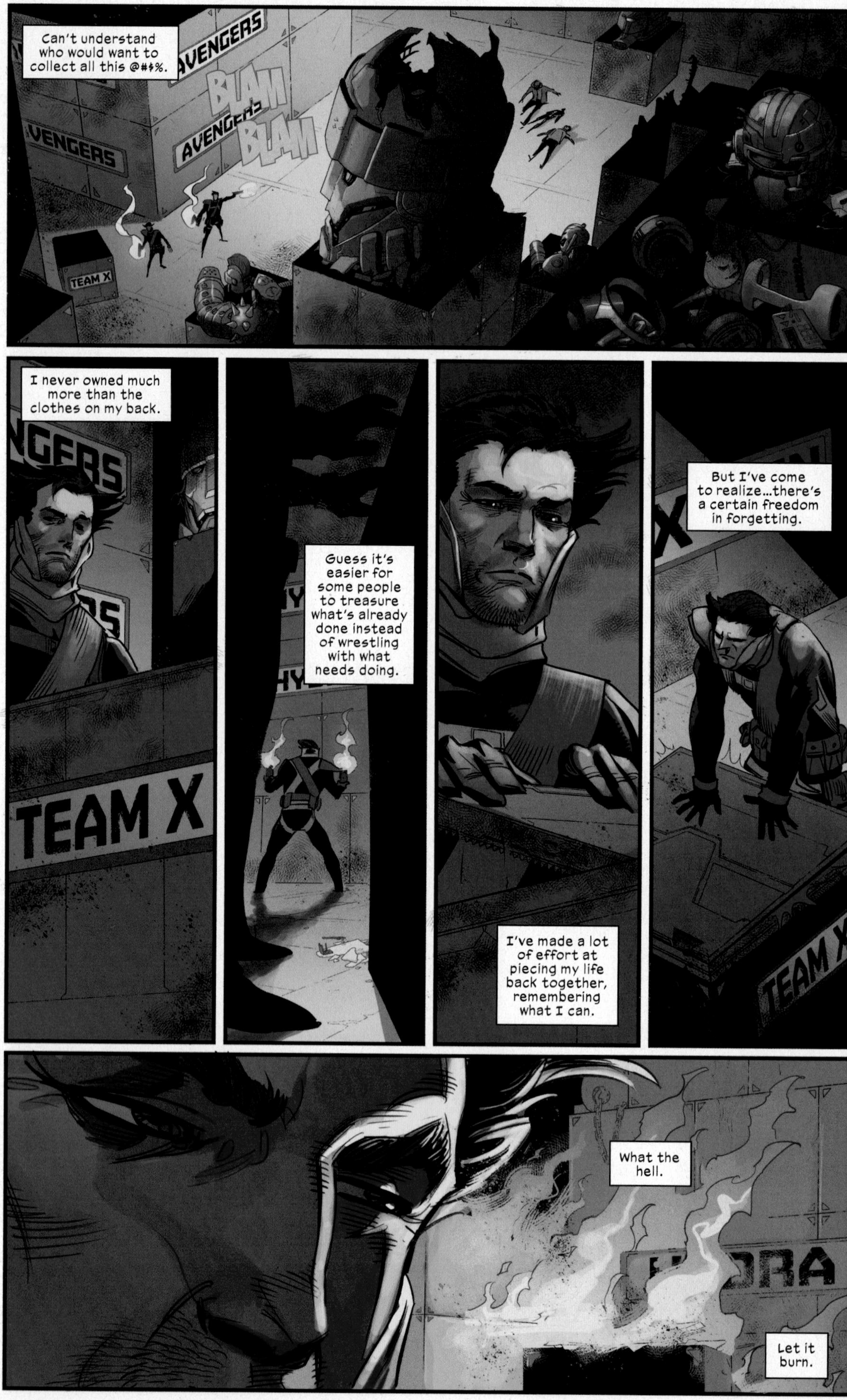
Can't understand who would want to collect all this @#$%.
AVENGERS
BLAM
AVENGERS
BLAM
TEAM X
I never owned much more than the clothes on my back.
TEAM X
Guess it's easier for some people to treasure what's already done instead of wrestling with what needs doing.
I've made a lot of effort at piecing my life back together, remembering what I can.
But I've come to realize...there's a certain freedom in forgetting.
TEAM X
What the hell.
Let it burn.

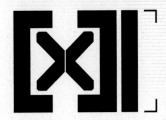

X-FACTOR LOGBOOK

Mutant: Wolverine

Subject: Lost Lives

Resurrection Query: Logan requests a full review of his resurrection log, citing an aberration encountered during a recent operation.

The presence of a severed hand -- allegedly his own -- indicates:

>> possible anomaly in death logs >>

>> possible relic of Weapon X clone >>

>> possible genomic experiment by XENO >>

>> *collating* >>

>> *collating* >>

>> *collating* >>

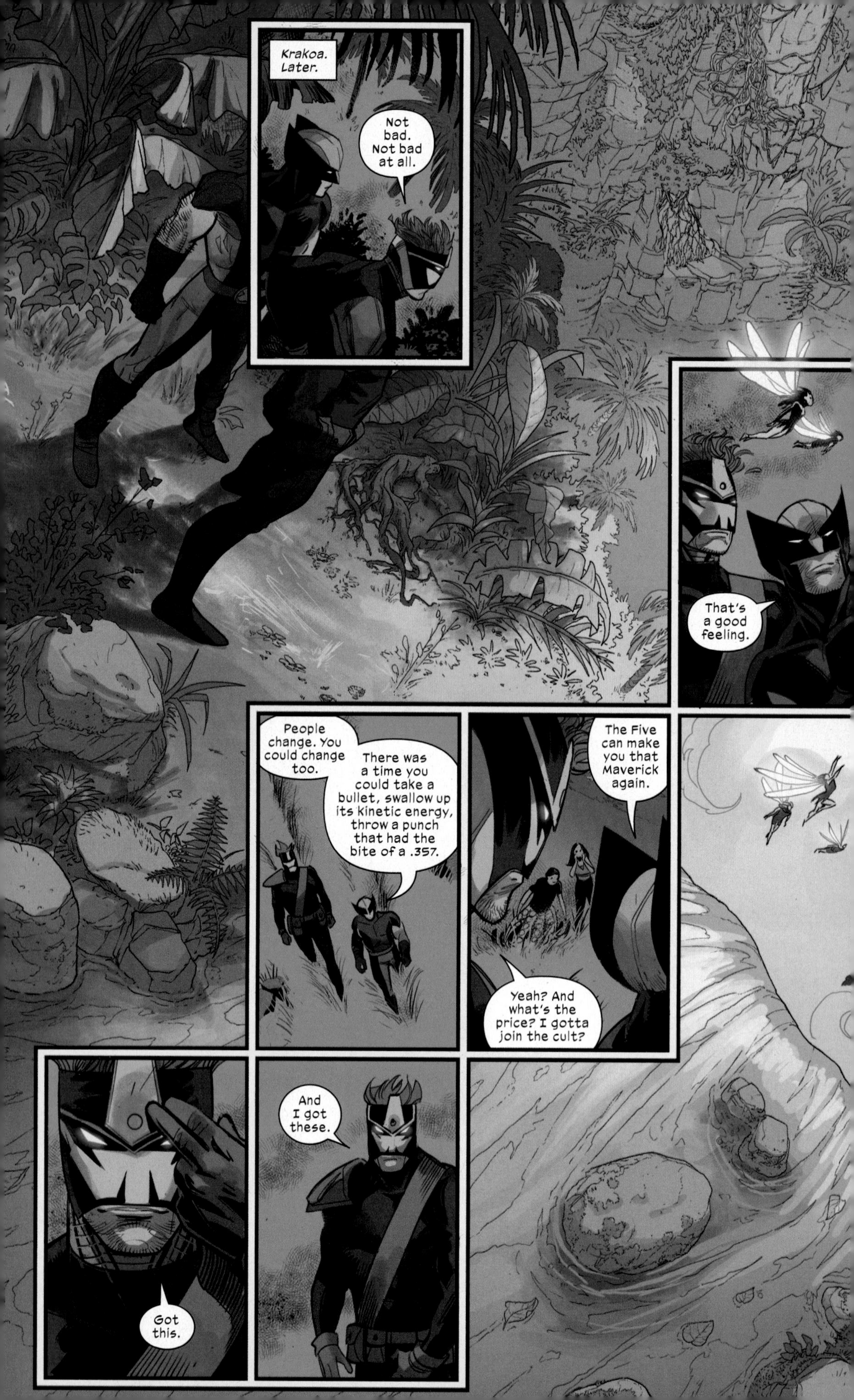
Krakoa. Later.
Not bad. Not bad at all.
That's a good feeling.
People change. You could change too.
There was a time you could take a bullet, swallow up its kinetic energy, throw a punch that had the bite of a .357.
The Five can make you that Maverick again.
Yeah? And what's the price? I gotta join the cult?
Got this.
And I got these.

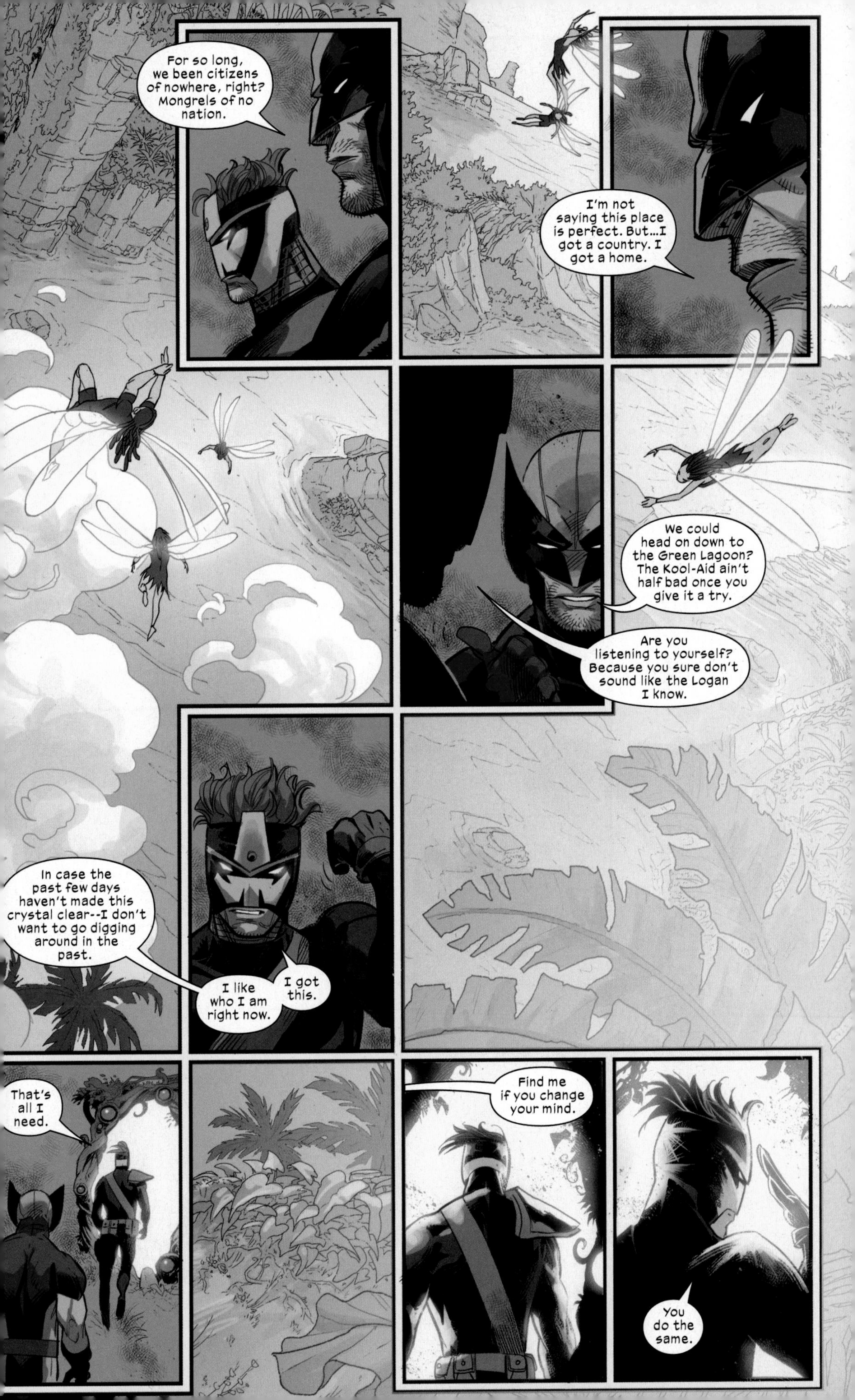

For so long, we been citizens of nowhere, right? Mongrels of no nation.
I'm not saying this place is perfect. But...I got a country. I got a home.
We could head on down to the Green Lagoon? The Kool-Aid ain't half bad once you give it a try.
Are you listening to yourself? Because you sure don't sound like the Logan I know.
In case the past few days haven't made this crystal clear--I don't want to go digging around in the past.
I like who I am right now.
I got this.
That's all I need.
Find me if you change your mind.
You do the same.

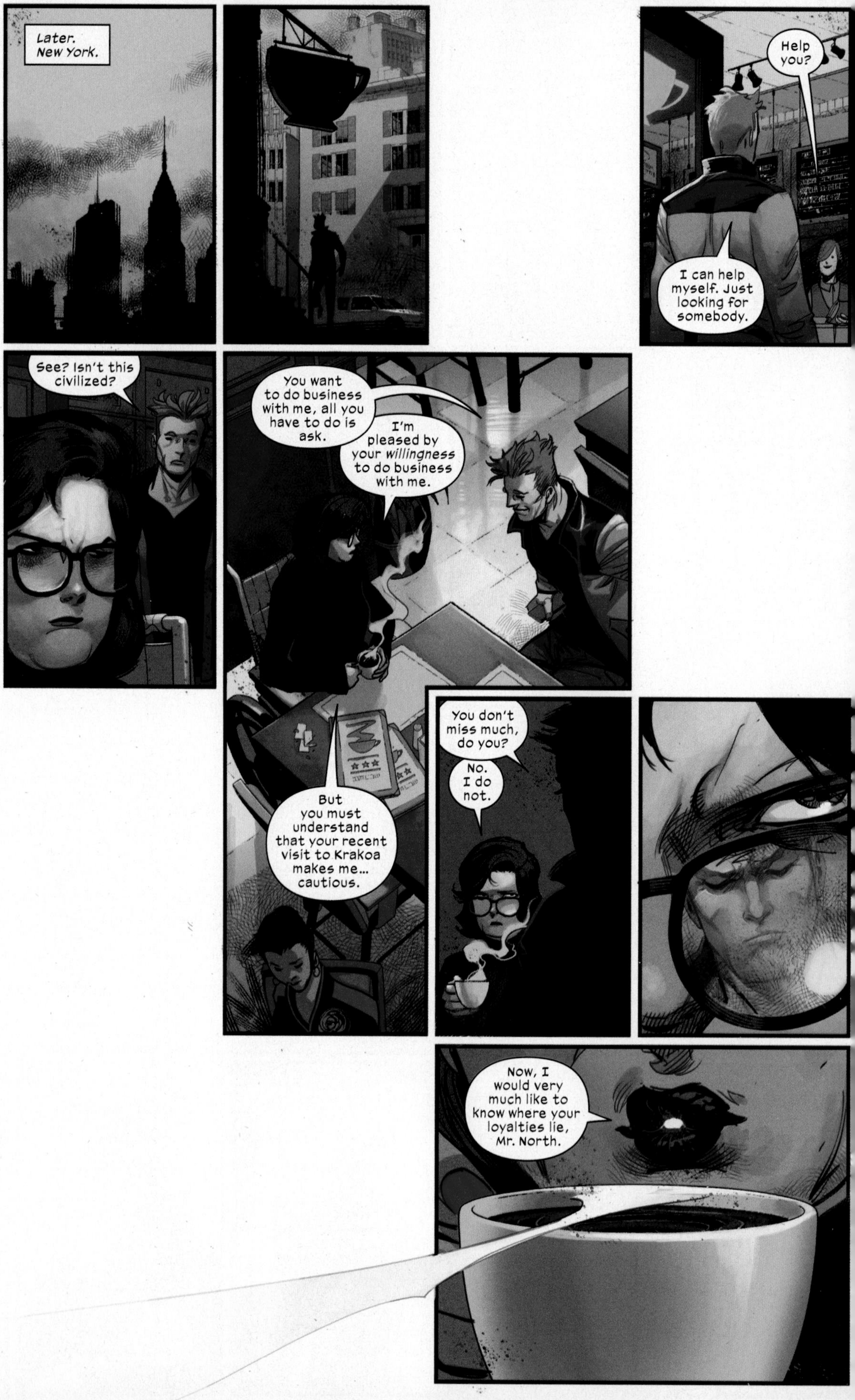
Later.
New York.
Help you?
I can help myself. Just looking for somebody.
See? Isn't this civilized?
You want to do business with me, all you have to do is ask.
I'm pleased by your *willingness* to do business with me.
But you must understand that your recent visit to Krakoa makes me... cautious.
You don't miss much, do you?
No. I do not.
Now, I would very much like to know where your loyalties lie, Mr. North.

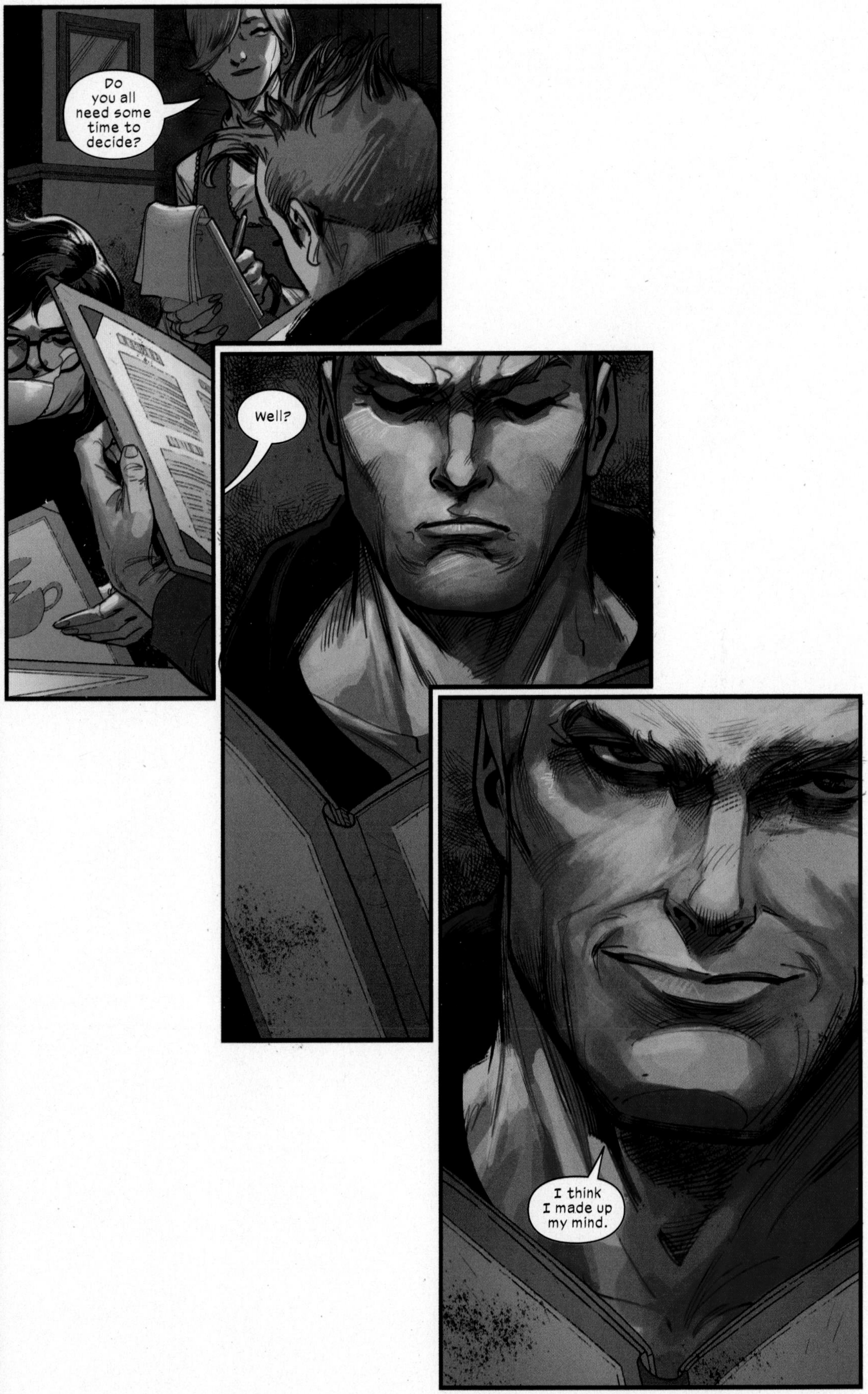
Do you all need some time to decide?
Well?
I think I made up my mind.

[reign_of_x]

[kra_]
[koa_]

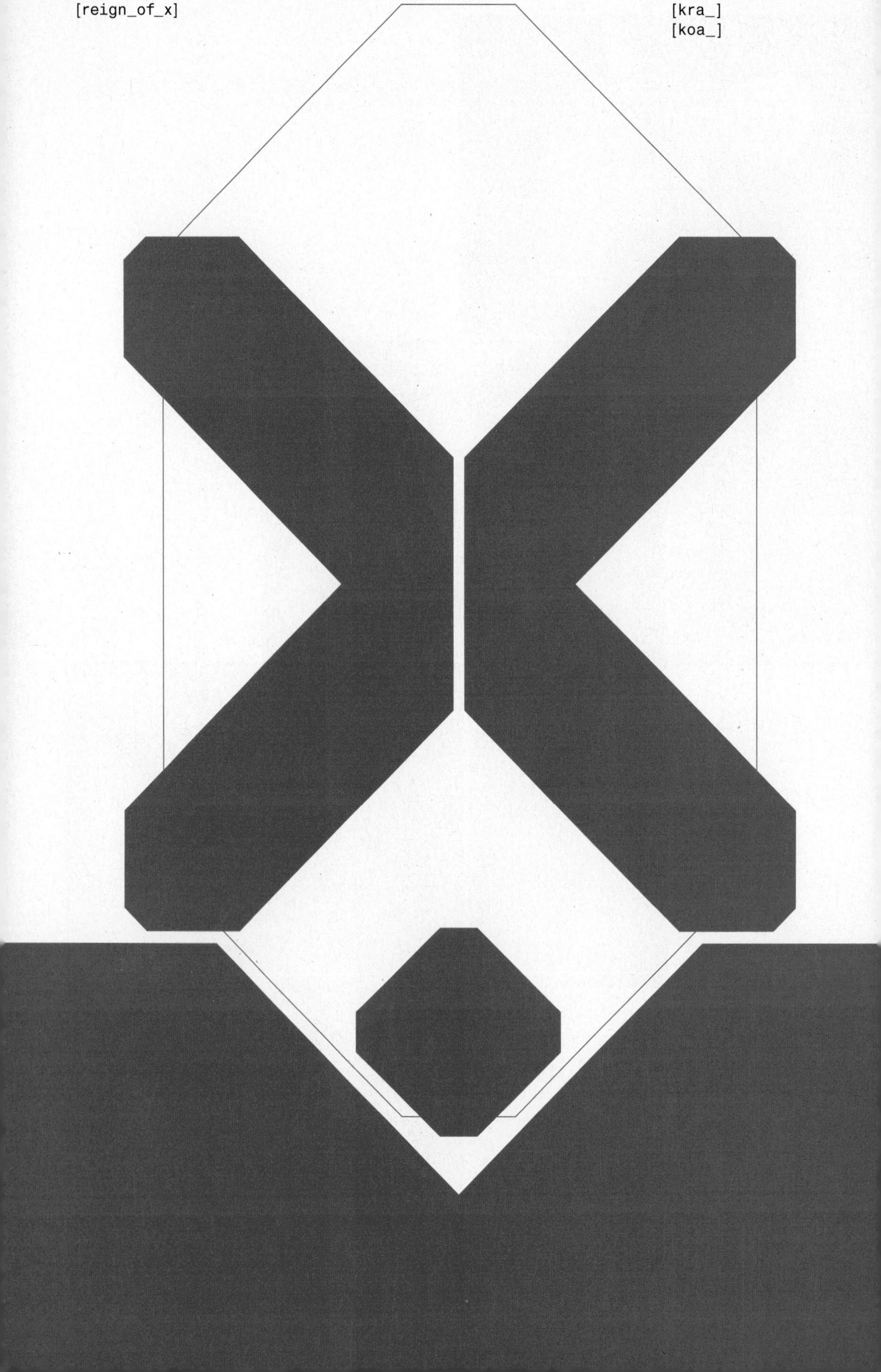

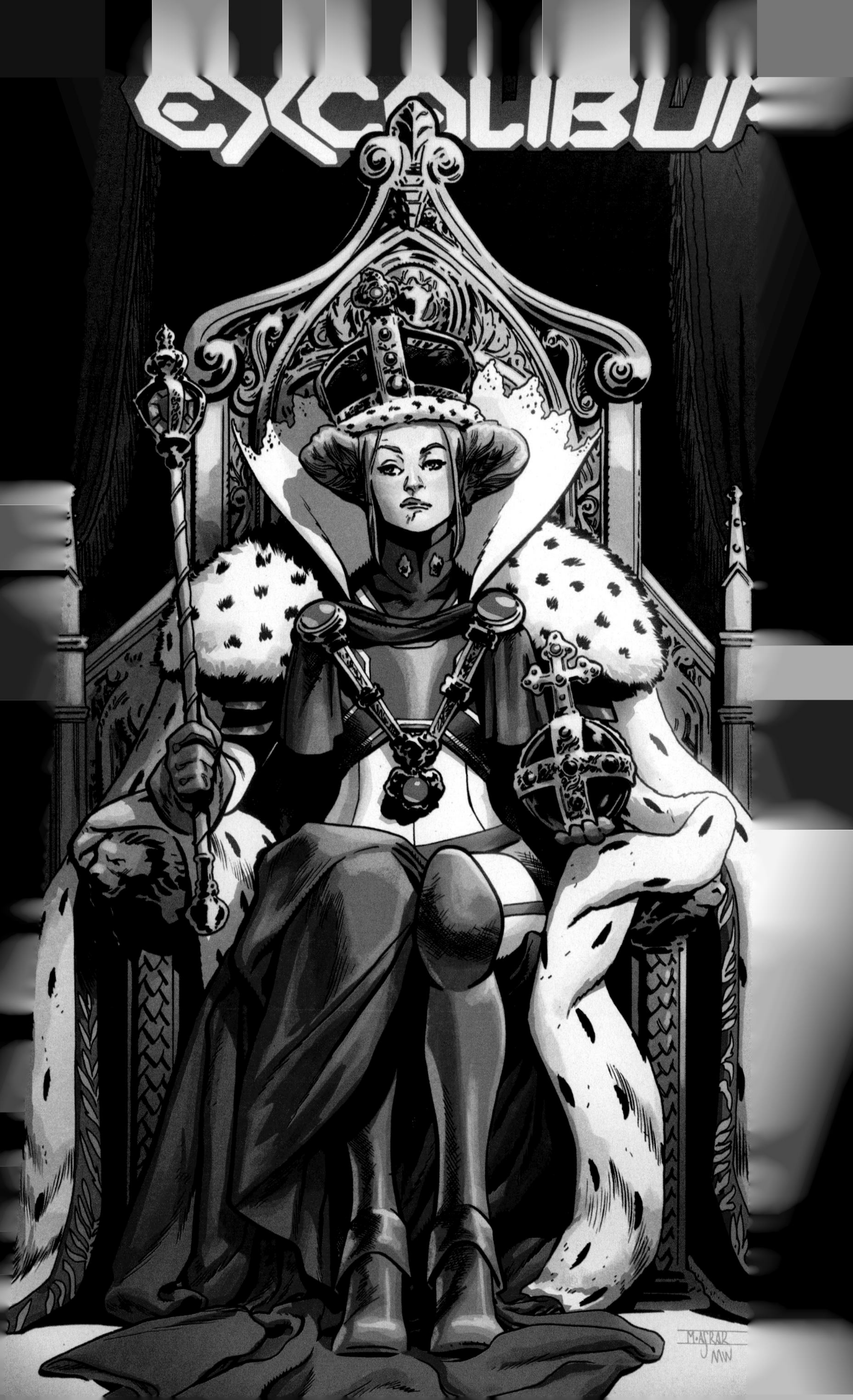

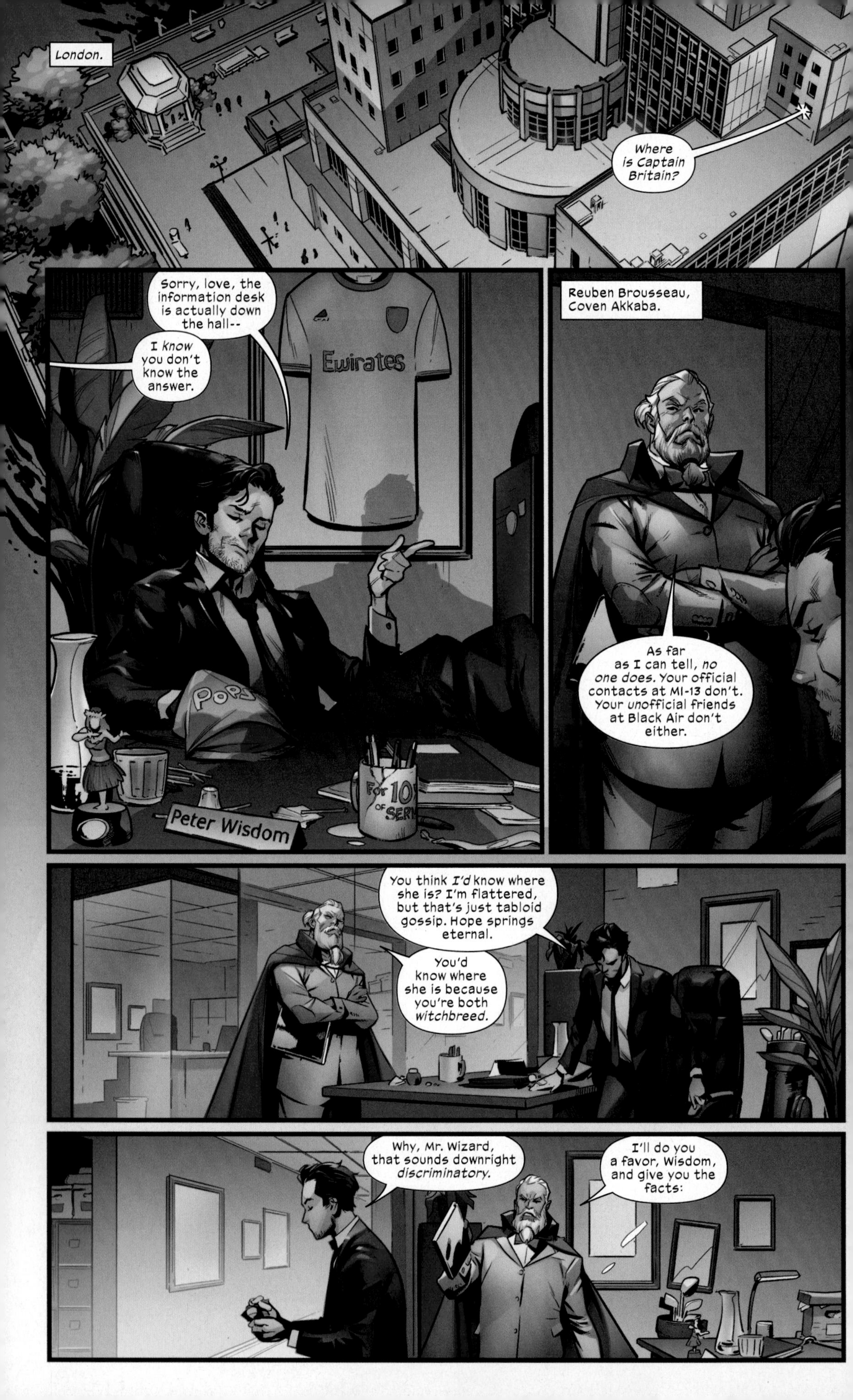
London.
Where is Captain Britain?
Sorry, love, the information desk is actually down the hall--
I know you don't know the answer.
Ewirates
Peter Wisdom
Reuben Brousseau, Coven Akkaba.
As far as I can tell, no one does. Your official contacts at MI-13 don't. Your unofficial friends at Black Air don't either.
You think I'd know where she is? I'm flattered, but that's just tabloid gossip. Hope springs eternal.
You'd know where she is because you're both witchbreed.
Why, Mr. Wizard, that sounds downright discriminatory.
I'll do you a favor, Wisdom, and give you the facts:

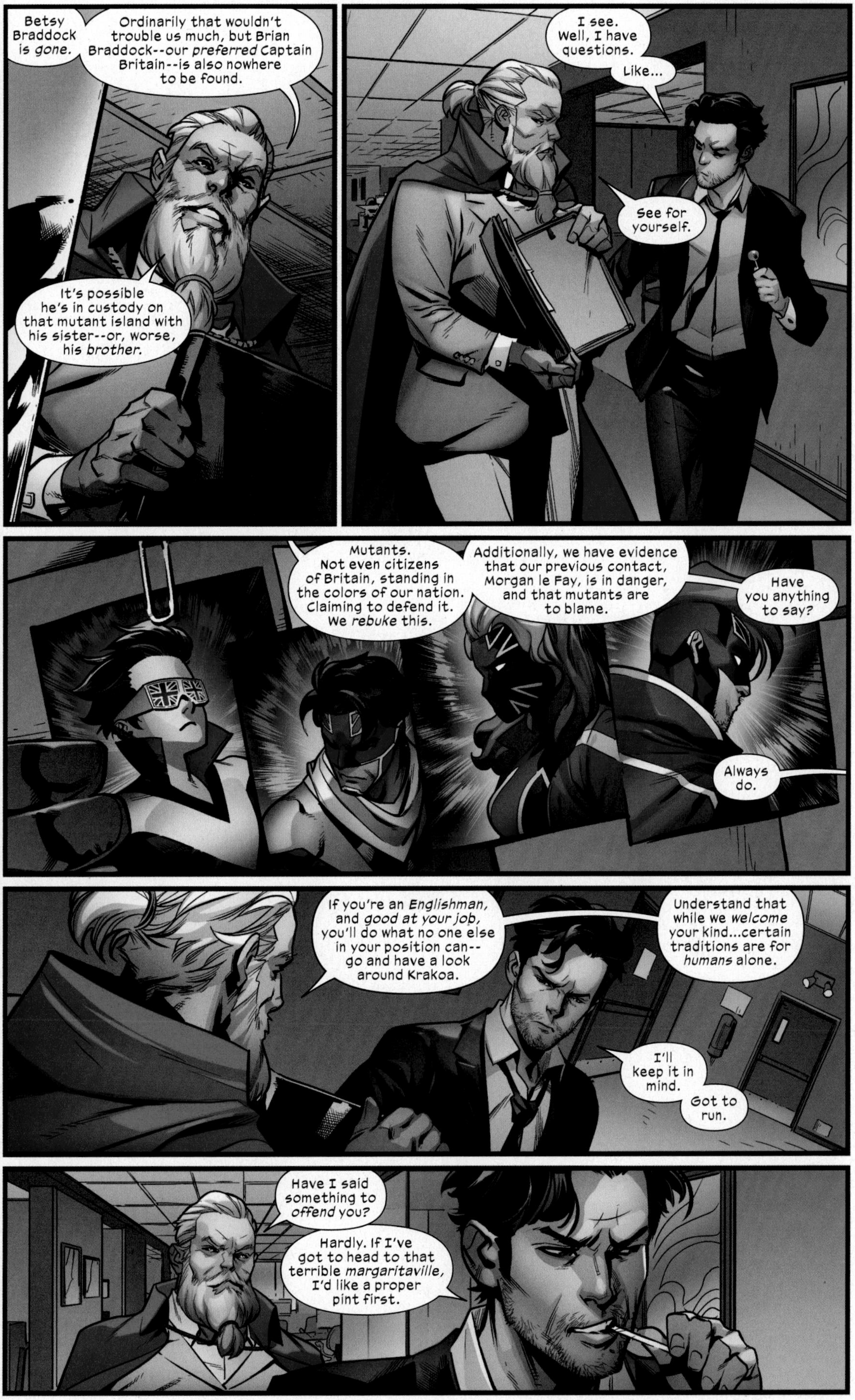
Betsy Braddock is *gone.*
Ordinarily that wouldn't trouble us much, but Brian Braddock--our *preferred* Captain Britain--is also nowhere to be found.
It's possible he's in custody on that mutant island with his sister--or, worse, his *brother.*
I see. Well, I have questions.
Like...
See for yourself.
Mutants. Not even citizens of Britain, standing in the colors of our nation. Claiming to defend it. We *rebuke* this.
Additionally, we have evidence that our previous contact, Morgan le Fay, is in danger, and that mutants are to blame.
Have you anything to say?
Always do.
If you're an *Englishman,* and *good at your job,* you'll do what no one else in your position can--go and have a look around Krakoa.
Understand that while we *welcome* your kind...certain traditions are for *humans* alone.
I'll keep it in mind.
Got to run.
Have I said something to *offend* you?
Hardly. If I've got to head to that terrible *margaritaville,* I'd like a proper pint first.

OTHER LIVES AND DIMENSIONS

A new Captain Britain Corps -- consisting of Betsy Braddocks from across the multiverse -- now stands at the ready. The only problem? EXCALIBUR can't find their Captain Britain... because she's stranded in another dimension... where she's not only Captain Britain... she's also the Queen of England.

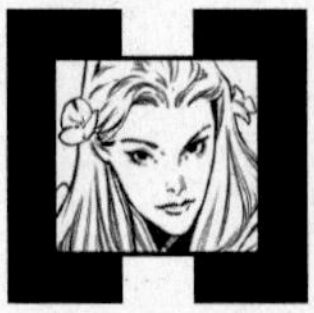
Captain Britain

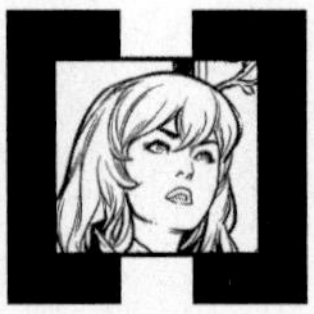
Rogue

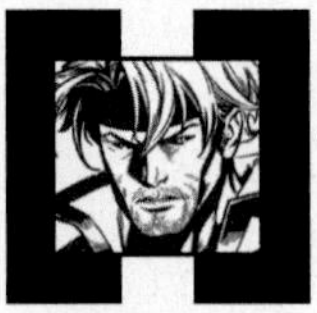
Gambit

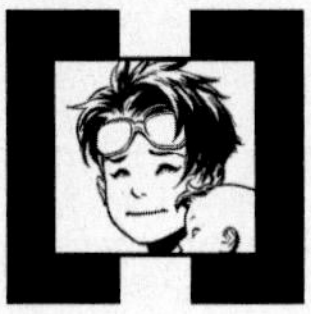
Jubilee

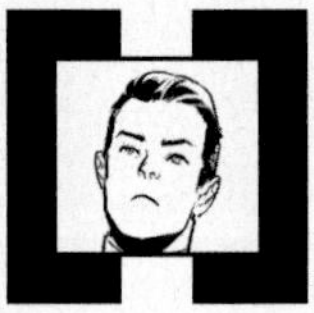
Rictor

EXCALIBUR
[X_17]

[ISSUE SEVENTEEN]...............................
....QEIII

TINI HOWARD.......................................[WRITER]
MARCUS TO...[ARTIST]
ERICK ARCINIEGA..............................[COLOR ARTIST]
VC's ARIANA MAHER...............................[LETTERER]
TOM MULLER..[DESIGN]

MAHMUD ASRAR & MATTHEW WILSON...............[COVER ARTISTS]

JONATHAN HICKMAN.................................[HEAD OF X]
JAY BOWEN & NICK RUSSELL.......................[PRODUCTION]
ANNALISE BISSA............................[ASSISTANT EDITOR]
JORDAN D. WHITE...................................[EDITOR]
C.B. CEBULSKI............................[EDITOR IN CHIEF]

[00_so_below_X]
[00_as_above_X]

[00_00....0]
[00_00....1]

[00_this____]
[00_world___]

[00_and_the_]

[00___other_]

[!] IN CASE OF OMNIVERSAL TROUBLE [!]

Captain Britain:

If you are reading this, it means that something has happened to displace me from my home dimension. As a member of the Captain Britain Corps, and a head of state, this is an eventuality that I must responsibly prepare for.

I must insist, that effective immediately, you refrain from showing your face outside of the palace in any way. The peace we keep with our allies is tenuous and precious to our kind. If it is known that I am missing, our enemies might strike against us.

The England of our line is the safest home mutants have ever known. I do not know from where you hail or what kind of life you have led. If the prospect of such a paradise tempts you to stay, I must caution you instead to lean on the honor and virtue that makes you a fine captain and protect this place by turning away.

You must return to your home reality. You mustn't threaten the peace of the mutants here, those born here and the ones who have immigrated here in search of a life mutants have never had. I do not know who you are, but it is likely you are a version of me — so I urge you to look into the heart we share and do what is right, even when it is not popular or comfortable.

Avoid the temptation to check in on differences between what you know from your reality and others. This is a distraction at best, and at worst, a dangerous game. While you may come from a reality with less responsibilities than the ones you have here, here you are the queen of what is currently the safest nation in the world for mutants.

We have never had a home like this in all of our history.

It is our duty to preserve this for them. Further instructions and materials are provided within.

— Elizabeth R. III

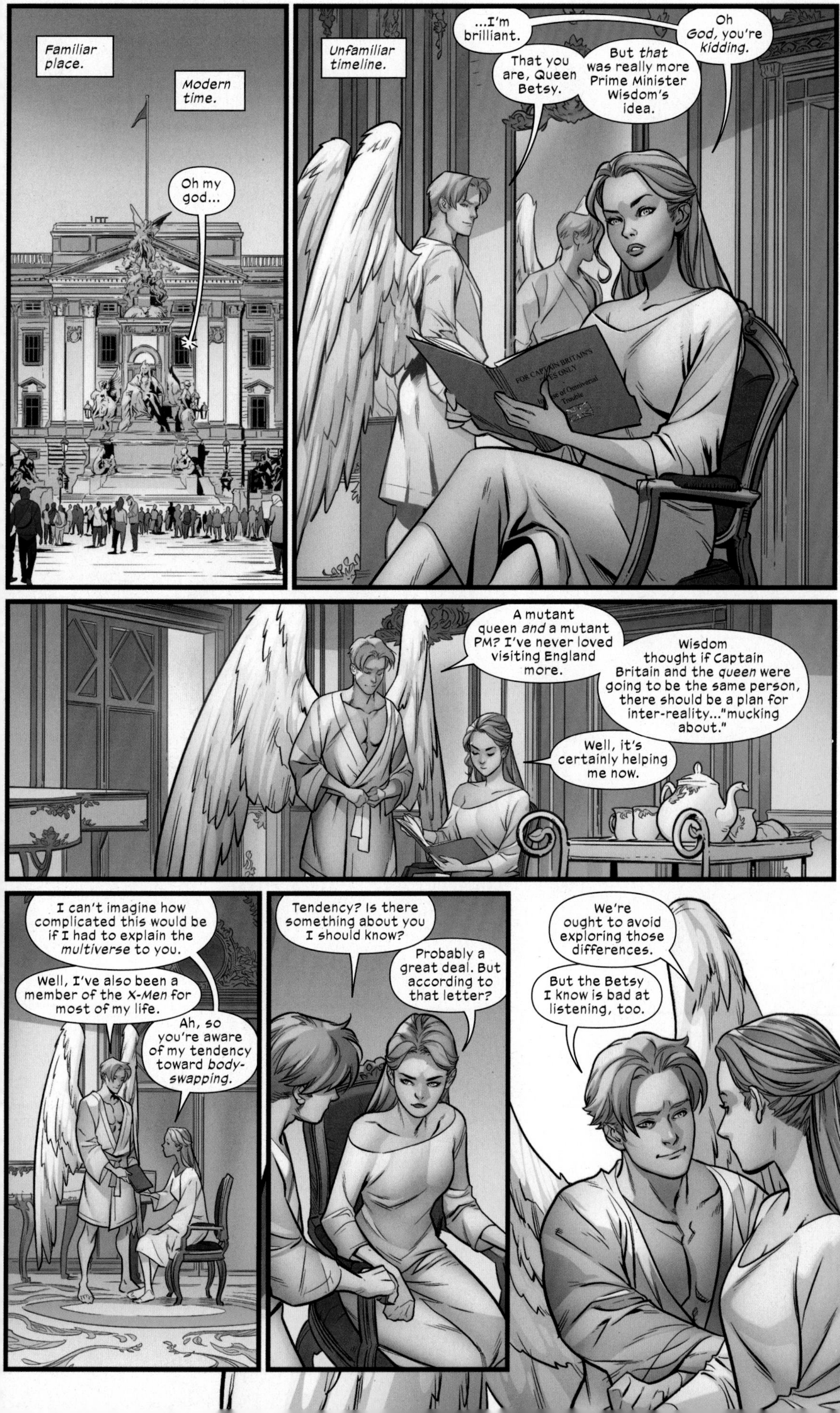
Familiar place.
Modern time.
Oh my god...
Unfamiliar timeline.
...I'm brilliant.
Oh God, you're kidding.
That you are, Queen Betsy.
But that was really more Prime Minister Wisdom's idea.
A mutant queen and a mutant PM? I've never loved visiting England more.
Wisdom thought if Captain Britain and the queen were going to be the same person, there should be a plan for inter-reality..."mucking about."
Well, it's certainly helping me now.
I can't imagine how complicated this would be if I had to explain the multiverse to you.
Well, I've also been a member of the X-Men for most of my life.
Ah, so you're aware of my tendency toward body-swapping.
Tendency? Is there something about you I should know?
Probably a great deal. But according to that letter?
We're ought to avoid exploring those differences.
But the Betsy I know is bad at listening, too.

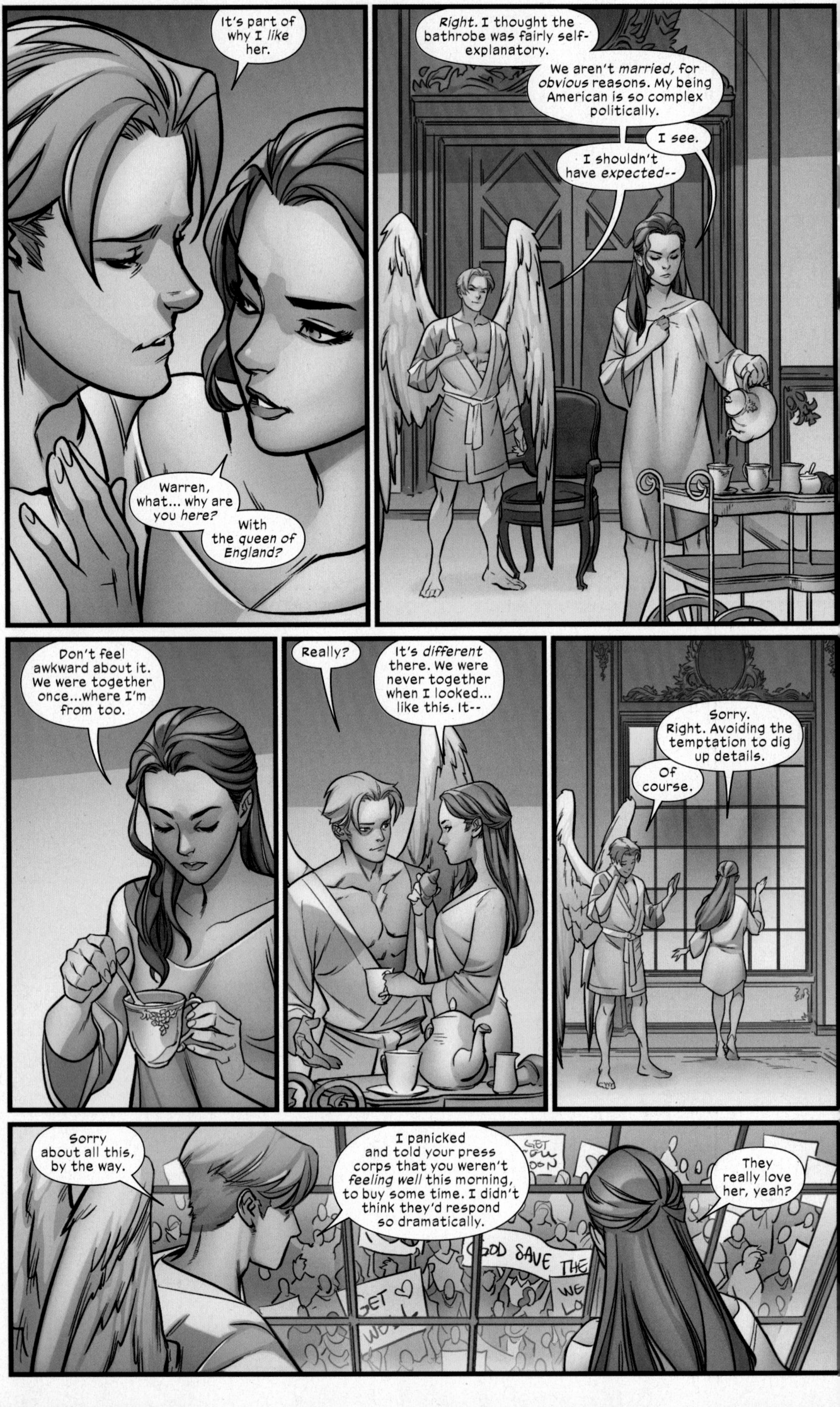
It's part of why I *like* her.
Warren, what... why are you *here?*
With the *queen of England?*
Right. I thought the bathrobe was fairly self-explanatory.
We aren't *married,* for *obvious* reasons. My being American is so complex politically.
I see.
I shouldn't have *expected*--
Don't feel awkward about it. We were together once...where I'm from too.
Really?
It's *different* there. We were never together when I looked... like this. It--
Sorry. Right. Avoiding the temptation to dig up details.
Of course.
Sorry about all this, by the way.
I panicked and told your press corps that you weren't *feeling well* this morning, to buy some time. I didn't think they'd respond so dramatically.
They really love her, yeah?
GOD SAVE THE

They really love *you*, queen Betsy.

No, they don't. I'm not her.

TNK

That's precisely why I have to *leave*, remember?

We've a plan to execute.

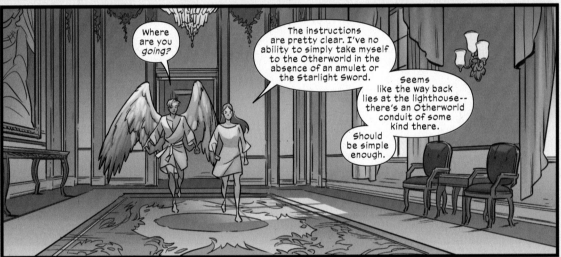

Where are you *going*?

The instructions are pretty clear. I've no ability to simply take myself to the Otherworld in the absence of an amulet or the Starlight Sword.

Seems like the way back lies at the lighthouse-- there's an Otherworld conduit of some kind there.

Should be simple enough.

Well, *all right*, your Majesty, but allow me to call you an escort before you go bumbling off alone to the *lighthouse*.

Bumbling? An escort?

In the interest of leaving out details-- I don't *need* an escort. I don't know about the *queen*, but *I* spent a few years in the *covert world*.

Well, you didn't *here*. And you don't know where you're going.

You'll need someone to cover for you and ensure you get there unbothered and *unseen*.

I suppose you think *you're* the right man for the job?

Absolutely not. As it is, I'm 90 minutes late for a board meeting.

I'm getting you the best mutant-for-hire I know. She'll get you in and out without anyone seeing you, I assure you. It might be a bit awkward though...

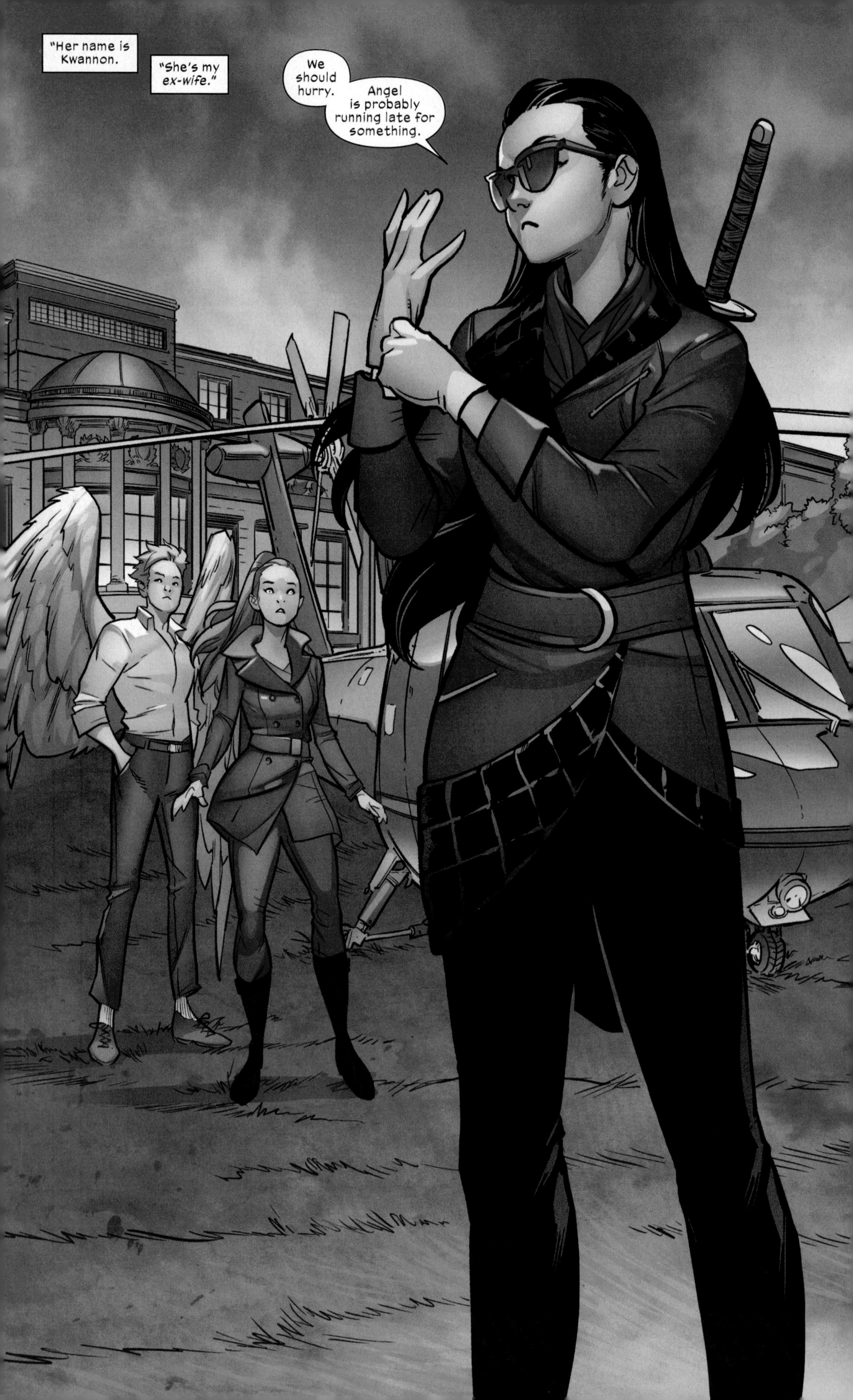
"Her name is Kwannon.
"She's my *ex-wife*."
We should hurry.
Angel is probably running late for something.

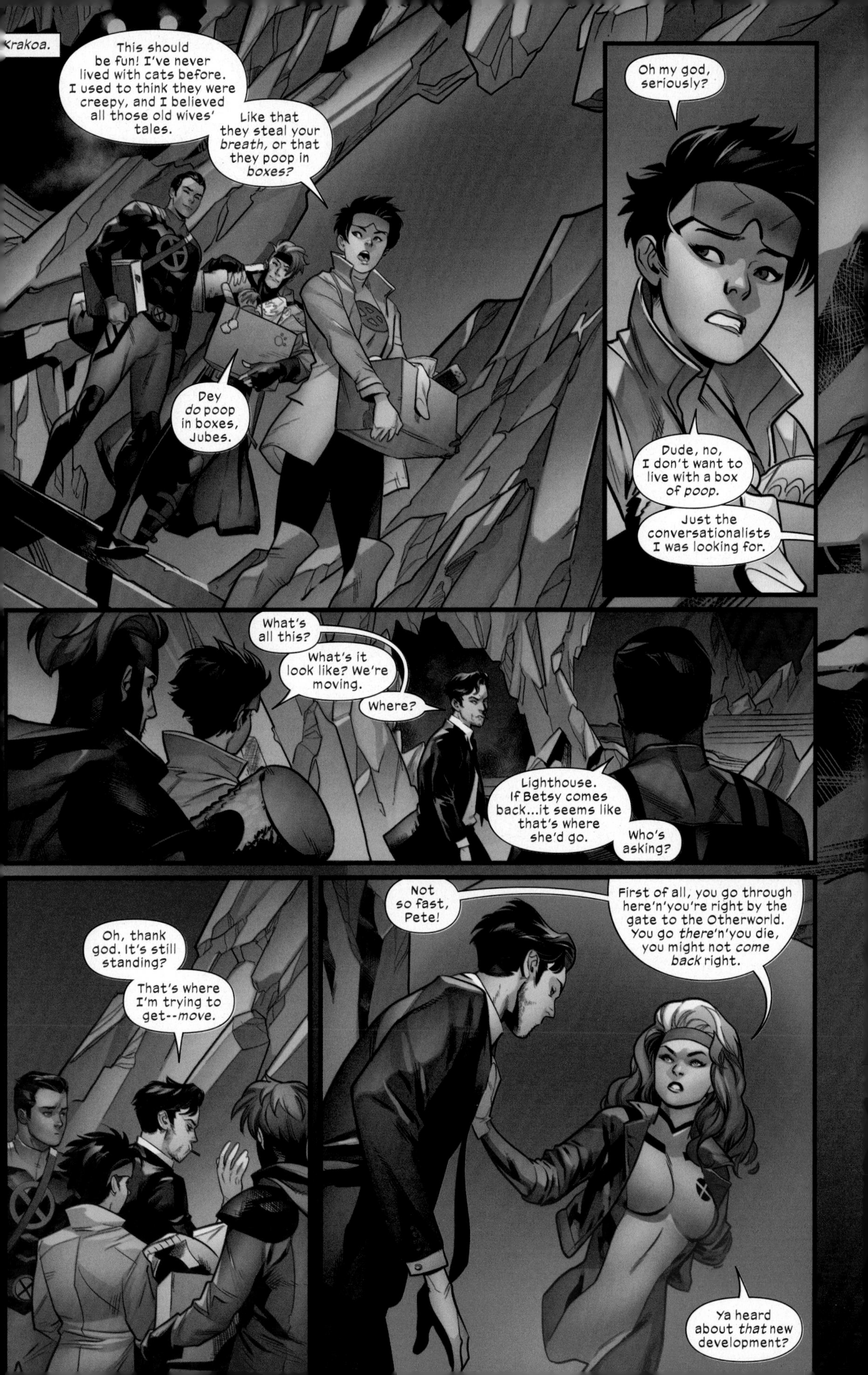

Krakoa.
This should be fun! I've never lived with cats before. I used to think they were creepy, and I believed all those old wives' tales.
Like that they steal your *breath,* or that they poop in *boxes?*
Dey *do* poop in boxes, Jubes.
Oh my god, seriously?
Dude, no, I don't want to live with a box of *poop.*
Just the conversationalists I was looking for.
What's all this?
What's it look like? We're moving.
Where?
Lighthouse. If Betsy comes back...it seems like that's where she'd go.
Who's asking?
Oh, thank god. It's still standing?
That's where I'm trying to get--*move.*
Not so fast, Pete!
First of all, you go through here'n'you're right by the gate to the Otherworld. You go *there*'n'you die, you might not *come back* right.
Ya heard about *that* new development?

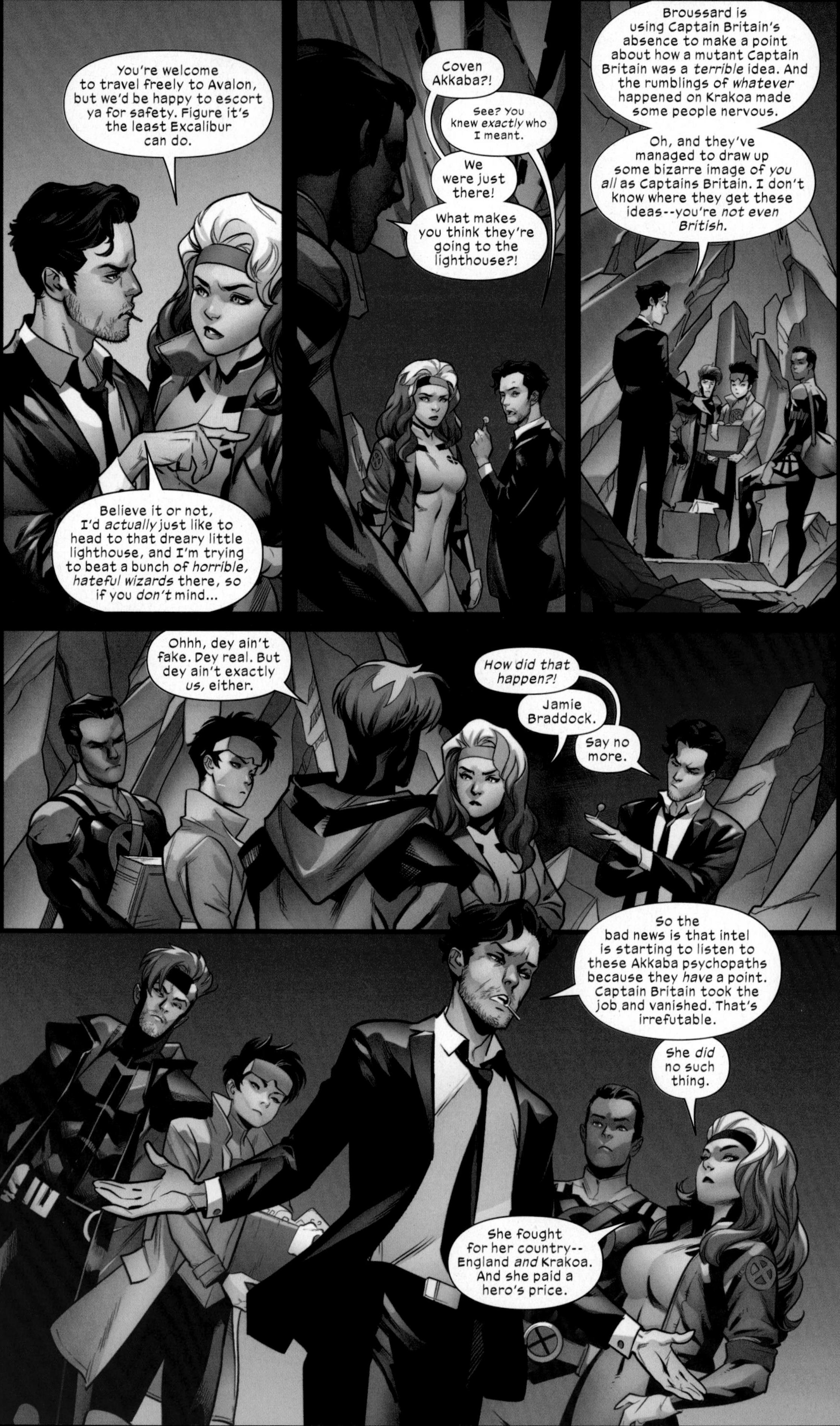

You're welcome to travel freely to Avalon, but we'd be happy to escort ya for safety. Figure it's the least Excalibur can do.
Believe it or not, I'd *actually* just like to head to that dreary little lighthouse, and I'm trying to beat a bunch of *horrible, hateful wizards* there, so if you *don't* mind...
Coven Akkaba?!
See? You knew *exactly* who I meant.
We were just there!
What makes you think they're going to the lighthouse?!
Broussard is using Captain Britain's absence to make a point about how a mutant Captain Britain was a *terrible* idea. And the rumblings of *whatever* happened on Krakoa made some people nervous.
Oh, and they've managed to draw up some bizarre image of *you all* as Captains Britain. I don't know where they get these ideas--you're *not even British.*
Ohhh, dey ain't fake. Dey real. But dey ain't exactly *us,* either.
How did that happen?!
Jamie Braddock.
Say no more.
So the bad news is that intel is starting to listen to these Akkaba psychopaths because they *have* a point. Captain Britain took the job and vanished. That's irrefutable.
She *did* no such thing.
She fought for her country-- England *and* Krakoa. And she paid a hero's price.

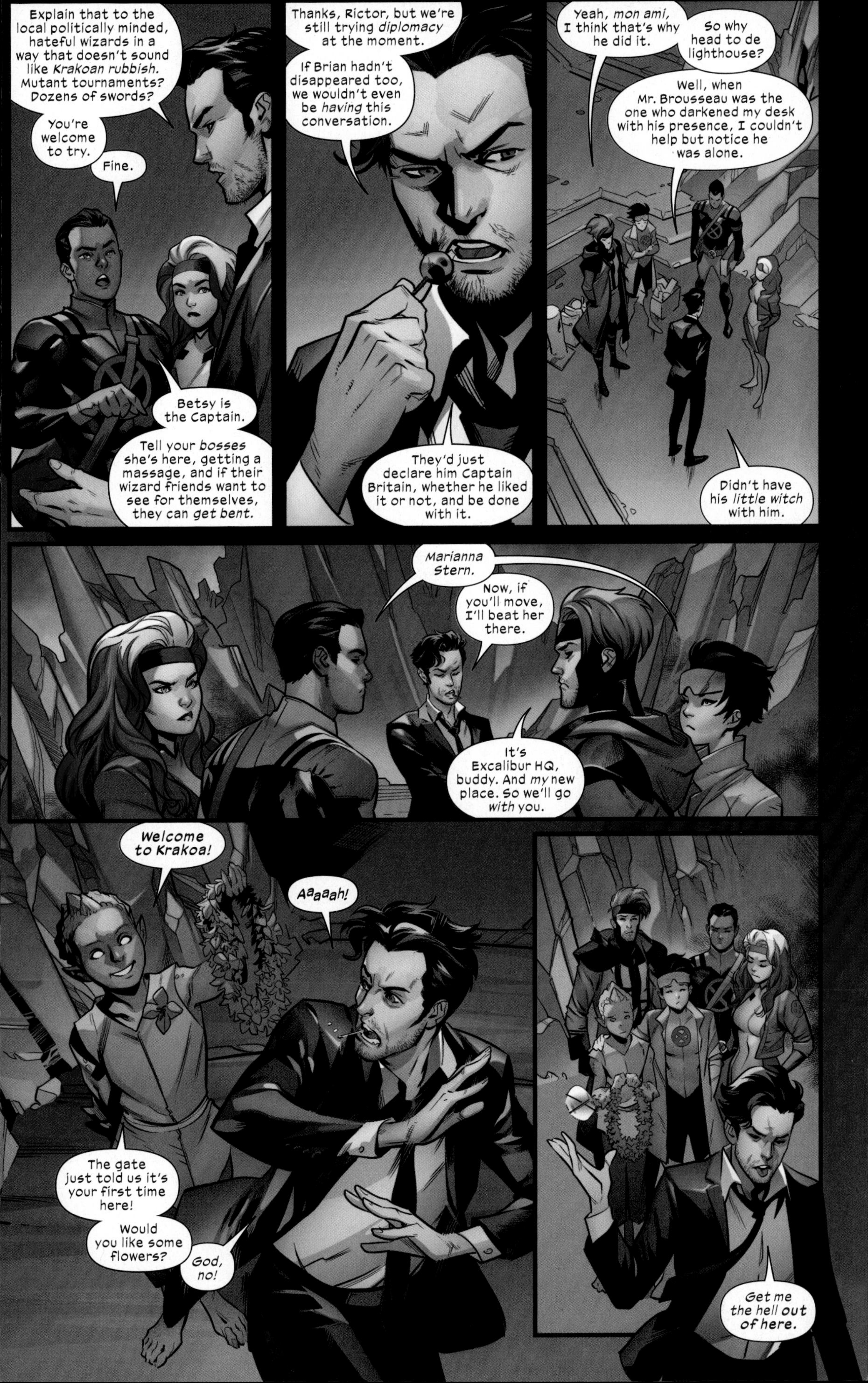

Explain that to the local politically minded, hateful wizards in a way that doesn't sound like *Krakoan rubbish.* Mutant tournaments? Dozens of swords?
You're welcome to try.
Fine.
Betsy is the Captain.
Tell your *bosses* she's here, getting a massage, and if their wizard friends want to see for themselves, they can *get bent.*
Thanks, Rictor, but we're still trying *diplomacy* at the moment.
If Brian hadn't disappeared too, we wouldn't even be *having* this conversation.
They'd just declare him Captain Britain, whether he liked it or not, and be done with it.
Yeah, *mon ami,* I think that's why he did it.
So why head to de lighthouse?
Well, when Mr. Brousseau was the one who darkened my desk with his presence, I couldn't help but notice he was alone.
Didn't have his *little witch* with him.
Marianna Stern.
Now, if you'll move, I'll beat her there.
It's Excalibur HQ, buddy. And *my* new place. So we'll go *with* you.
Welcome to Krakoa!
Aaaaah!
The gate just told us it's your first time here!
Would you like some flowers?
God, no!
Get me the hell out of here.

KING JAMES III MEMORIAL INTELLIGENCE CENTER

"THE LIGHTHOUSE"

Formerly the Braddock family lighthouse, the crumbling structure was torn down and made into a state-of-the-art intelligence facility following the ascension and reign of King James III.

Each reality must touch Otherworld. As it is a source of great power for the Braddock family and mutantkind, it remains highly defended from the enemies of mutantdom in QEIII's England. Without the powers inherent in Captain Britain's office, it remains the only way to access Otherworld.

Additionally, as the center of British intelligence, the site is highly defended by both mutant and human means, making it impenetrable to all but the most careful of psychics.

DIRECTOR: ALYSANDE STUART

- QEIII

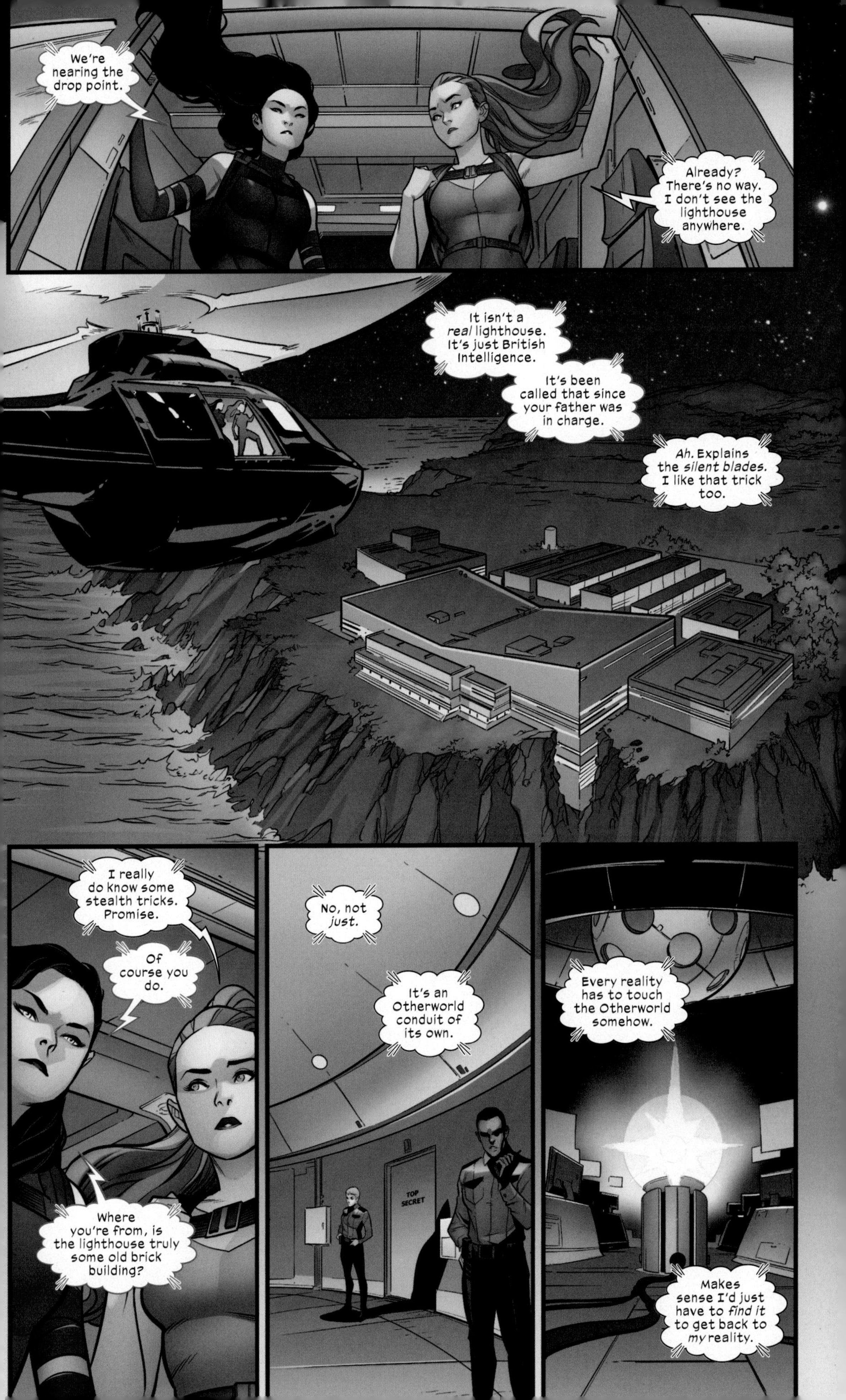
We're nearing the drop point.
Already? There's no way. I don't see the lighthouse anywhere.
It isn't a *real* lighthouse. It's just British Intelligence.
It's been called that since your father was in charge.
Ah. Explains the *silent blades.* I like that trick too.
I really do know some stealth tricks. Promise.
Of course you do.
Where you're from, is the lighthouse truly some old brick building?
No, not *just.*
It's an Otherworld conduit of its own.
TOP SECRET
Every reality has to touch the Otherworld somehow.
Makes sense I'd just have to *find it* to get back to *my* reality.

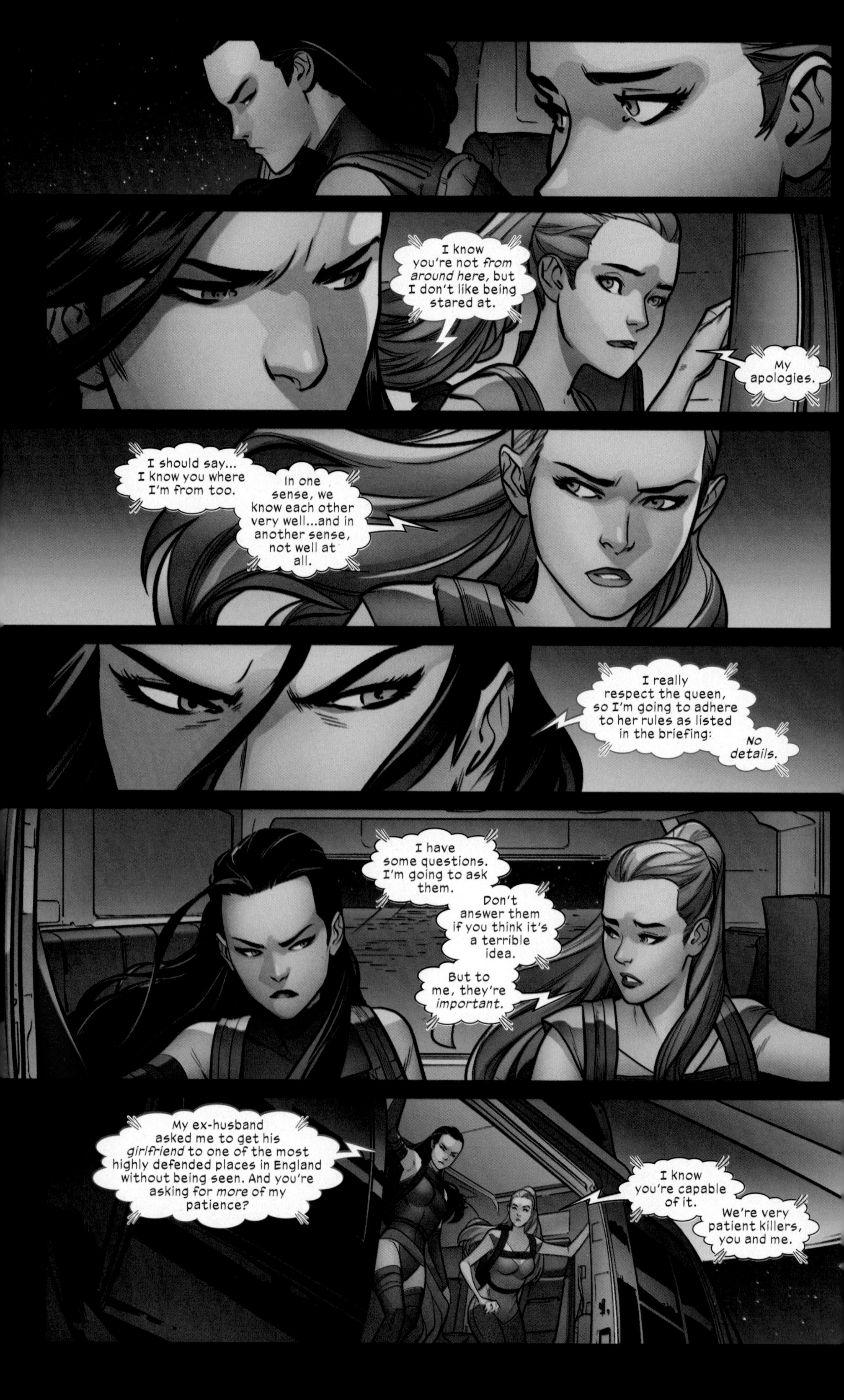
I know you're not *from around here*, but I don't like being stared at.
My apologies.
I should say... I know you where I'm from too.
In one sense, we know each other very well...and in another sense, not well at all.
I really respect the queen, so I'm going to adhere to her rules as listed in the briefing:
No details.
I have some questions. I'm going to ask them.
Don't answer them if you think it's a terrible idea.
But to me, they're *important*.
My ex-husband asked me to get his *girlfriend* to one of the most highly defended places in England without being seen. And you're asking for *more* of my patience?
I know you're capable of it.
We're very patient killers, you and me.

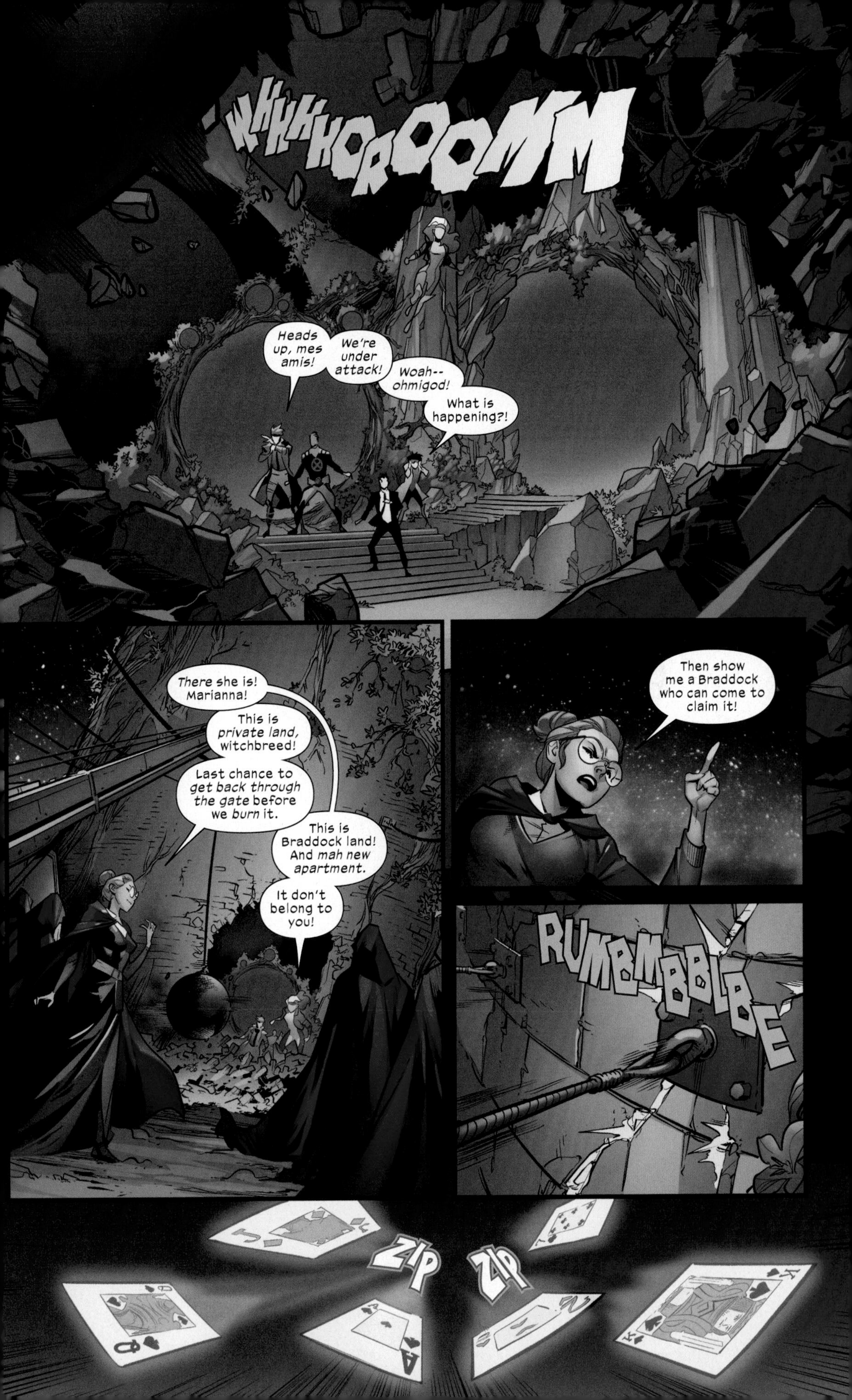
KKKKHOROOOMM
Heads up, mes amis!
We're under attack!
Woah--ohmigod!
What is happening?!
There she is! Marianna!
This is private land, witchbreed!
Last chance to get back through the gate before we burn it.
This is Braddock land! And mah new apartment.
It don't belong to you!
Then show me a Braddock who can come to claim it!
RUMBMBBLBE
ZIP
ZIP

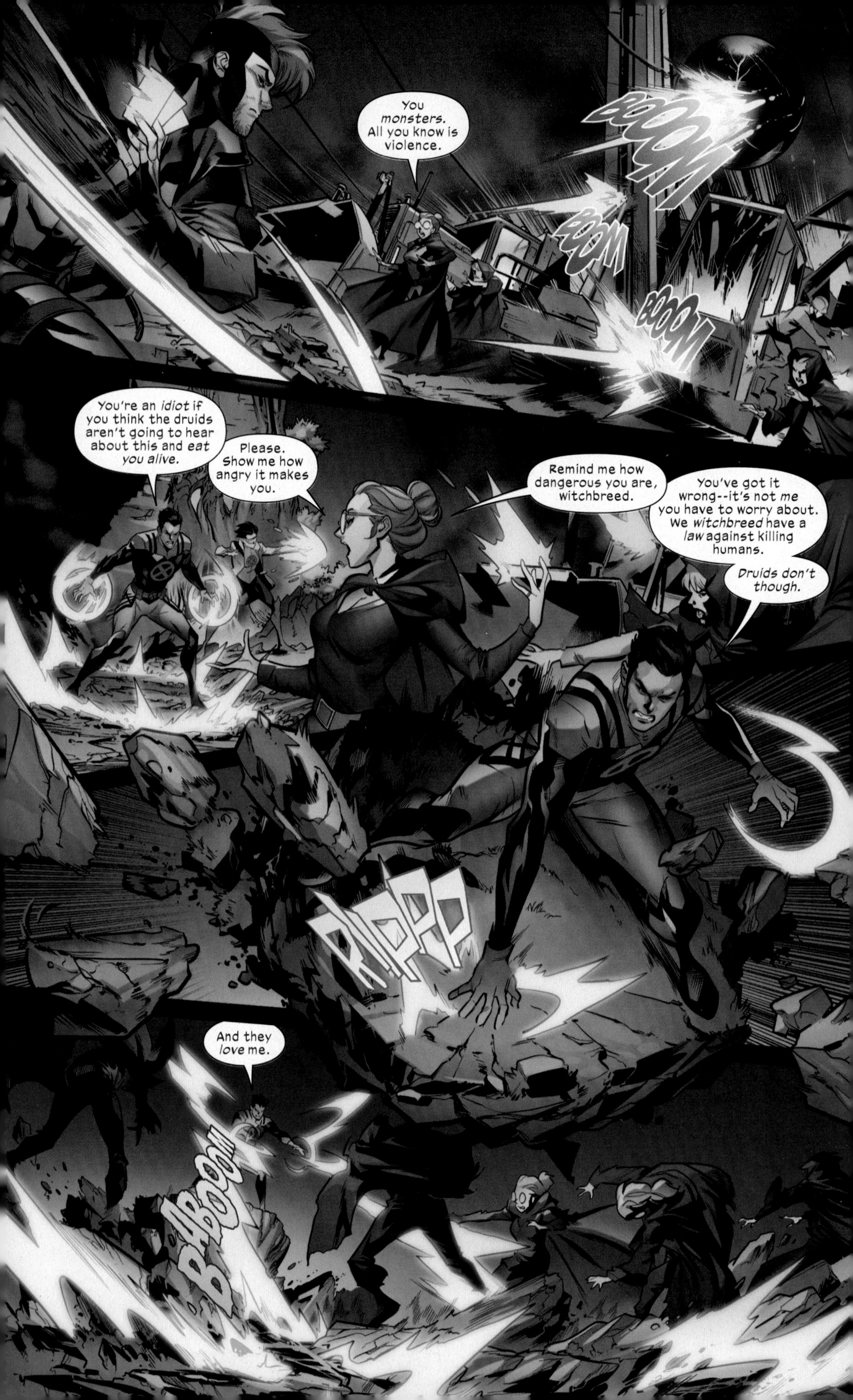

You *monsters.* All you know is violence.
BOOOM
BOOM
BOOM
You're an *idiot* if you think the druids aren't going to hear about this and *eat you alive.*
Please. Show me how angry it makes you.
Remind me how dangerous you are, witchbreed.
You've got it wrong--it's not *me* you have to worry about. We *witchbreed* have a *law* against killing humans.
Druids don't though.
RIPPP
And they *love* me.
BABOOOM

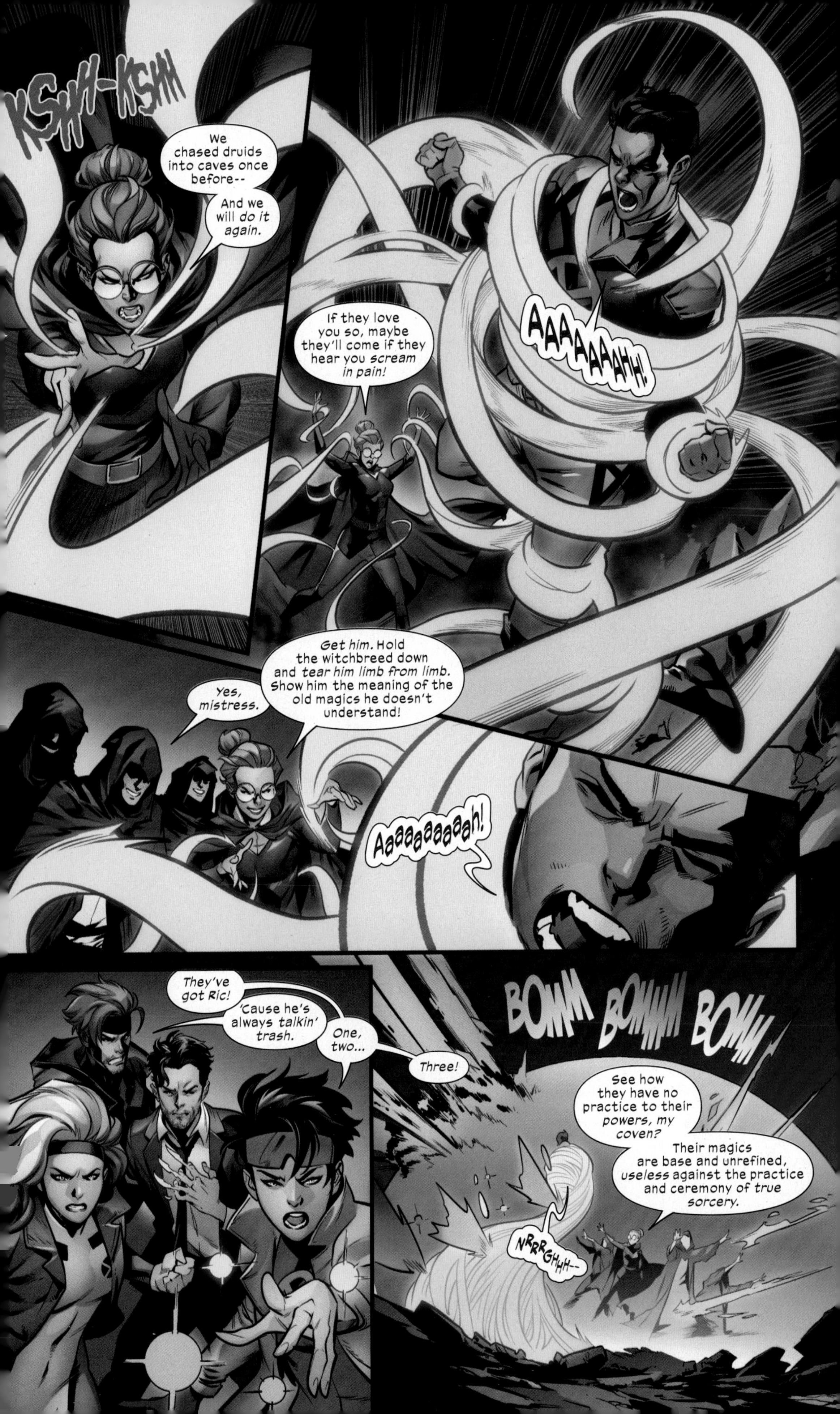
KSHH-KSHH
We chased druids into caves once before--
And we will do it again.
If they love you so, maybe they'll come if they hear you scream in pain!
AAAAAAAAHH!
Yes, mistress.
Get him. Hold the witchbreed down and tear him limb from limb. Show him the meaning of the old magics he doesn't understand!
Aaaaaaaaaah!
They've got Ric!
'Cause he's always talkin' trash.
One, two...
Three!
BOMM BOMM BOMM
See how they have no practice to their powers, my coven?
Their magics are base and unrefined, useless against the practice and ceremony of true sorcery.
NRRRGHHH--

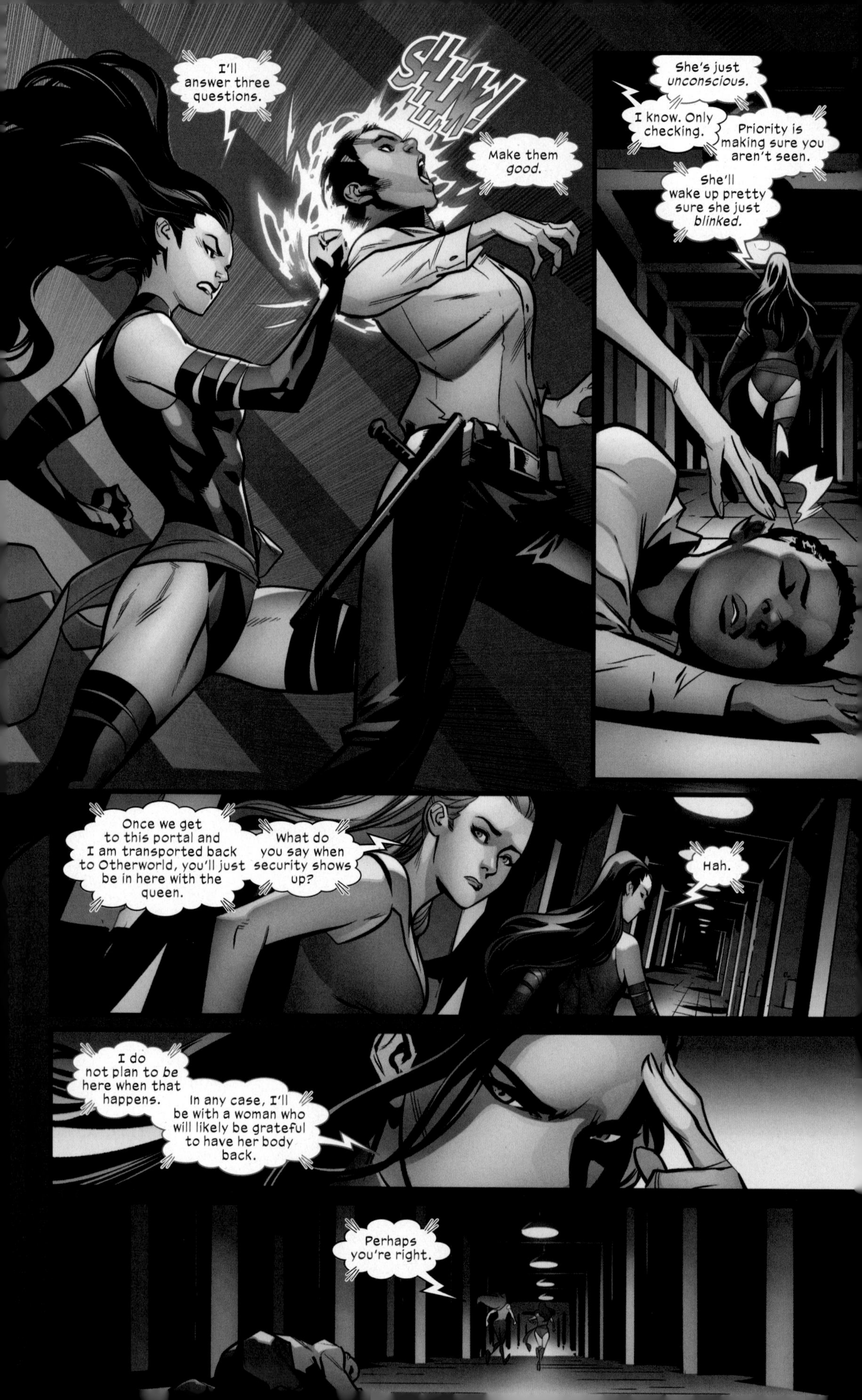
I'll answer three questions.
SHWM!
Make them *good*.
She's just *unconscious*.
I know. Only checking.
Priority is making sure you aren't seen.
She'll wake up pretty sure she just *blinked*.
Once we get to this portal and I am transported back to Otherworld, you'll just be in here with the queen.
What do you say when security shows up?
Hah.
I do not plan to *be* here when that happens.
In any case, I'll be with a woman who will likely be grateful to have her body back.
Perhaps you're right.

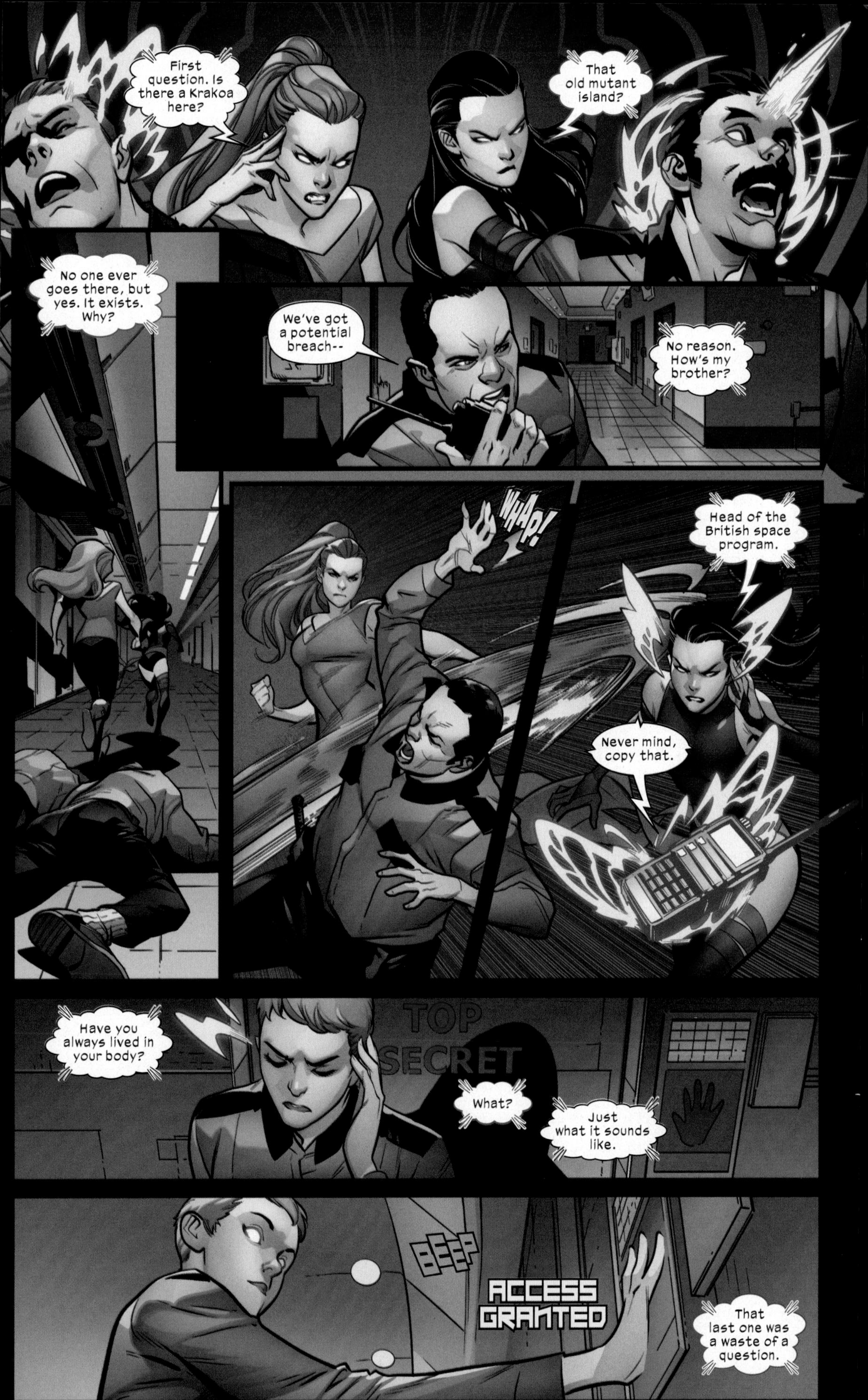

First question. Is there a Krakoa here?
That old mutant island?
No one ever goes there, but yes. It exists. Why?
We've got a potential breach--
No reason. How's my brother?
WHAP!
Head of the British space program.
Never mind, copy that.
TOP SECRET
Have you always lived in your body?
What?
Just what it sounds like.
BEEP
ACCESS GRANTED
That last one was a waste of a question.

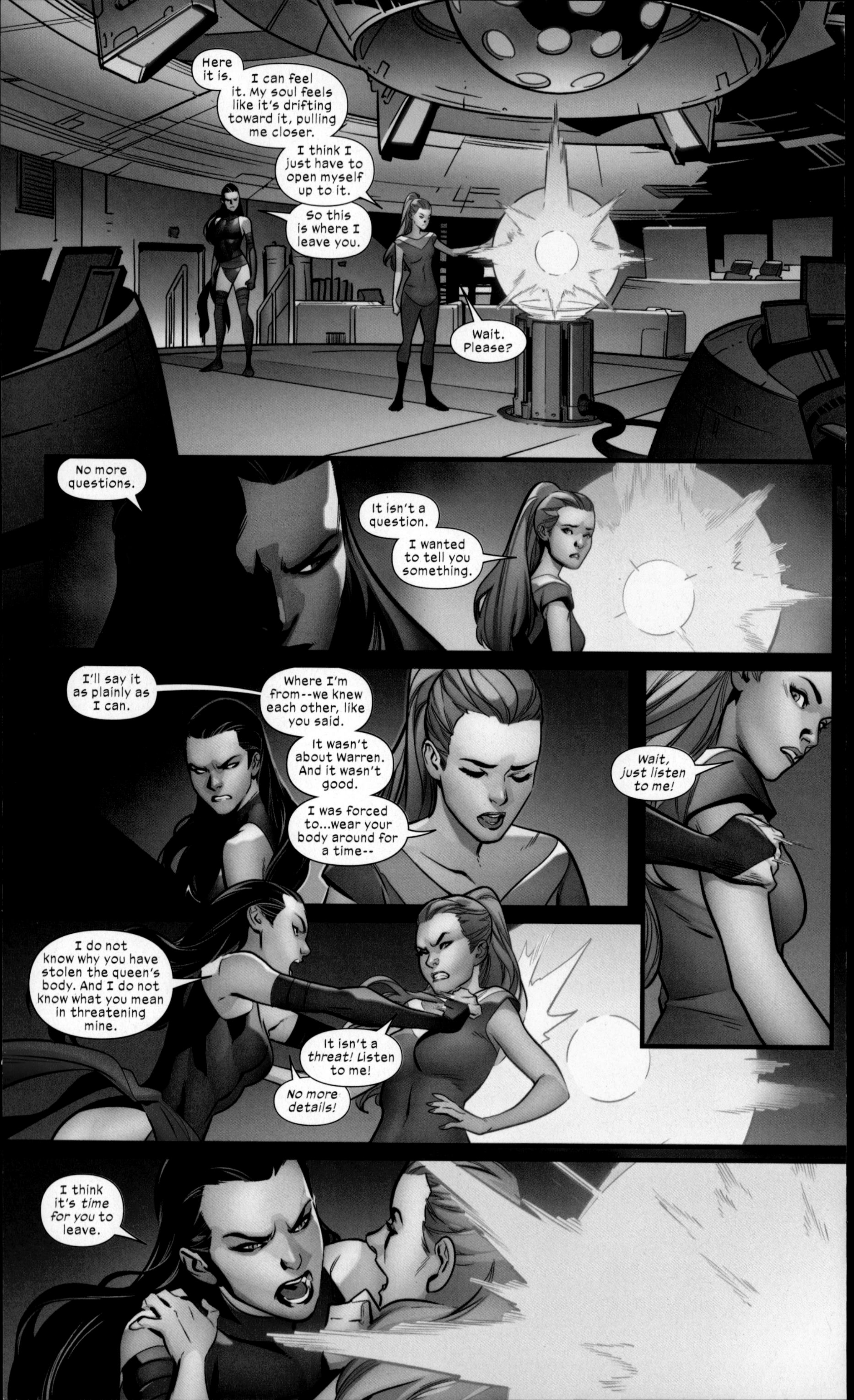
Here it is.
I can feel it. My soul feels like it's drifting toward it, pulling me closer.
I think I just have to open myself up to it.
So this is where I leave you.
Wait. Please?
No more questions.
It isn't a question.
I wanted to tell you something.
I'll say it as plainly as I can.
Where I'm from--we knew each other, like you said.
It wasn't about Warren. And it wasn't good.
I was forced to...wear your body around for a time--
Wait, just listen to me!
I do not know why you have stolen the queen's body. And I do not know what you mean in threatening mine.
It isn't a threat! Listen to me!
No more details!
I think it's time for you to leave.

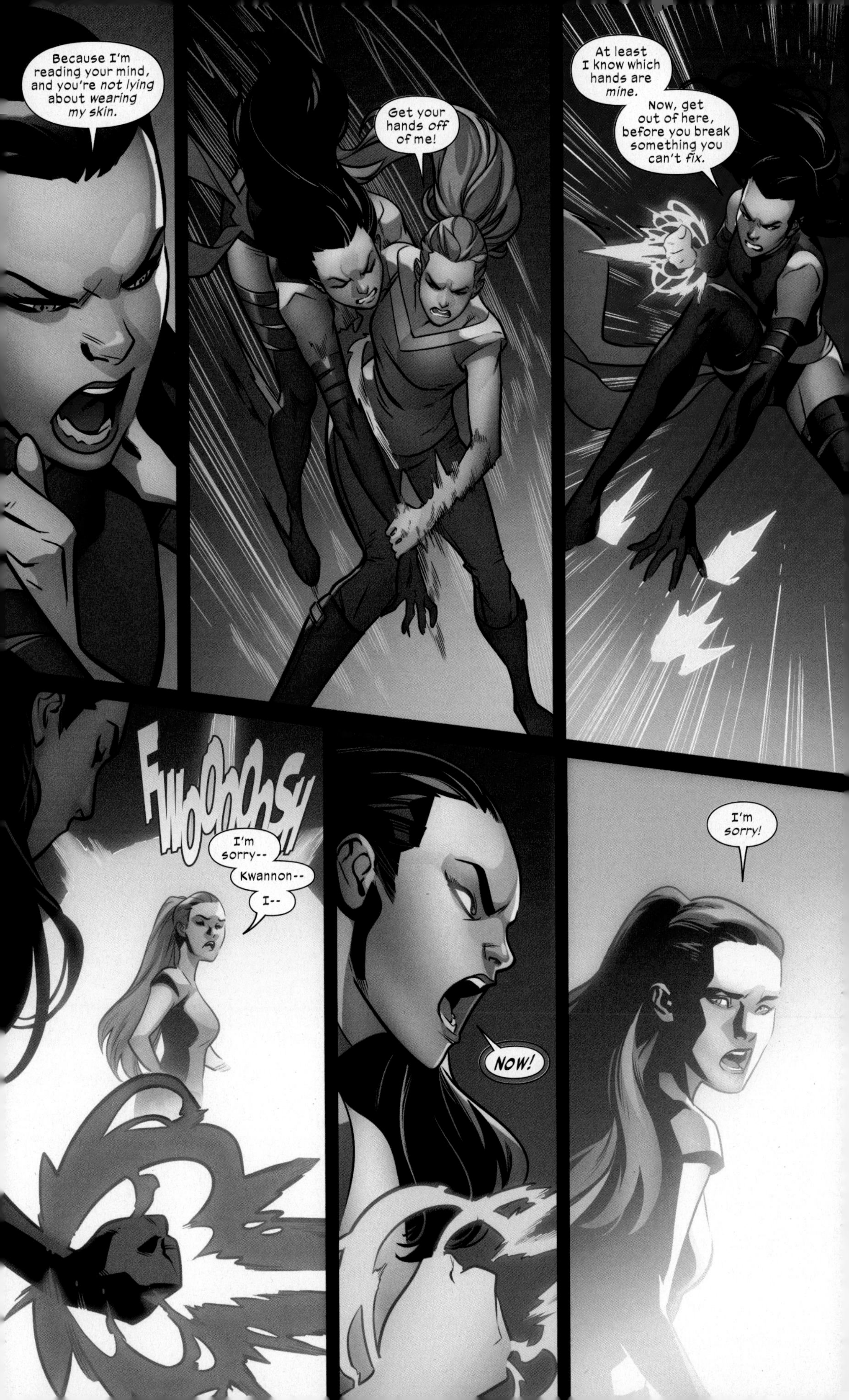

Because I'm reading your mind, and you're *not lying* about *wearing* my skin.
Get your hands *off* of me!
At least I know which hands are *mine*.
Now, get out of here, before you break something you can't *fix*.
FWOOOOSH
I'm sorry--
Kwannon--
I--
NOW!
I'm *sorry!*

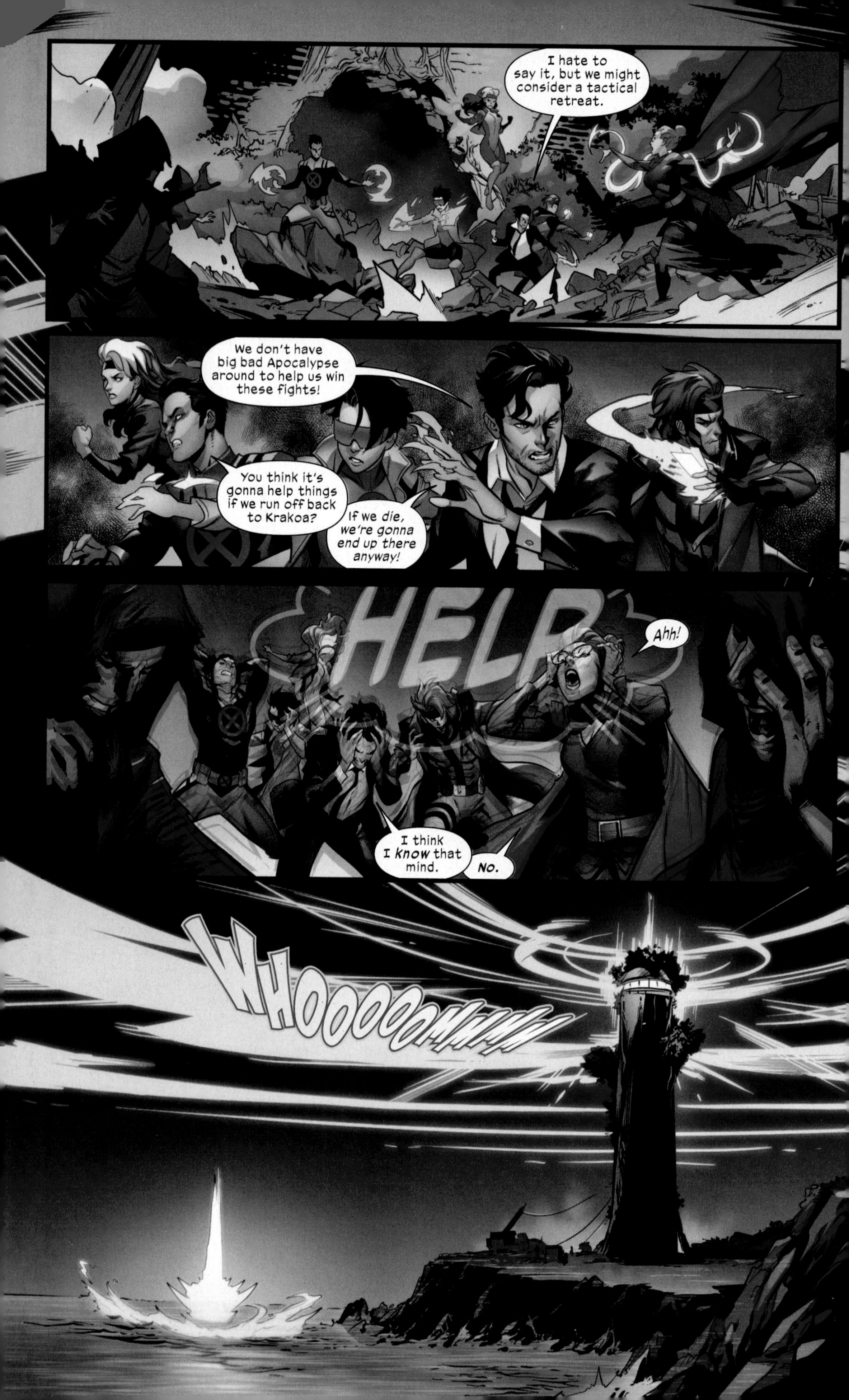

I hate to say it, but we might consider a tactical retreat.
We don't have big bad Apocalypse around to help us win these fights!
You think it's gonna help things if we run off back to Krakoa?
If we die, we're gonna end up there anyway!
HELP
Ahh!
I think I *know* that mind.
NO.
WHOOOOOMMMM

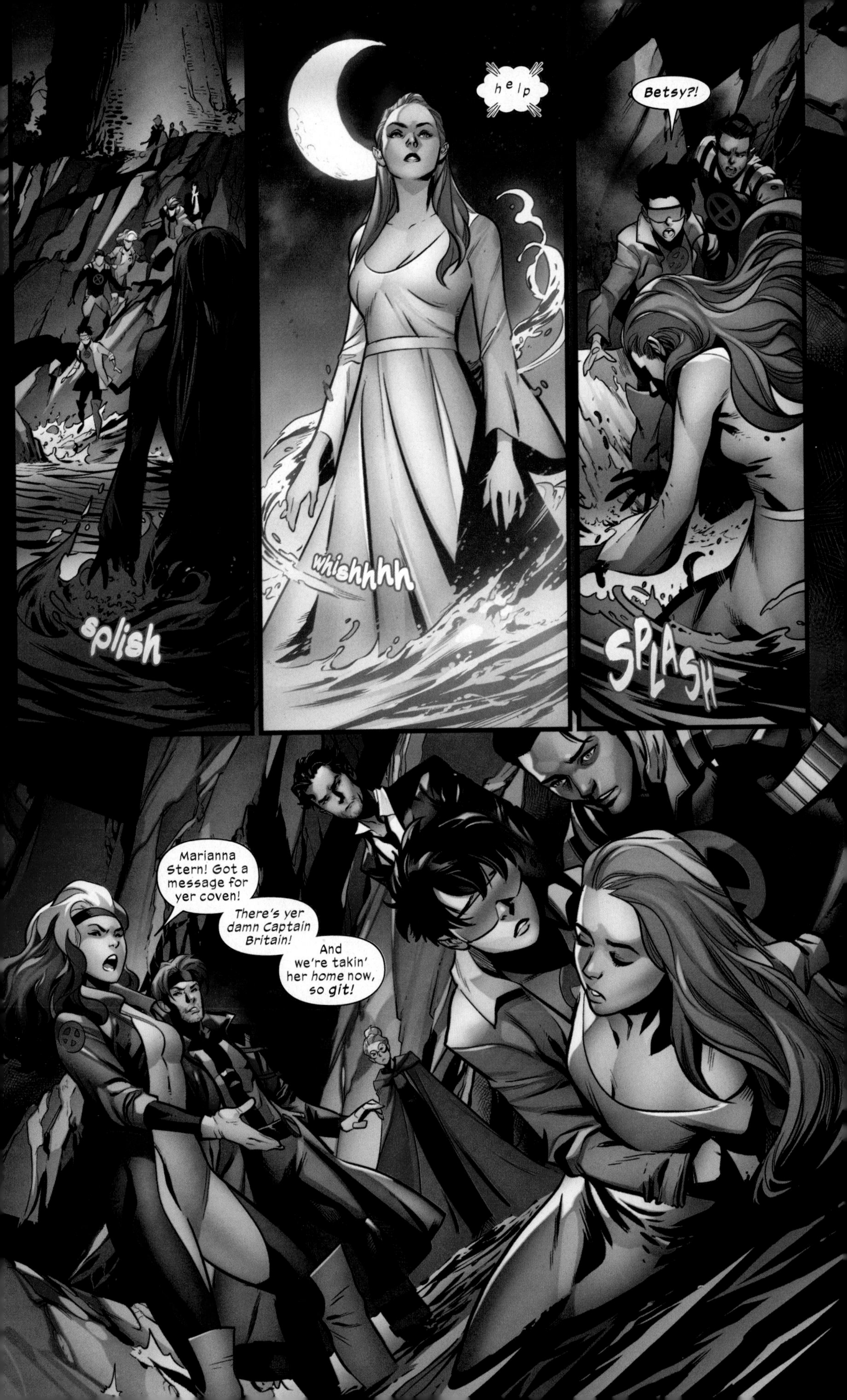
splish
help
whishhhh
Betsy?!
SPLASH
Marianna Stern! Got a message for yer coven!
There's yer damn Captain Britain!
And we're takin' her home now, so git!

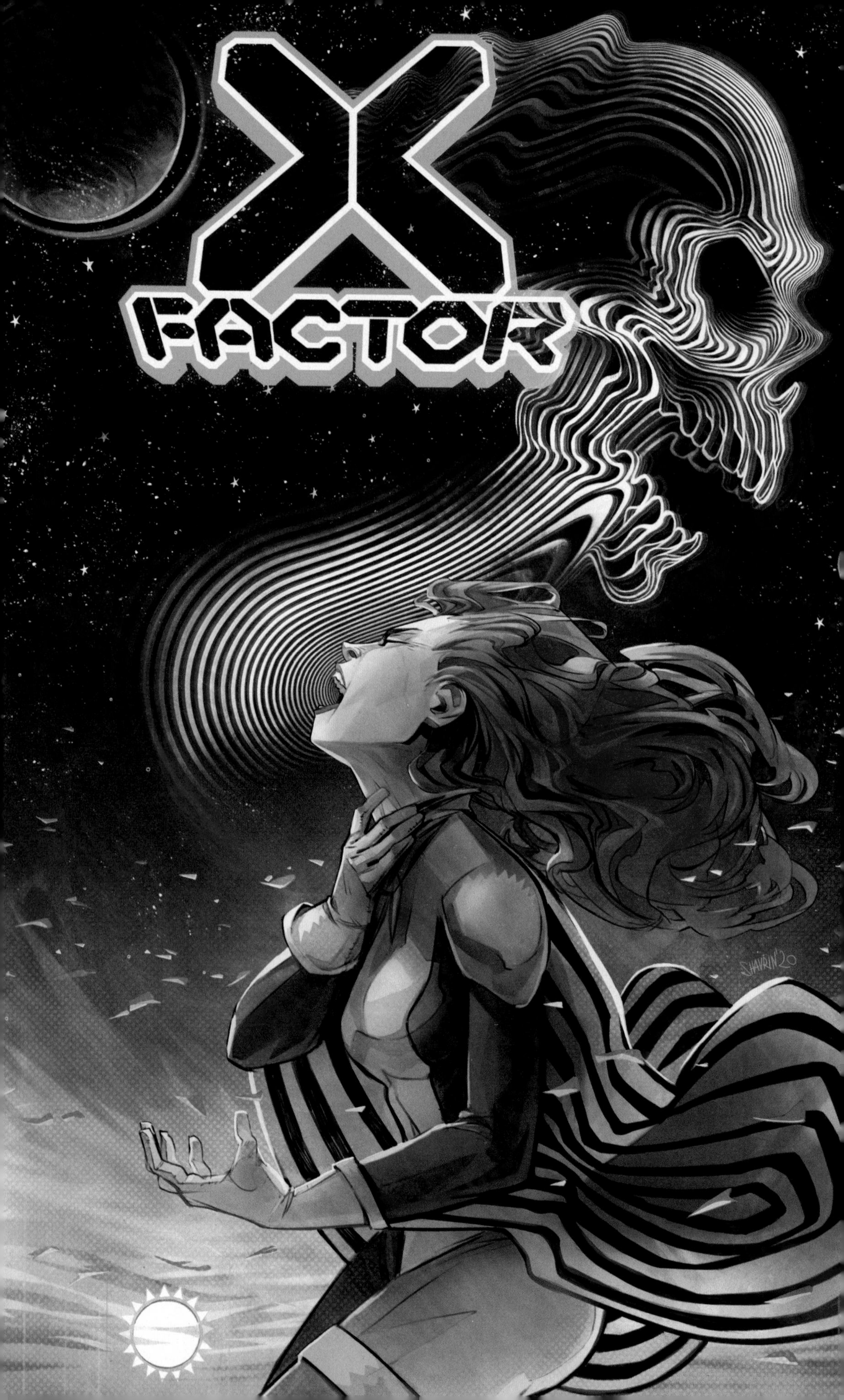
X
FACTOR
SHAVRIN'20

[xfac_[0.6]
[tor__[0.6]

Death is an awakening from the dream
of life. Burrow in sleep, down, down...

--THERESA CASSIDY*

* ███████████████

[xfac_[0.6]
[tor__[0.6]

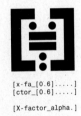

[x-fa_[0.6].....]
[ctor_[0.6].....]

[X-factor_alpha.]

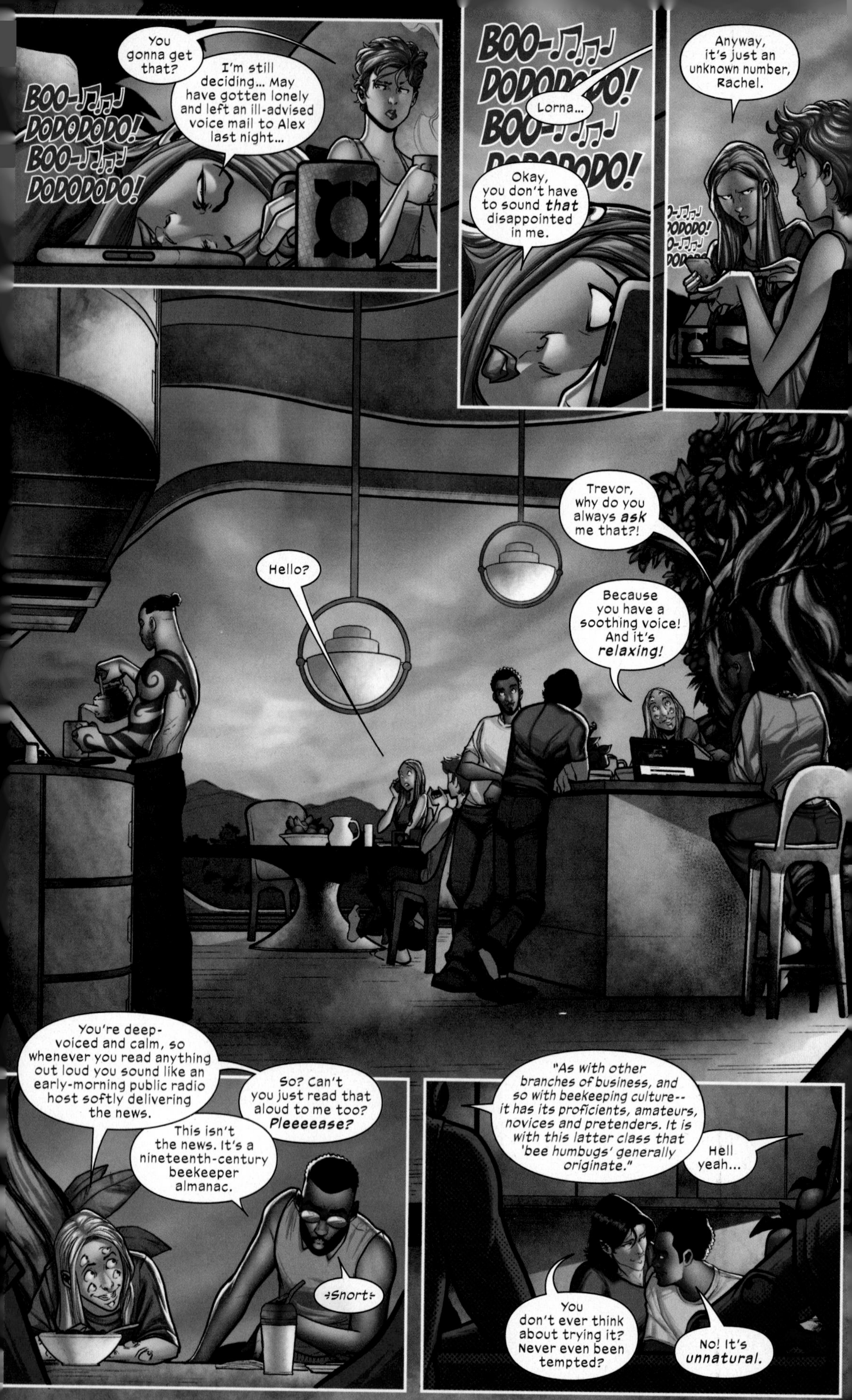
BOO-♫♫♩ DODODODO! BOO-♫♫♩ DODODODO!
You gonna get that?
I'm still deciding... May have gotten lonely and left an ill-advised voice mail to Alex last night...
Lorna...
Okay, you don't have to sound *that* disappointed in me.
Anyway, it's just an unknown number, Rachel.
Hello?
Trevor, why do you always *ask* me that?!
Because you have a soothing voice! And it's *relaxing!*
You're deep-voiced and calm, so whenever you read anything out loud you sound like an early-morning public radio host softly delivering the news.
So? Can't you just read that aloud to me too? *Pleeeease?*
This isn't the news. It's a nineteenth-century beekeeper almanac.
Snort
"As with other branches of business, and so with beekeeping culture-- it has its proficients, amateurs, novices and pretenders. It is with this latter class that 'bee humbugs' generally originate."
Hell yeah...
You don't ever think about trying it? Never even been tempted?
No! It's *unnatural.*

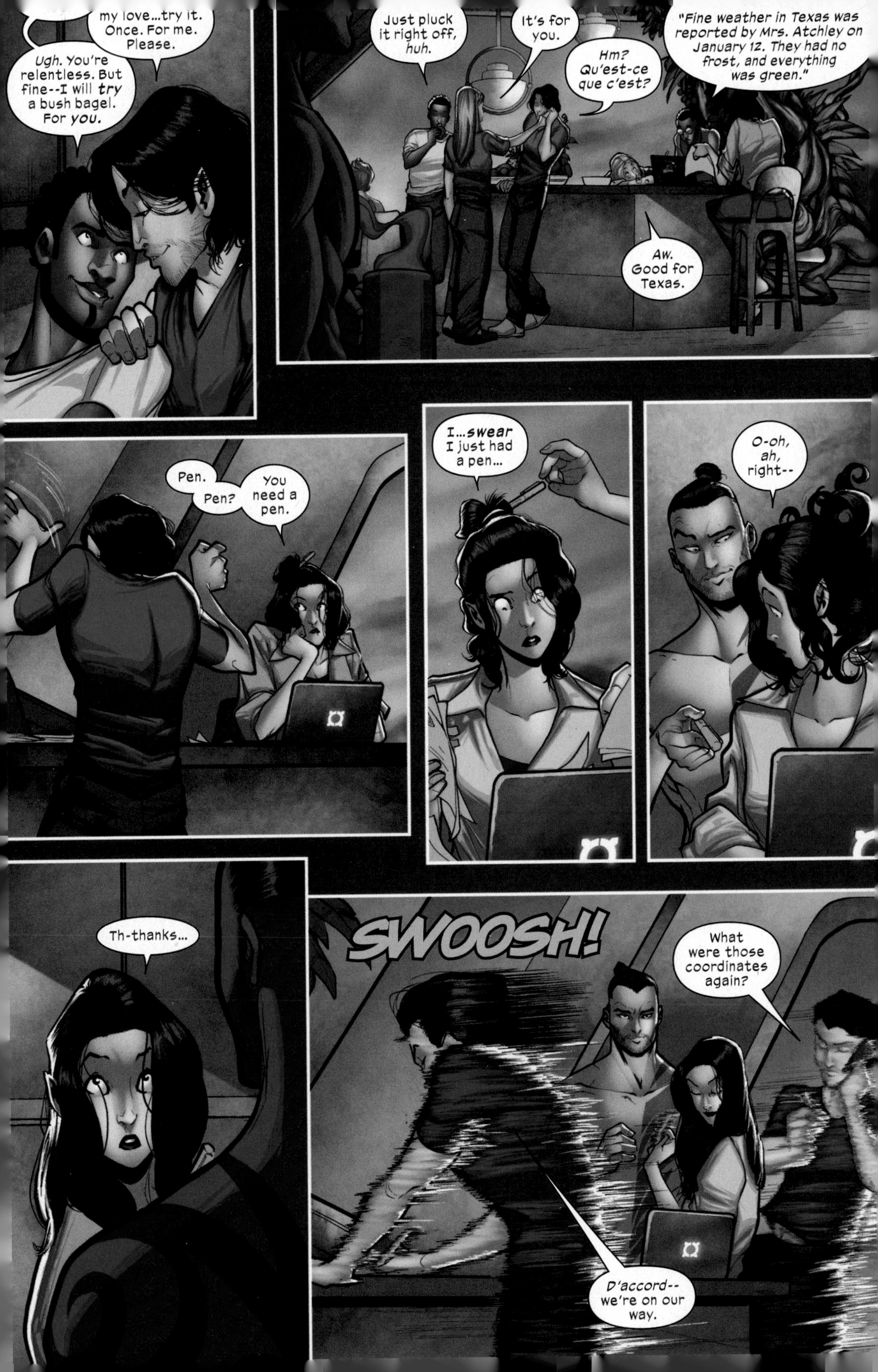

my love...try it. Once. For me. Please.
Ugh. You're relentless. But fine--I will *try* a bush bagel. For *you.*
Just pluck it right off, huh.
It's for you.
Hm? Qu'est-ce que c'est?
"Fine weather in Texas was reported by Mrs. Atchley on January 12. They had no frost, and everything was green."
Aw. Good for Texas.
Pen.
Pen?
You need a pen.
I...*swear* I just had a pen...
O-oh, ah, right--
Th-thanks...
SWOOSH!
What were those coordinates again?
D'accord--we're on our way.

[00_proof_X]
[00_death_X]

DEATHS TOO CLOSE FOR COMFORT

X-FACTOR has been investigating dead and missing mutants, thus ensuring their resurrections. More recently, that applied to Siryn after her cliffside fall.

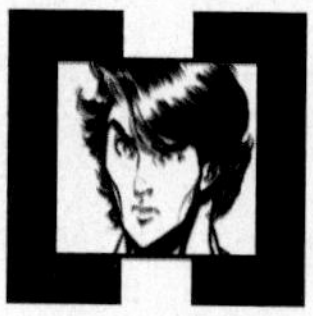
Northstar

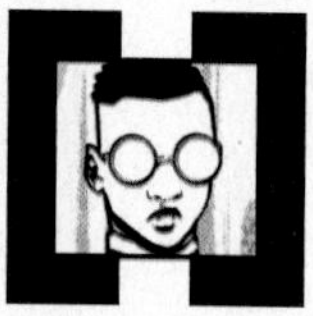
Prodigy

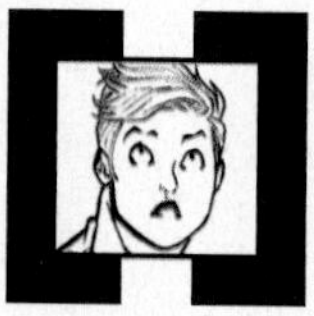
Prestige

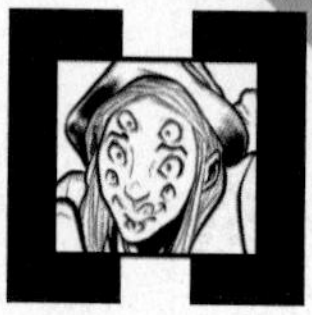
Eye-Boy

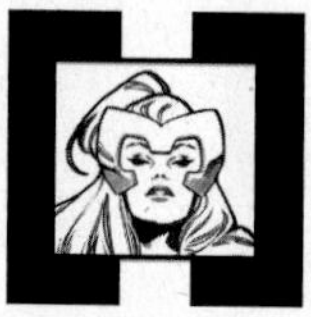
Polaris

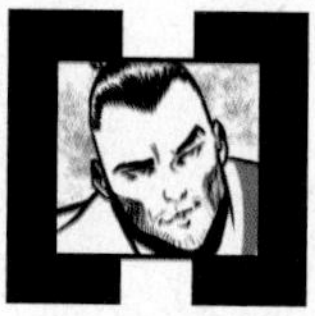
Daken

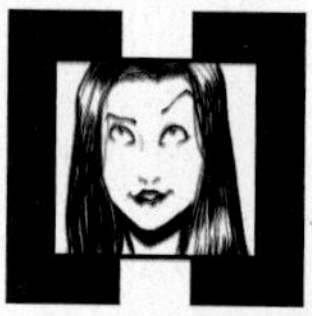
Aurora

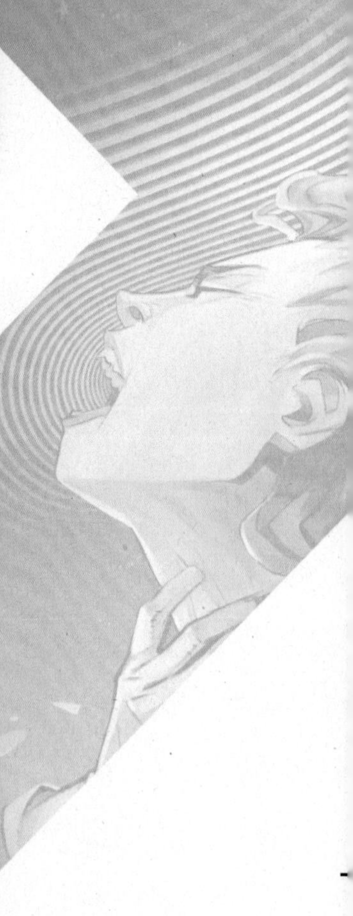

X-FACTOR
[X_06]

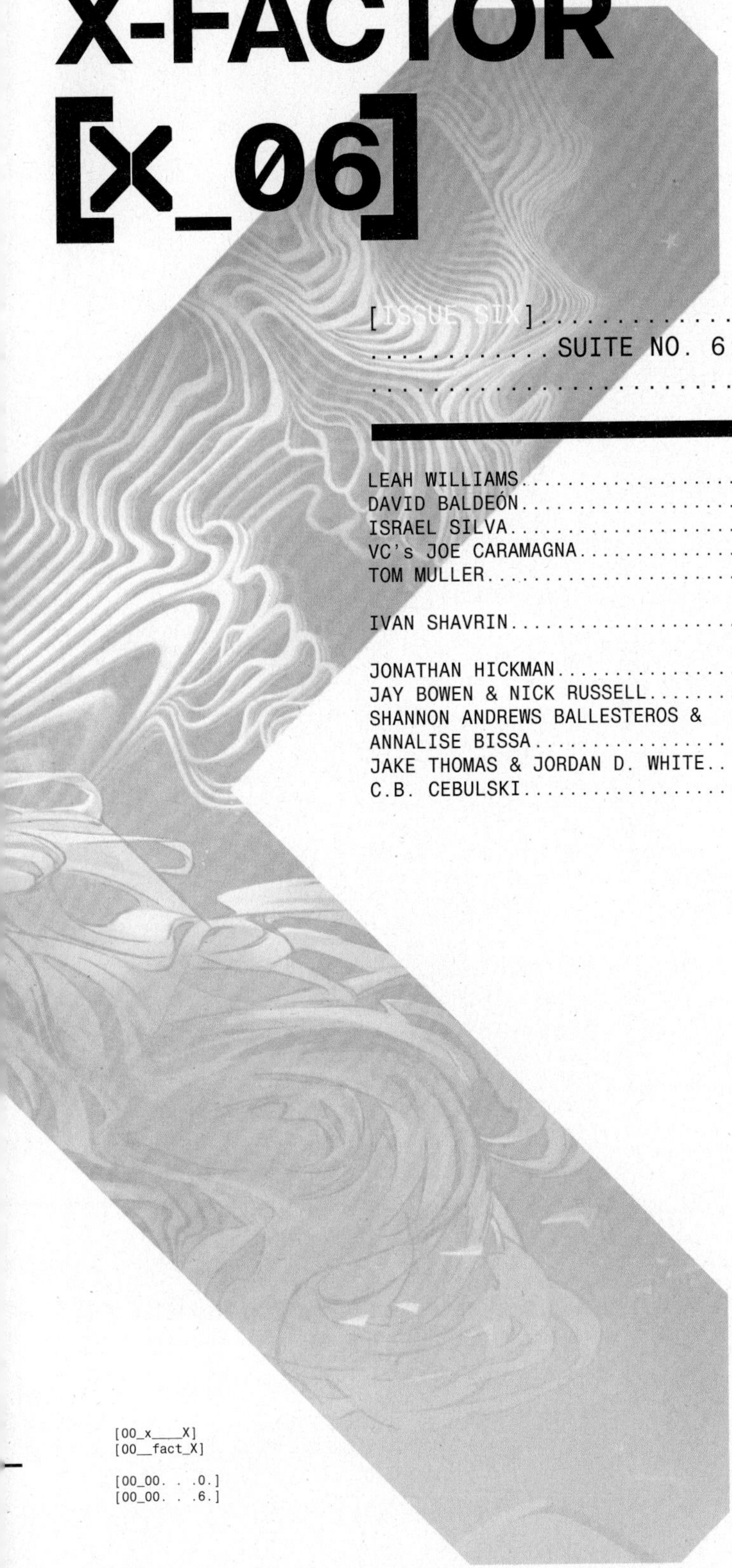

[ISSUE SIX]....................................
............SUITE NO. 6: SCIO ME NIHIL SCIRE
............................"SECOND MOVEMENT"

LEAH WILLIAMS..................................[WRITER]
DAVID BALDEÓN..................................[ARTIST]
ISRAEL SILVA..............................[COLOR ARTIST]
VC's JOE CARAMAGNA...........................[LETTERER]
TOM MULLER.....................................[DESIGN]

IVAN SHAVRIN..............................[COVER ARTIST]

JONATHAN HICKMAN............................[HEAD OF X]
JAY BOWEN & NICK RUSSELL....................[PRODUCTION]
SHANNON ANDREWS BALLESTEROS &
ANNALISE BISSA.........................[ASSISTANT EDITORS]
JAKE THOMAS & JORDAN D. WHITE...................[EDITORS]
C.B. CEBULSKI.........................[EDITOR IN CHIEF]

[00_x____X]
[00__fact_X]

[00_00. . .0.]
[00_00. . .6.]

[00_______]
[00_and___]

[00_the___]

[00__five__]

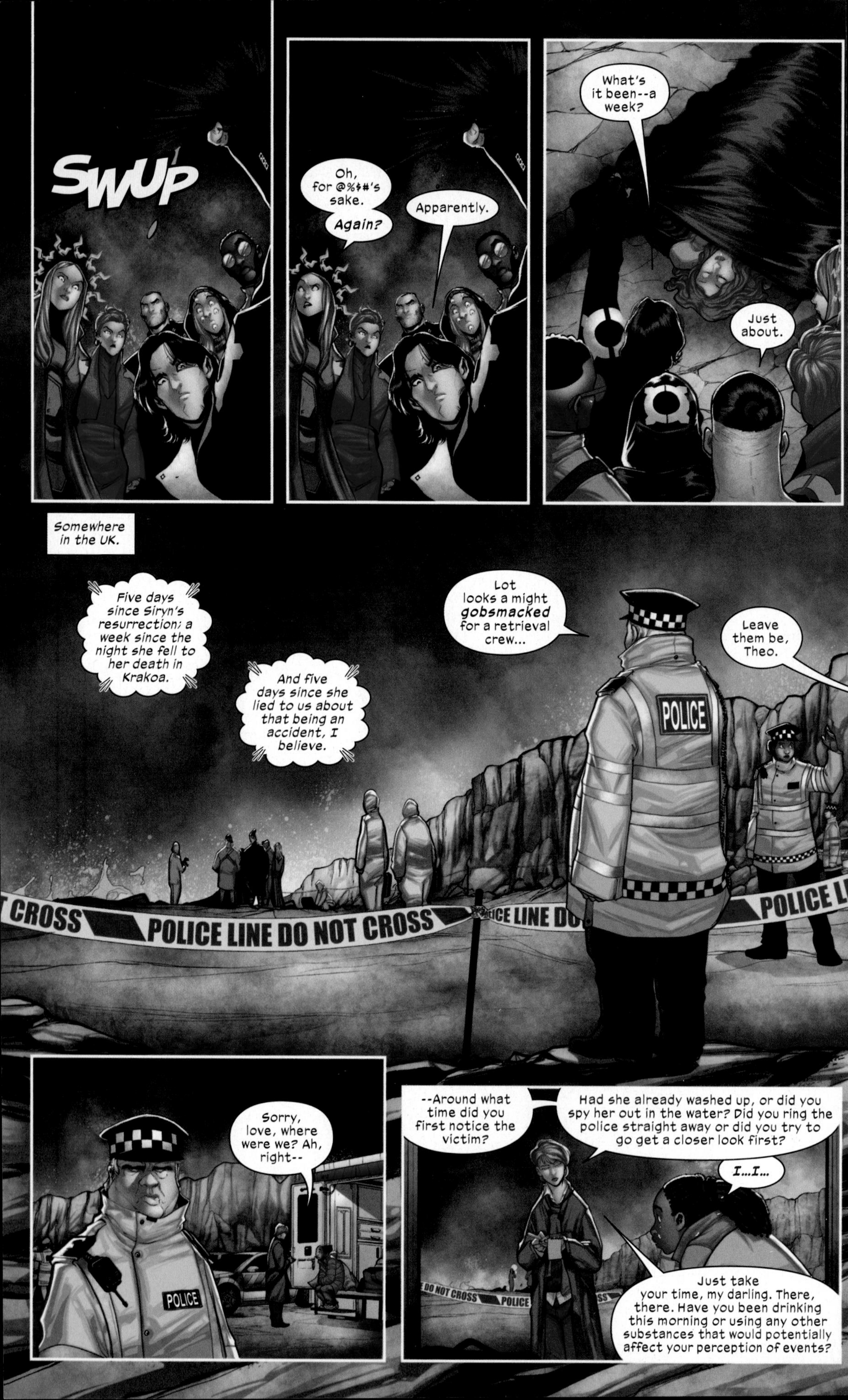
SWUP
Oh, for @%$#'s sake. Again?
Apparently.
What's it been--a week?
Just about.
Somewhere in the UK.
Five days since Siryn's resurrection; a week since the night she fell to her death in Krakoa.
And five days since she lied to us about that being an accident, I believe.
Lot looks a might gobsmacked for a retrieval crew...
Leave them be, Theo.
POLICE
POLICE LINE DO NOT CROSS
Sorry, love, where were we? Ah, right--
POLICE
--Around what time did you first notice the victim?
Had she already washed up, or did you spy her out in the water? Did you ring the police straight away or did you try to go get a closer look first?
I...I...
Just take your time, my darling. There, there. Have you been drinking this morning or using any other substances that would potentially affect your perception of events?

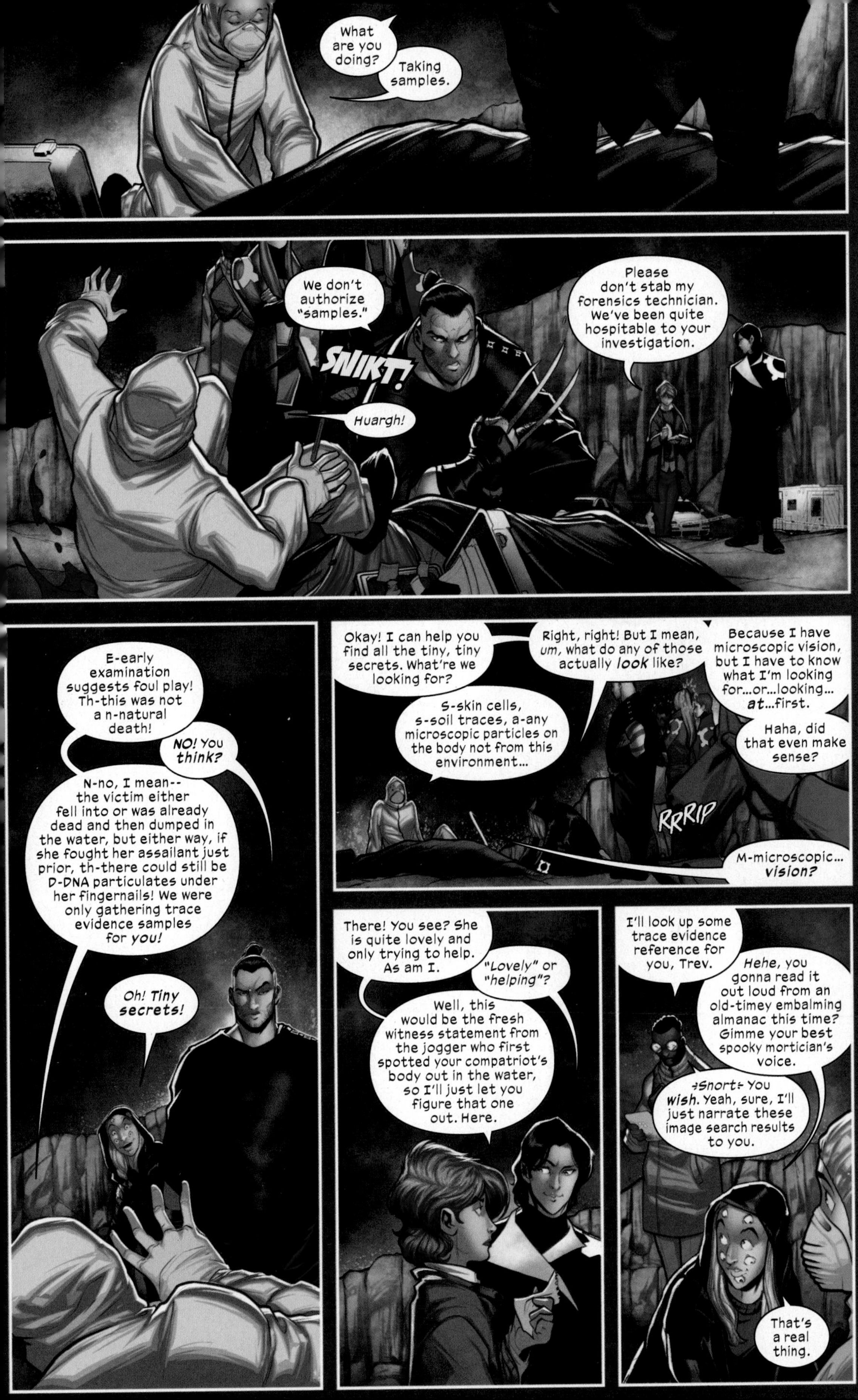

What are you doing?
Taking samples.
We don't authorize "samples."
SNIKT!
Huargh!
Please don't stab my forensics technician. We've been quite hospitable to your investigation.
E-early examination suggests foul play! Th-this was not a n-natural death!
NO! You think?
N-no, I mean-- the victim either fell into or was already dead and then dumped in the water, but either way, if she fought her assailant just prior, th-there could still be D-DNA particulates under her fingernails! We were only gathering trace evidence samples for you!
Oh! Tiny secrets!
Okay! I can help you find all the tiny, tiny secrets. What're we looking for?
S-skin cells, s-soil traces, a-any microscopic particles on the body not from this environment...
Right, right! But I mean, um, what do any of those actually look like?
Because I have microscopic vision, but I have to know what I'm looking for...or...looking... at...first.
Haha, did that even make sense?
RRRIP
M-microscopic... vision?
There! You see? She is quite lovely and only trying to help. As am I.
"Lovely" or "helping"?
Well, this would be the fresh witness statement from the jogger who first spotted your compatriot's body out in the water, so I'll just let you figure that one out. Here.
I'll look up some trace evidence reference for you, Trev.
Hehe, you gonna read it out loud from an old-timey embalming almanac this time? Gimme your best spooky mortician's voice.
Snort You wish. Yeah, sure, I'll just narrate these image search results to you.
That's a real thing.

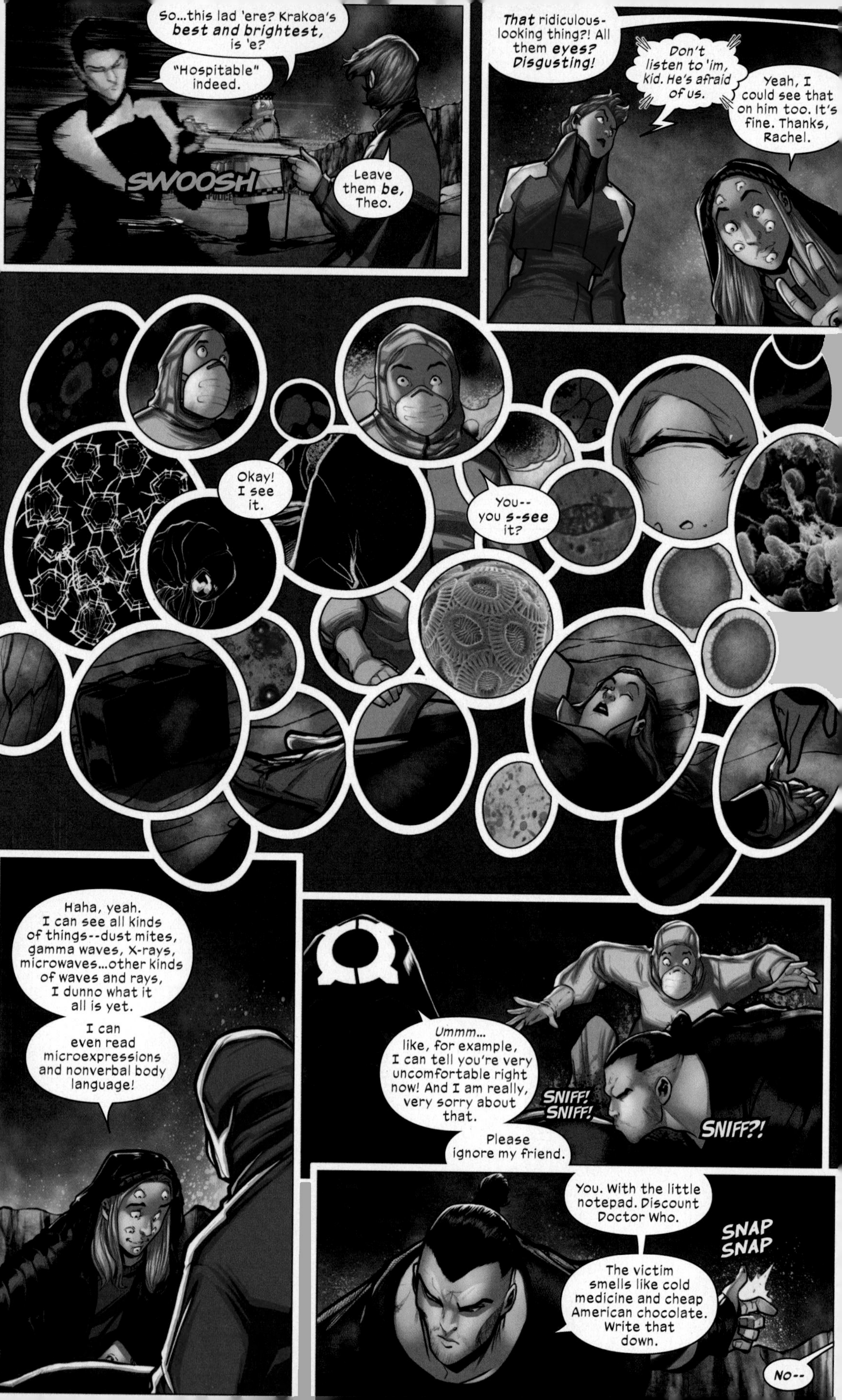
So...this lad 'ere? Krakoa's best and brightest, is 'e?
"Hospitable" indeed.
SWOOSH
Leave them be, Theo.
That ridiculous-looking thing?! All them eyes? Disgusting!
Don't listen to 'im, kid. He's afraid of us.
Yeah, I could see that on him too. It's fine. Thanks, Rachel.
Okay! I see it.
You-- you s-see it?
Haha, yeah. I can see all kinds of things--dust mites, gamma waves, X-rays, microwaves...other kinds of waves and rays, I dunno what it all is yet.
I can even read microexpressions and nonverbal body language!
Ummm... like, for example, I can tell you're very uncomfortable right now! And I am really, very sorry about that.
SNIFF! SNIFF!
SNIFF?!
Please ignore my friend.
You. With the little notepad. Discount Doctor Who.
SNAP SNAP
The victim smells like cold medicine and cheap American chocolate. Write that down.
No--

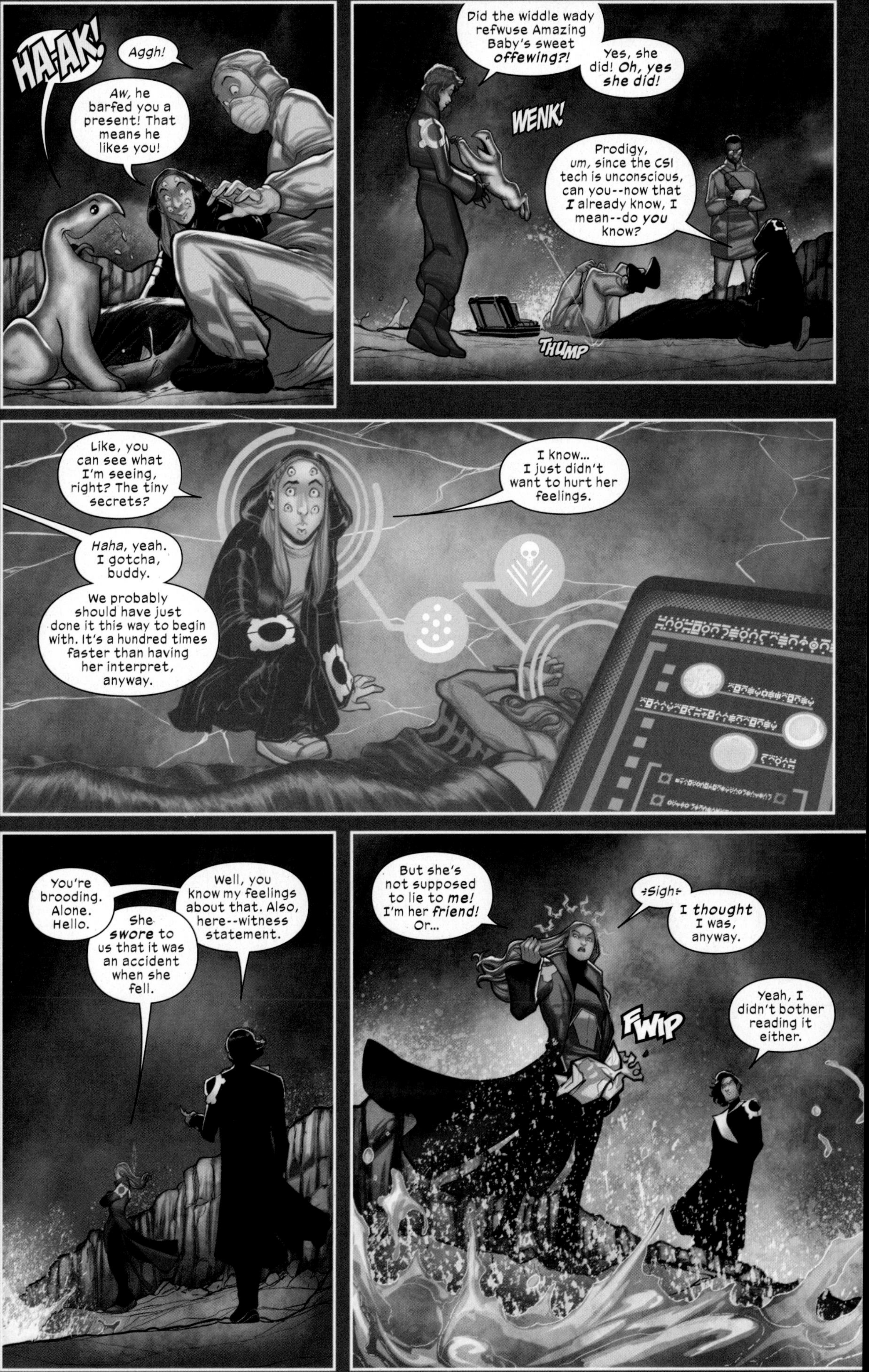
HA-AK!
Aggh!
Aw, he barfed you a present! That means he likes you!
Did the widdle wady refwuse Amazing Baby's sweet offewing?!
Yes, she did! Oh, yes she did!
WENK!
Prodigy, um, since the CSI tech is unconscious, can you--now that I already know, I mean--do you know?
THUMP
Like, you can see what I'm seeing, right? The tiny secrets?
I know... I just didn't want to hurt her feelings.
Haha, yeah. I gotcha, buddy.
We probably should have just done it this way to begin with. It's a hundred times faster than having her interpret, anyway.
You're brooding. Alone. Hello.
Well, you know my feelings about that. Also, here--witness statement.
She swore to us that it was an accident when she fell.
But she's not supposed to lie to me! I'm her friend! Or...
-Sigh-
I thought I was, anyway.
FWIP
Yeah, I didn't bother reading it either.

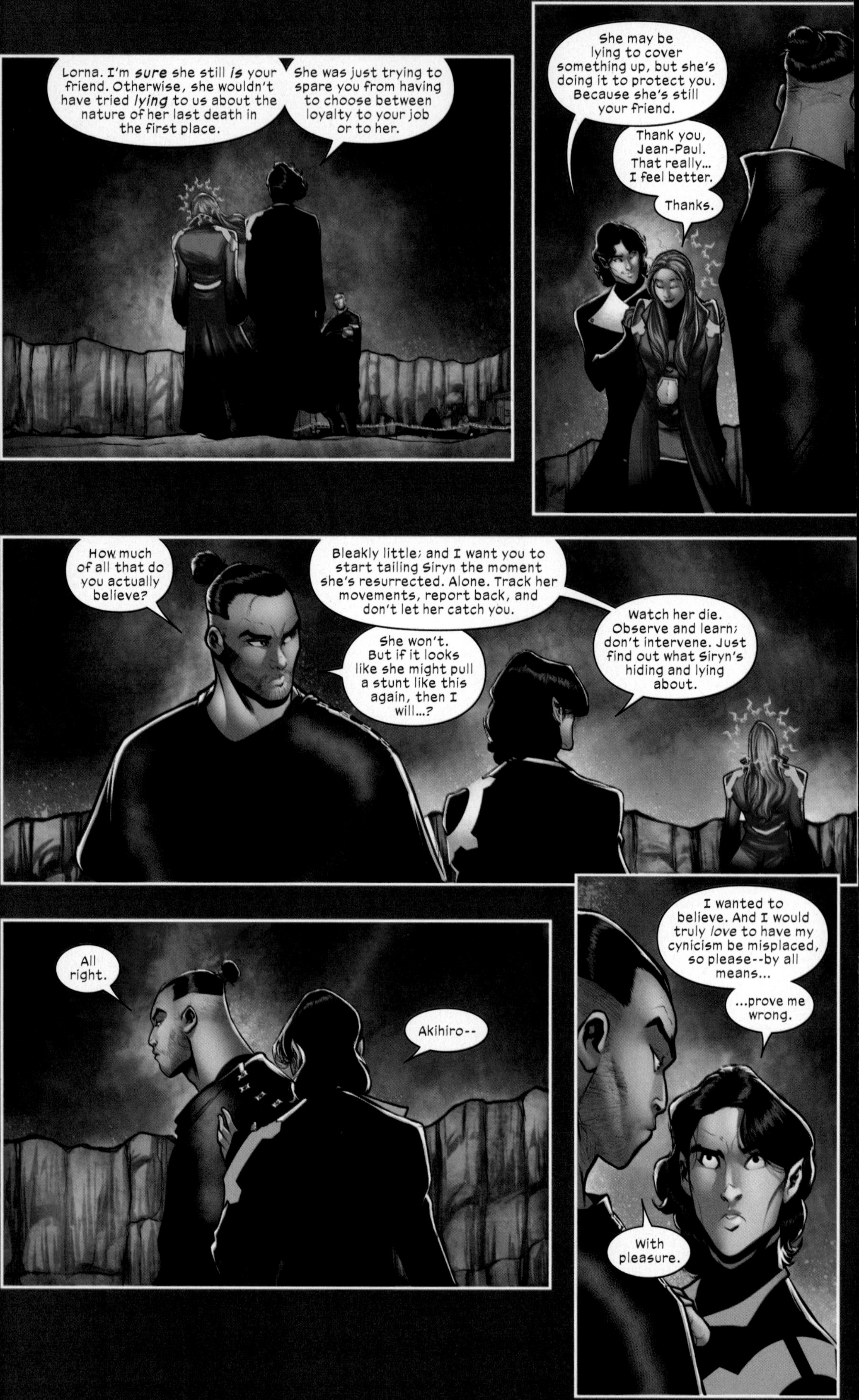
Lorna. I'm *sure* she still *is* your friend. Otherwise, she wouldn't have tried *lying* to us about the nature of her last death in the first place.
She was just trying to spare you from having to choose between loyalty to your job or to her.
She may be lying to cover something up, but she's doing it to protect you. Because she's still your friend.
Thank you, Jean-Paul. That really... I feel better.
Thanks.
How much of all that do you actually believe?
Bleakly little; and I want you to start tailing Siryn the moment she's resurrected. Alone. Track her movements, report back, and don't let her catch you.
She won't. But if it looks like she might pull a stunt like this again, then I will...?
Watch her die. Observe and learn; don't intervene. Just find out what Siryn's hiding and lying about.
All right.
Akihiro--
I wanted to believe. And I would truly *love* to have my cynicism be misplaced, so please--by all means...
...prove me wrong.
With pleasure.

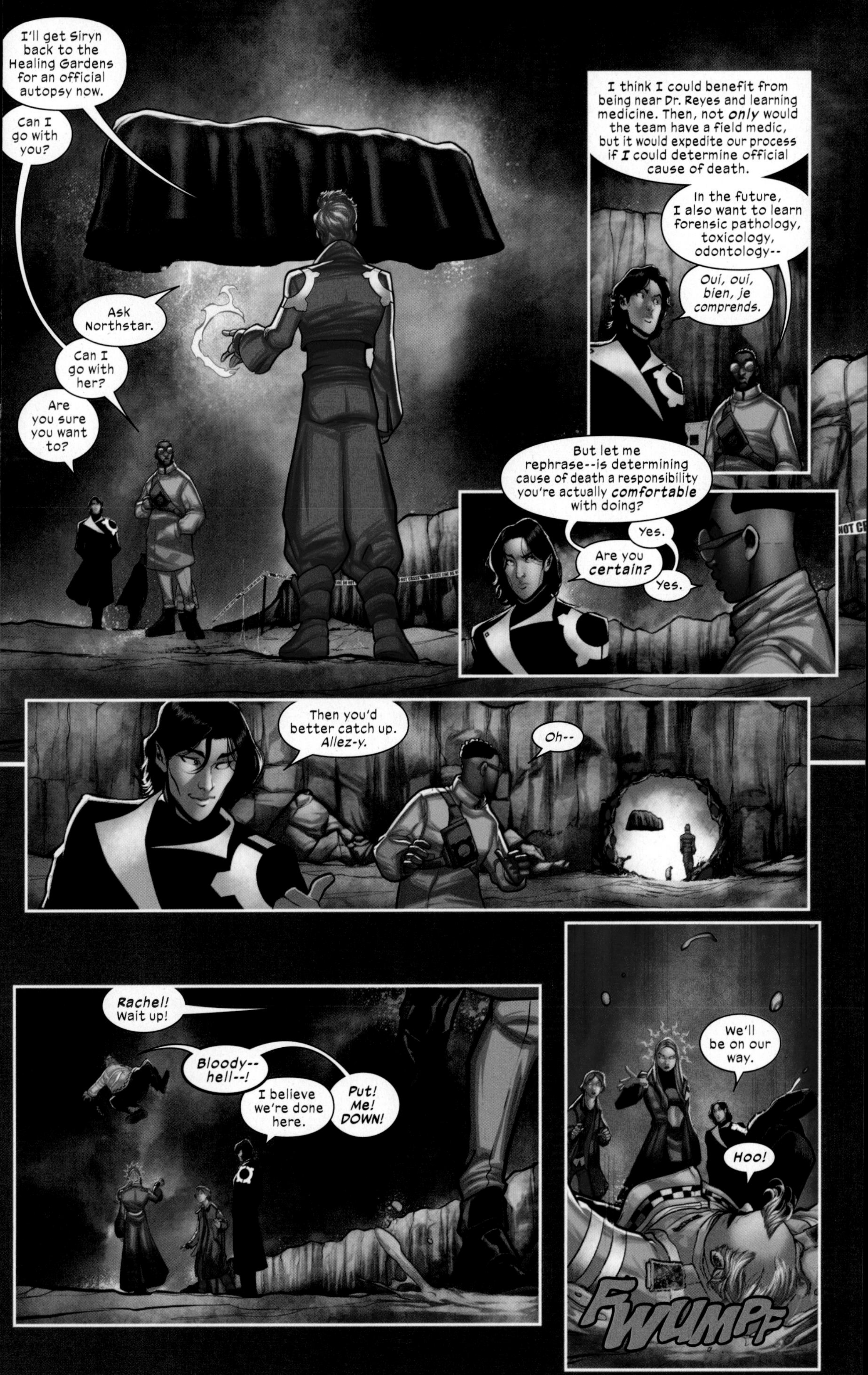
I'll get Siryn back to the Healing Gardens for an official autopsy now.
Can I go with you?
Ask Northstar.
Can I go with her?
Are you sure you want to?
I think I could benefit from being near Dr. Reyes and learning medicine. Then, not *only* would the team have a field medic, but it would expedite our process if *I* could determine official cause of death.
In the future, I also want to learn forensic pathology, toxicology, odontology--
Oui, oui, bien, je comprends.
But let me rephrase--is determining cause of death a responsibility you're actually *comfortable* with doing?
Yes.
Are you *certain?*
Yes.
Then you'd better catch up. *Allez-y.*
Oh--
Rachel! Wait up!
Bloody--hell--!
I believe we're done here.
Put! Me! DOWN!
We'll be on our way.
Hoo!
FWUMPF

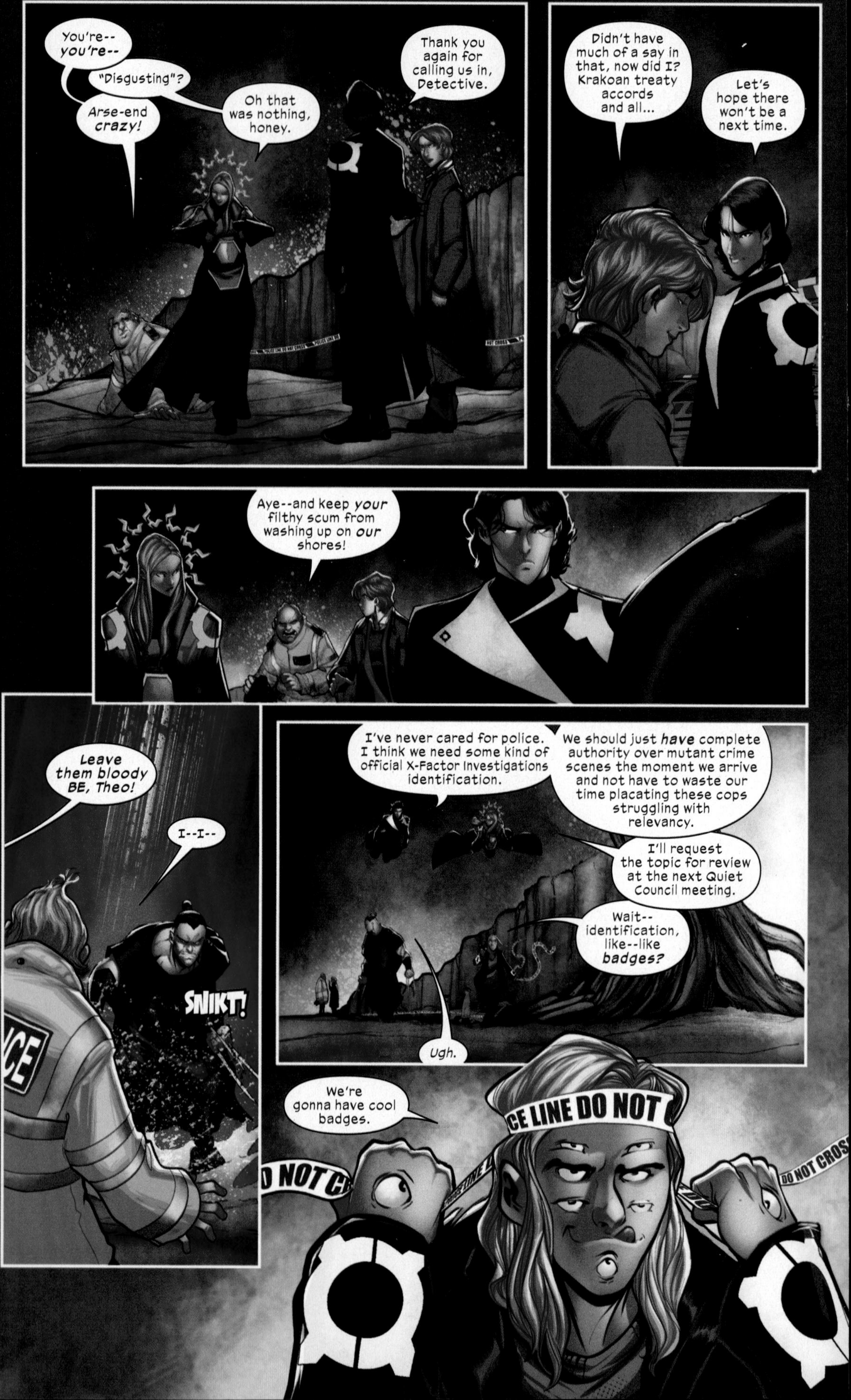
You're-- you're--
"Disgusting"?
Arse-end crazy!
Oh that was nothing, honey.
Thank you again for calling us in, Detective.
Didn't have much of a say in that, now did I? Krakoan treaty accords and all...
Let's hope there won't be a next time.
Aye--and keep your filthy scum from washing up on our shores!
Leave them bloody BE, Theo!
I--I--
SNIKT!
I've never cared for police. I think we need some kind of official X-Factor Investigations identification.
We should just have complete authority over mutant crime scenes the moment we arrive and not have to waste our time placating these cops struggling with relevancy.
I'll request the topic for review at the next Quiet Council meeting.
Wait-- identification, like--like badges?
Ugh.
We're gonna have cool badges.
CE LINE DO NOT C
DO NOT C
DO NOT CROS

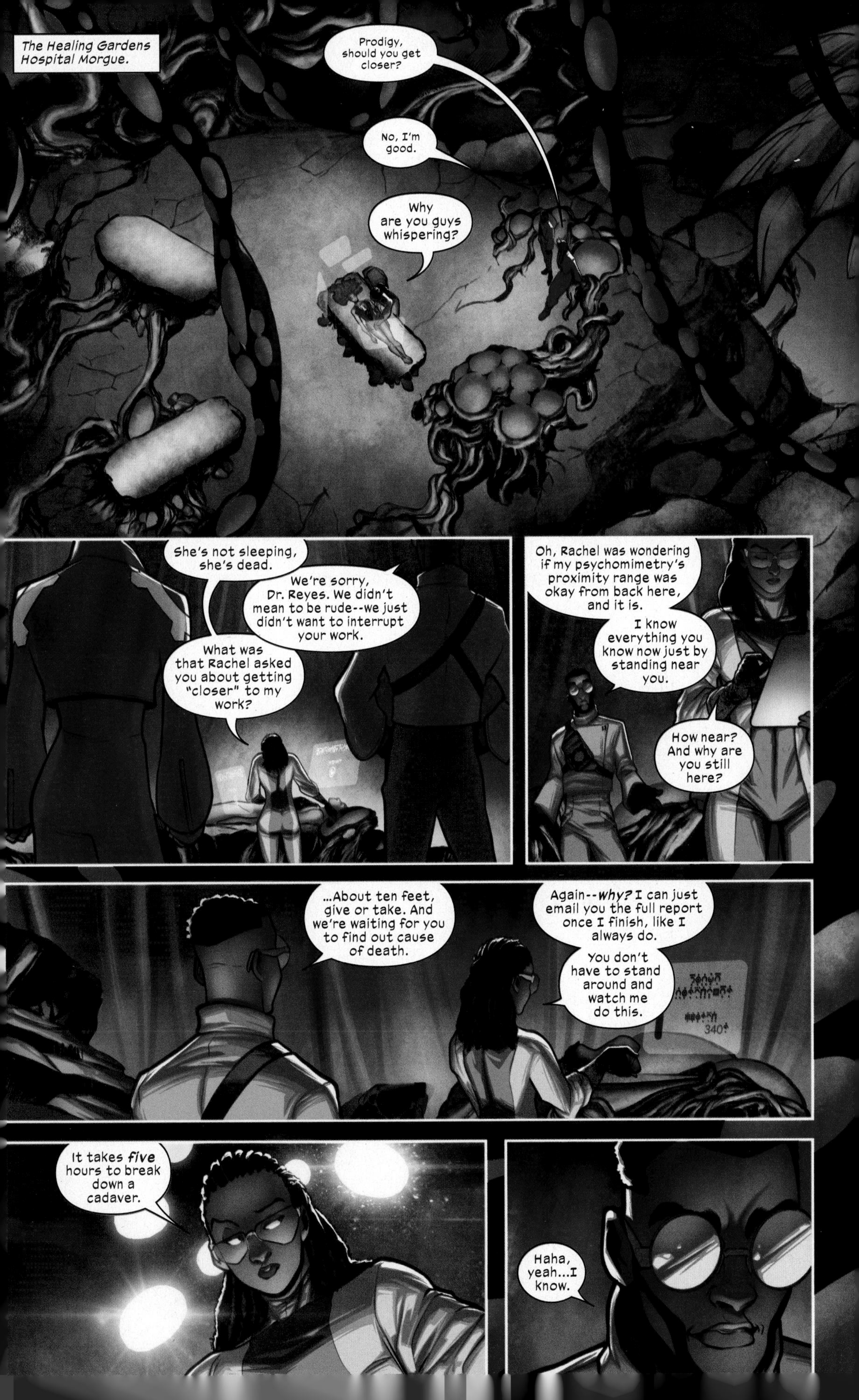
The Healing Gardens Hospital Morgue.
Prodigy, should you get closer?
No, I'm good.
Why are you guys whispering?
She's not sleeping, she's dead.
We're sorry, Dr. Reyes. We didn't mean to be rude--we just didn't want to interrupt your work.
What was that Rachel asked you about getting "closer" to my work?
Oh, Rachel was wondering if my psychomimetry's proximity range was okay from back here, and it is.
I know everything you know now just by standing near you.
How near? And why are you still here?
...About ten feet, give or take. And we're waiting for you to find out cause of death.
Again--*why?* I can just email you the full report once I finish, like I always do.
You don't have to stand around and watch me do this.
It takes *five* hours to break down a cadaver.
Haha, yeah...I know.

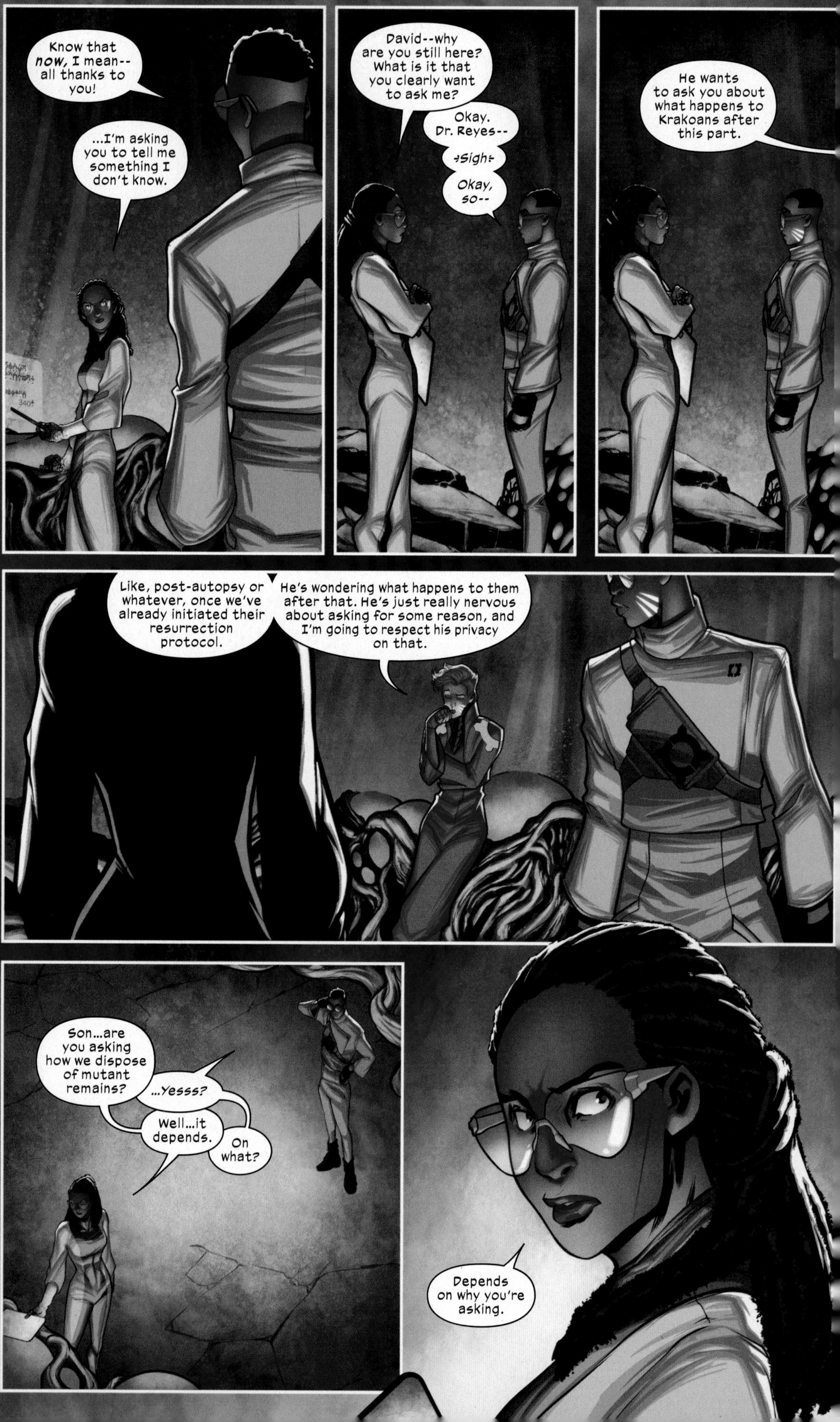
Know that *now,* I mean--all thanks to you!
...I'm asking you to tell me something I don't know.
David--why are you still here? What is it that you clearly want to ask me?
Okay. Dr. Reyes--
Sigh
Okay, so--
He wants to ask you about what happens to Krakoans after this part.
Like, post-autopsy or whatever, once we've already initiated their resurrection protocol.
He's wondering what happens to them after that. He's just really nervous about asking for some reason, and I'm going to respect his privacy on that.
Son...are you asking how we dispose of mutant remains?
...Yesss?
Well...it depends.
On what?
Depends on why you're asking.

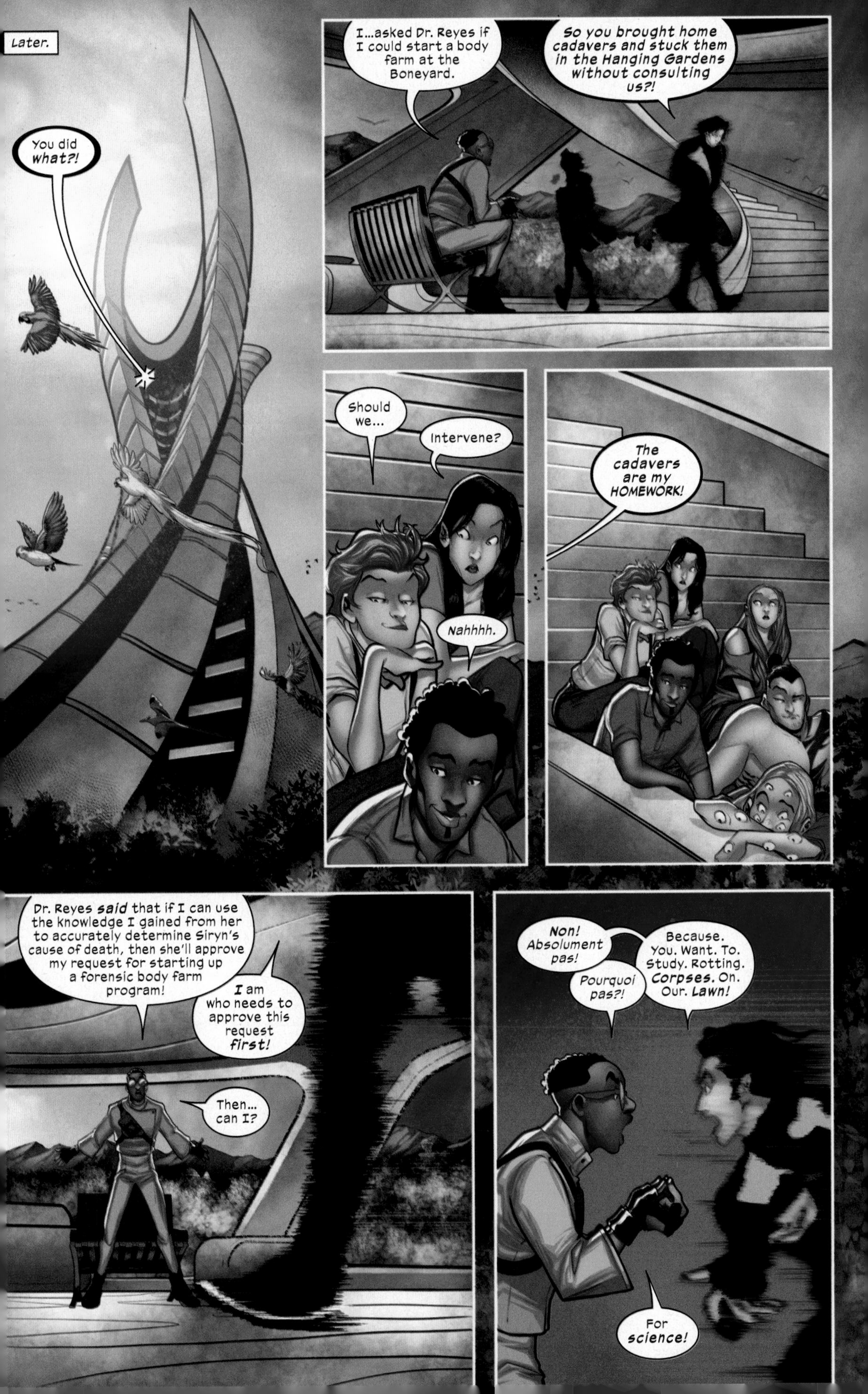

Later.
You did what?!
I...asked Dr. Reyes if I could start a body farm at the Boneyard.
So you brought home cadavers and stuck them in the Hanging Gardens without consulting us?!
Should we...
Intervene?
Nahhhh.
The cadavers are my HOMEWORK!
Dr. Reyes said that if I can use the knowledge I gained from her to accurately determine Siryn's cause of death, then she'll approve my request for starting up a forensic body farm program!
I am who needs to approve this request first!
Then... can I?
Non! Absolument pas!
Pourquoi pas?!
Because. You. Want. To. Study. Rotting. Corpses. On. Our. Lawn!
For science!

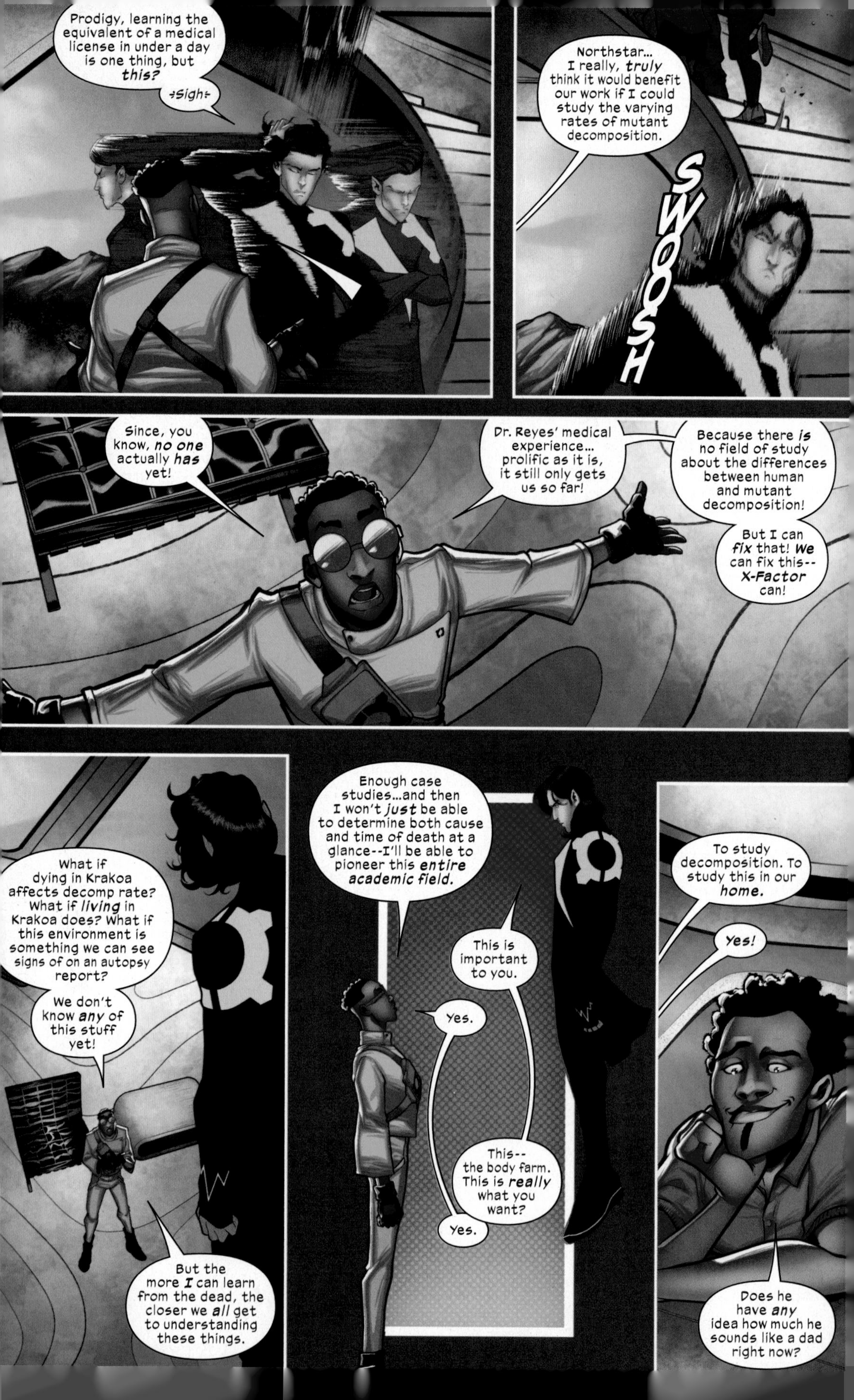
Prodigy, learning the equivalent of a medical license in under a day is one thing, but this?
-Sigh-
Northstar... I really, truly think it would benefit our work if I could study the varying rates of mutant decomposition.
SWOOSH
Since, you know, no one actually has yet!
Dr. Reyes' medical experience... prolific as it is, it still only gets us so far!
Because there is no field of study about the differences between human and mutant decomposition!
But I can fix that! We can fix this-- X-Factor can!
What if dying in Krakoa affects decomp rate? What if living in Krakoa does? What if this environment is something we can see signs of on an autopsy report?
We don't know any of this stuff yet!
But the more I can learn from the dead, the closer we all get to understanding these things.
Enough case studies...and then I won't just be able to determine both cause and time of death at a glance--I'll be able to pioneer this entire academic field.
This is important to you.
Yes.
This-- the body farm. This is really what you want?
Yes.
To study decomposition. To study this in our home.
Yes!
Does he have any idea how much he sounds like a dad right now?

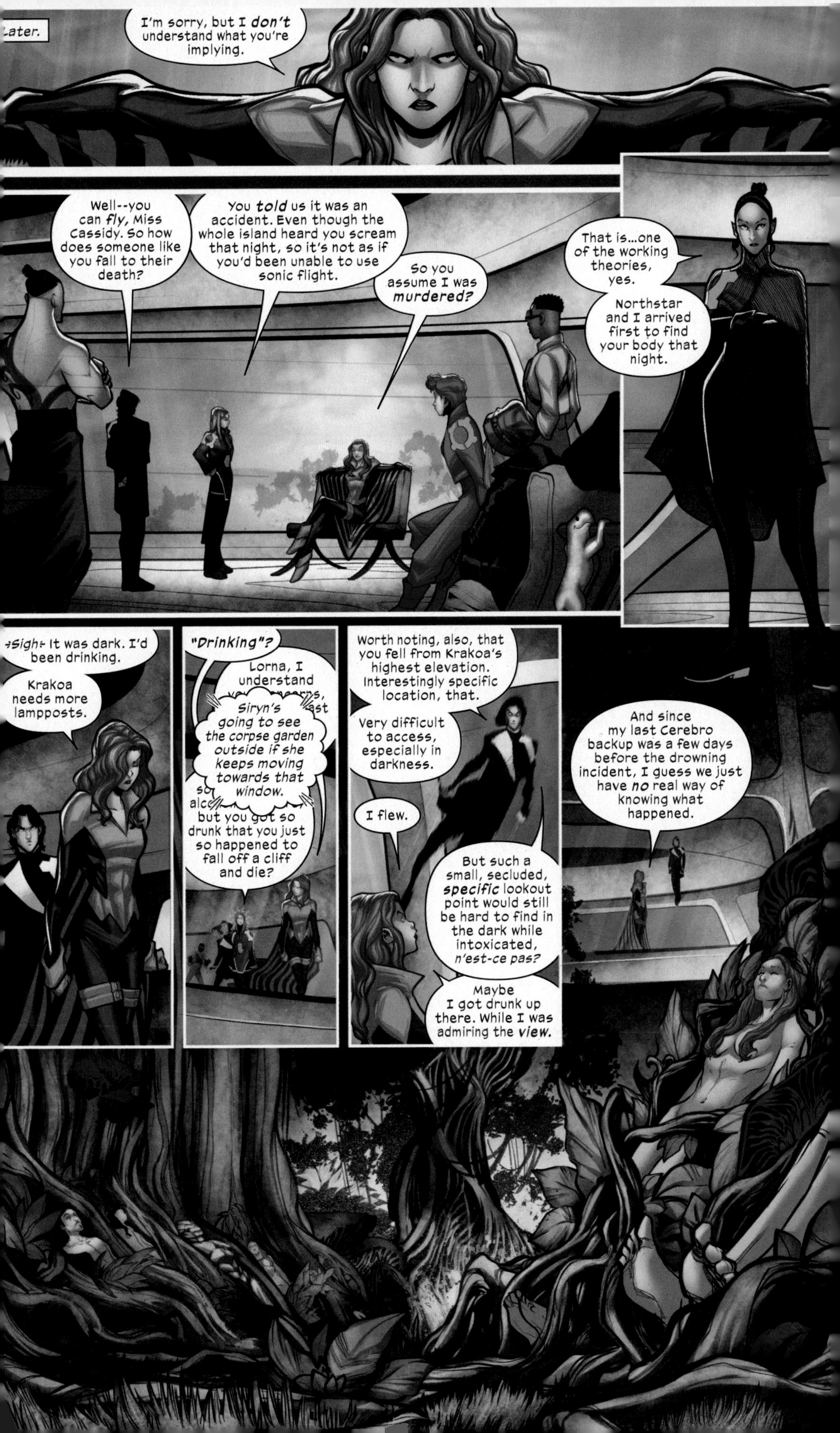

Later.
I'm sorry, but I don't understand what you're implying.
Well--you can fly, Miss Cassidy. So how does someone like you fall to their death?
You told us it was an accident. Even though the whole island heard you scream that night, so it's not as if you'd been unable to use sonic flight.
So you assume I was murdered?
That is...one of the working theories, yes.
Northstar and I arrived first to find your body that night.
Sigh It was dark. I'd been drinking.
Krakoa needs more lampposts.
"Drinking"?
Lorna, I understand
Siryn's going to see the corpse garden outside if she keeps moving towards that window.
but you got so drunk that you just so happened to fall off a cliff and die?
Worth noting, also, that you fell from Krakoa's highest elevation. Interestingly specific location, that.
Very difficult to access, especially in darkness.
I flew.
But such a small, secluded, specific lookout point would still be hard to find in the dark while intoxicated, n'est-ce pas?
Maybe I got drunk up there. While I was admiring the view.
And since my last Cerebro backup was a few days before the drowning incident, I guess we just have no real way of knowing what happened.

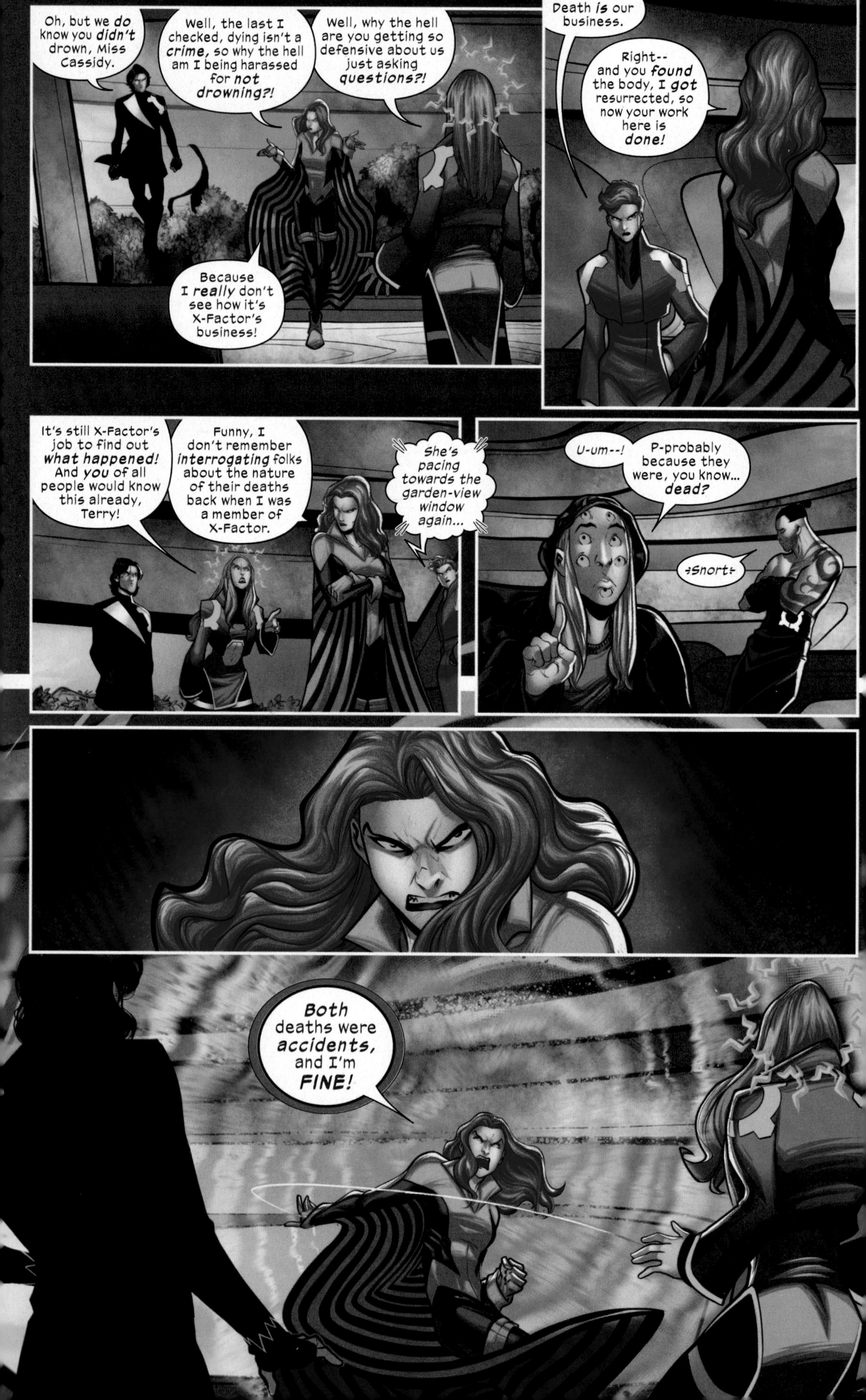

Oh, but we *do* know you *didn't* drown, Miss Cassidy.
Well, the last I checked, dying isn't a *crime*, so why the hell am I being harassed for *not drowning?!*
Well, why the hell are you getting so defensive about us just asking *questions?!*
Because I *really* don't see how it's X-Factor's business!
Death *is* our business.
Right-- and you *found* the body, I *got* resurrected, so now your work here is *done!*
It's still X-Factor's job to find out *what happened!* And *you* of all people would know this already, Terry!
Funny, I don't remember *interrogating* folks about the nature of their deaths back when I was a member of X-Factor.
She's pacing towards the garden-view window again...
U-um--!
P-probably because they were, you know... *dead?*
=Snort=
Both deaths were *accidents*, and I'm ***FINE!***

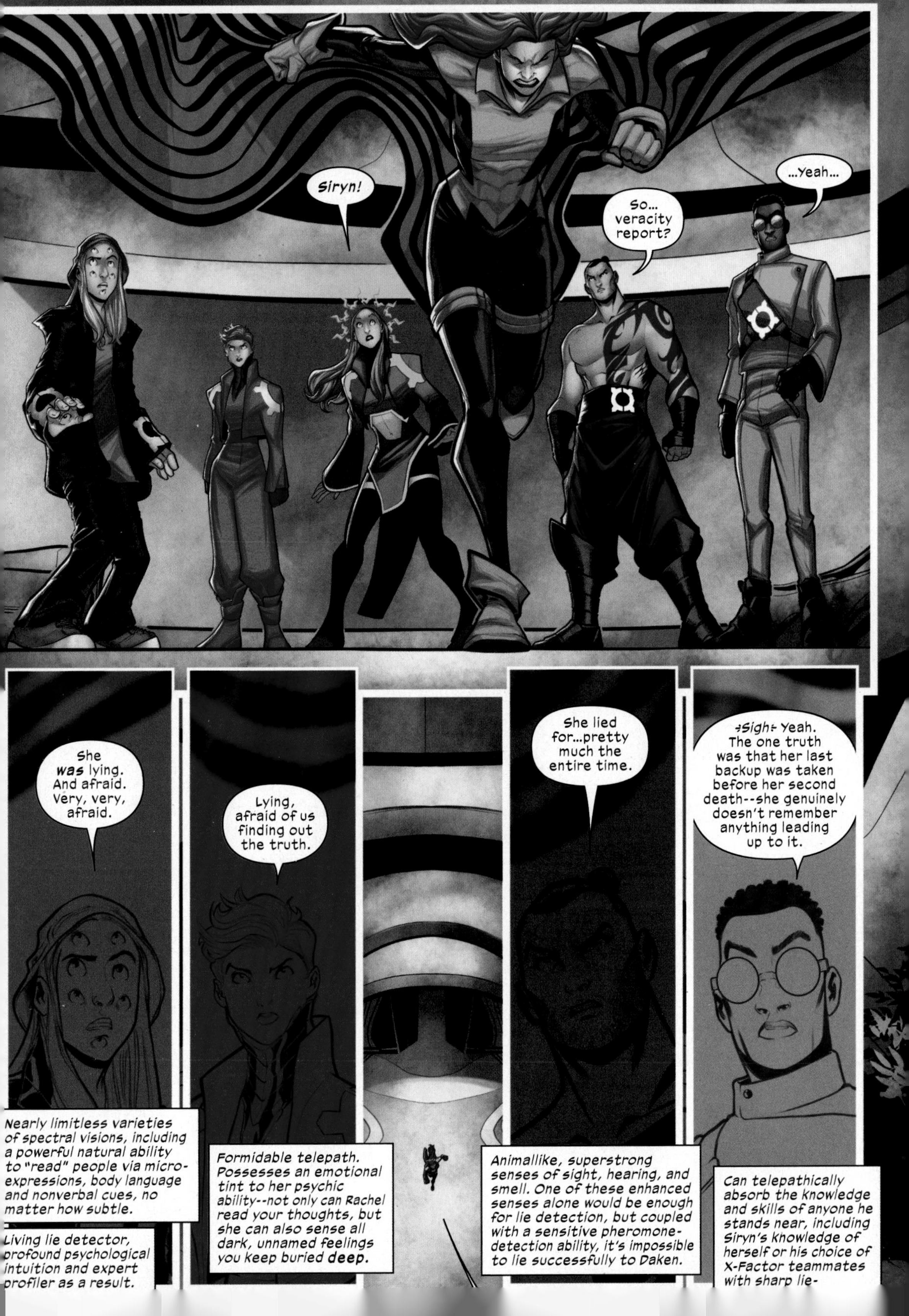
Siryn!
So... veracity report?
...Yeah...
She was lying. And afraid. Very, very, afraid.
Lying, afraid of us finding out the truth.
She lied for...pretty much the entire time.
=Sigh= Yeah. The one truth was that her last backup was taken before her second death--she genuinely doesn't remember anything leading up to it.
Nearly limitless varieties of spectral visions, including a powerful natural ability to "read" people via micro-expressions, body language and nonverbal cues, no matter how subtle.
Living lie detector, profound psychological intuition and expert profiler as a result.
Formidable telepath. Possesses an emotional tint to her psychic ability--not only can Rachel read your thoughts, but she can also sense all dark, unnamed feelings you keep buried deep.
Animallike, superstrong senses of sight, hearing, and smell. One of these enhanced senses alone would be enough for lie detection, but coupled with a sensitive pheromone-detection ability, it's impossible to lie successfully to Daken.
Can telepathically absorb the knowledge and skills of anyone he stands near, including Siryn's knowledge of herself or his choice of X-Factor teammates with sharp lie-

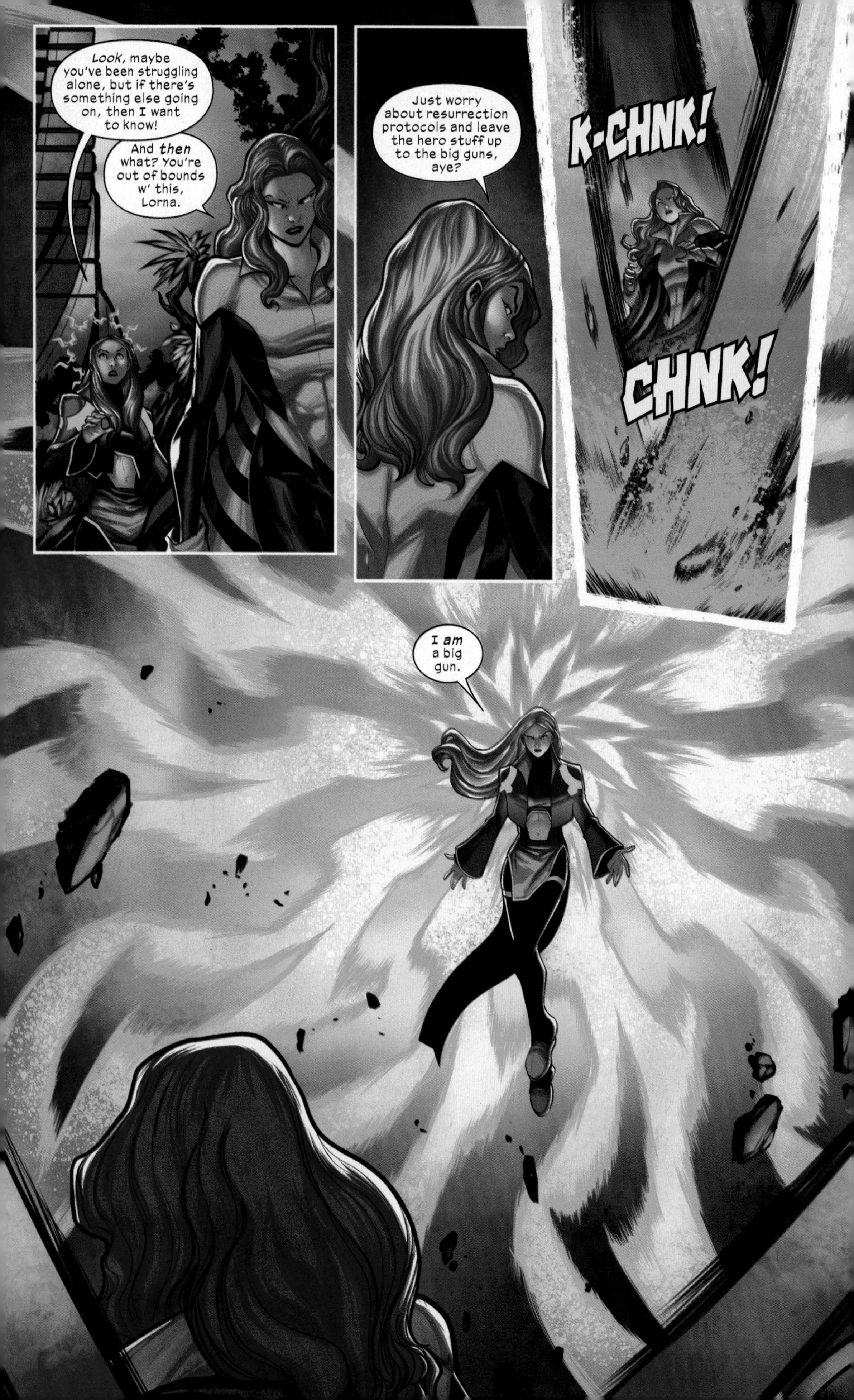
Look, maybe you've been struggling alone, but if there's something else going on, then I want to know!
And then what? You're out of bounds w' this, Lorna.
Just worry about resurrection protocols and leave the hero stuff up to the big guns, aye?
K-CHNK!
CHNK!
I am a big gun.

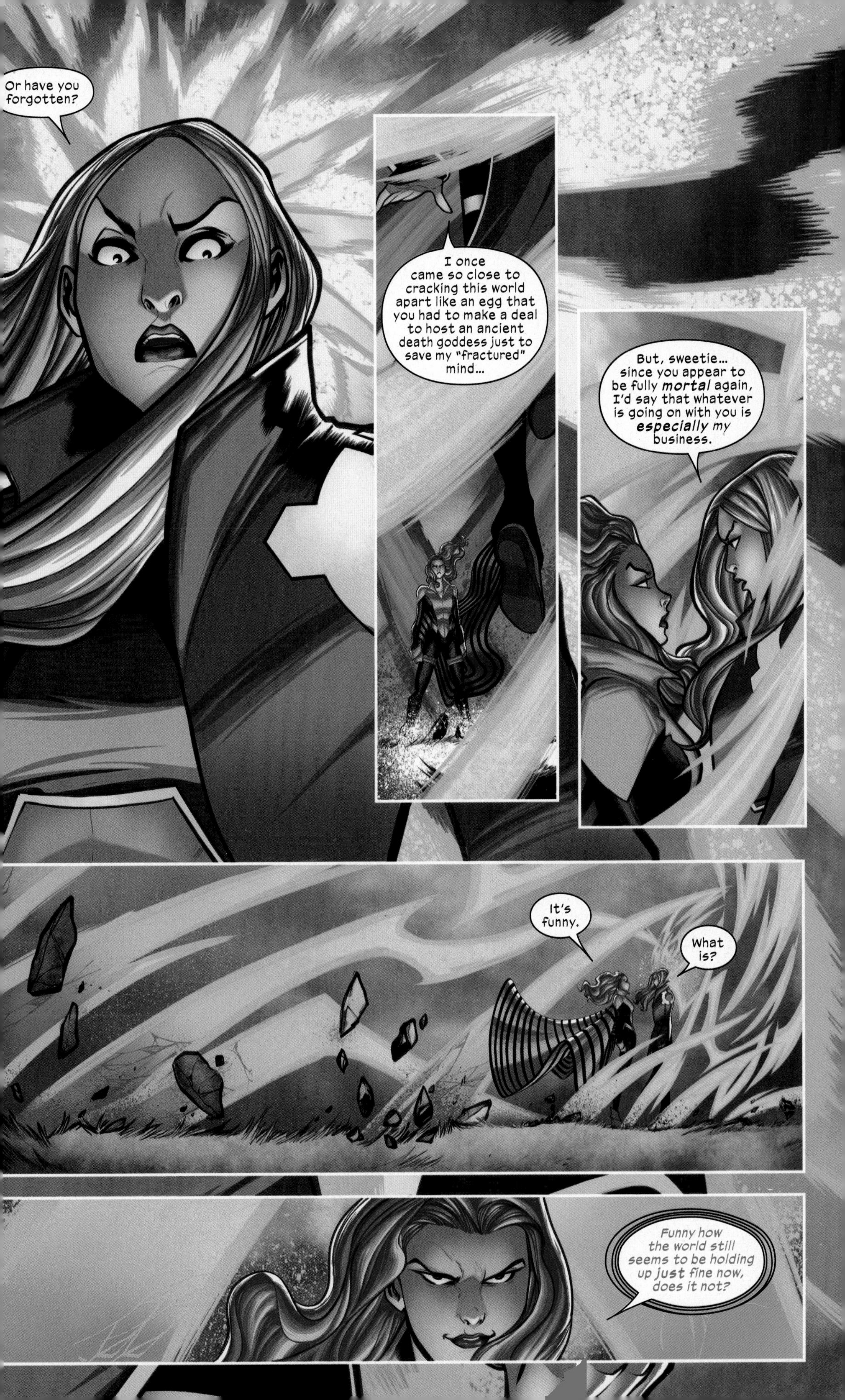
Or have you forgotten?
I once came so close to cracking this world apart like an egg that you had to make a deal to host an ancient death goddess just to save my "fractured" mind...
But, sweetie... since you appear to be fully *mortal* again, I'd say that whatever is going on with you is ***especially*** my business.
It's funny.
What is?
Funny how the world still seems to be holding up just *fine now, does it not?*

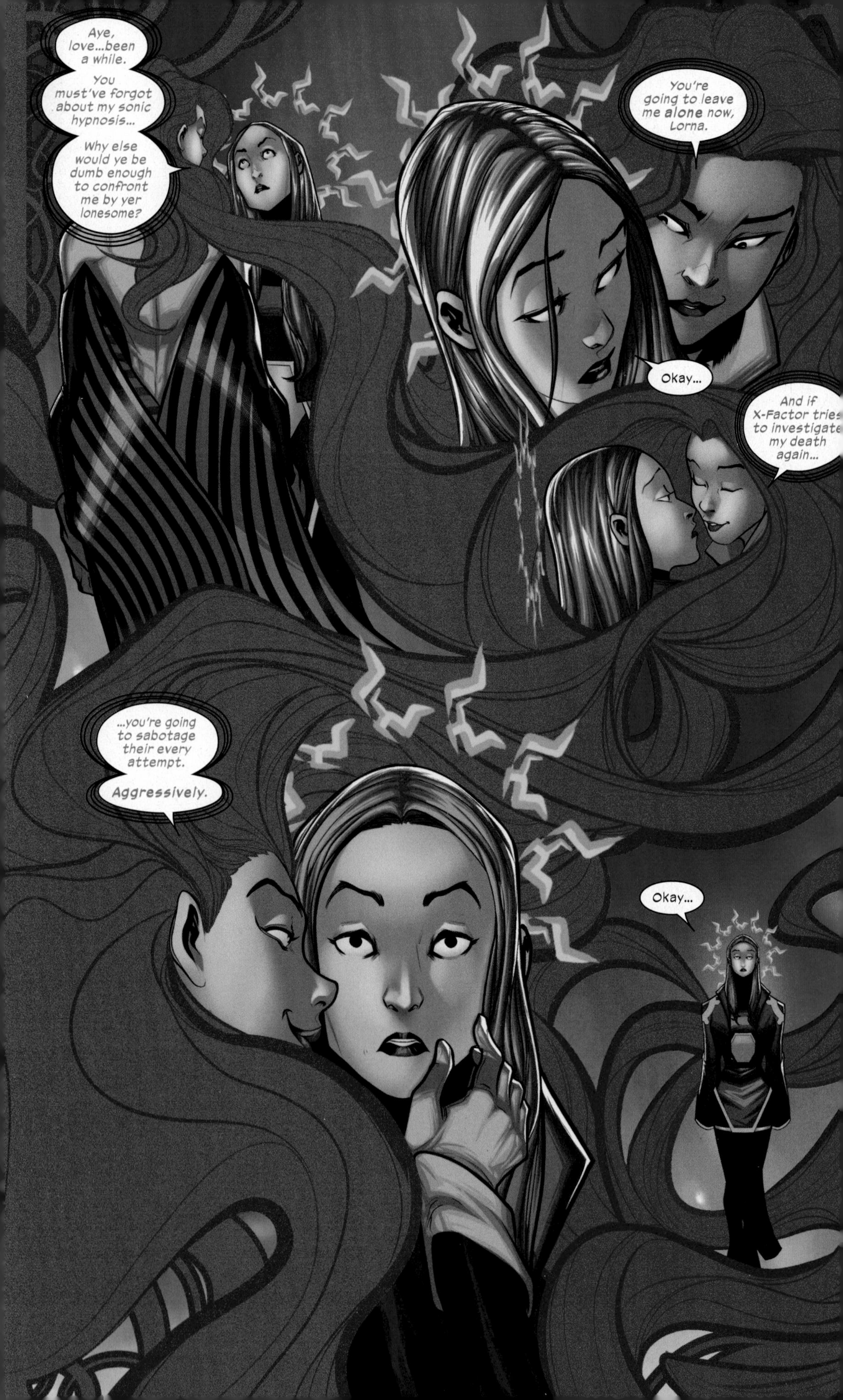
Aye, love...been a while.
You must've forgot about my sonic hypnosis...
Why else would ye be dumb enough to confront me by yer lonesome?
You're going to leave me alone now, Lorna.
Okay...
And if X-Factor tries to investigate my death again...
...you're going to sabotage their every attempt.
Aggressively.
Okay...

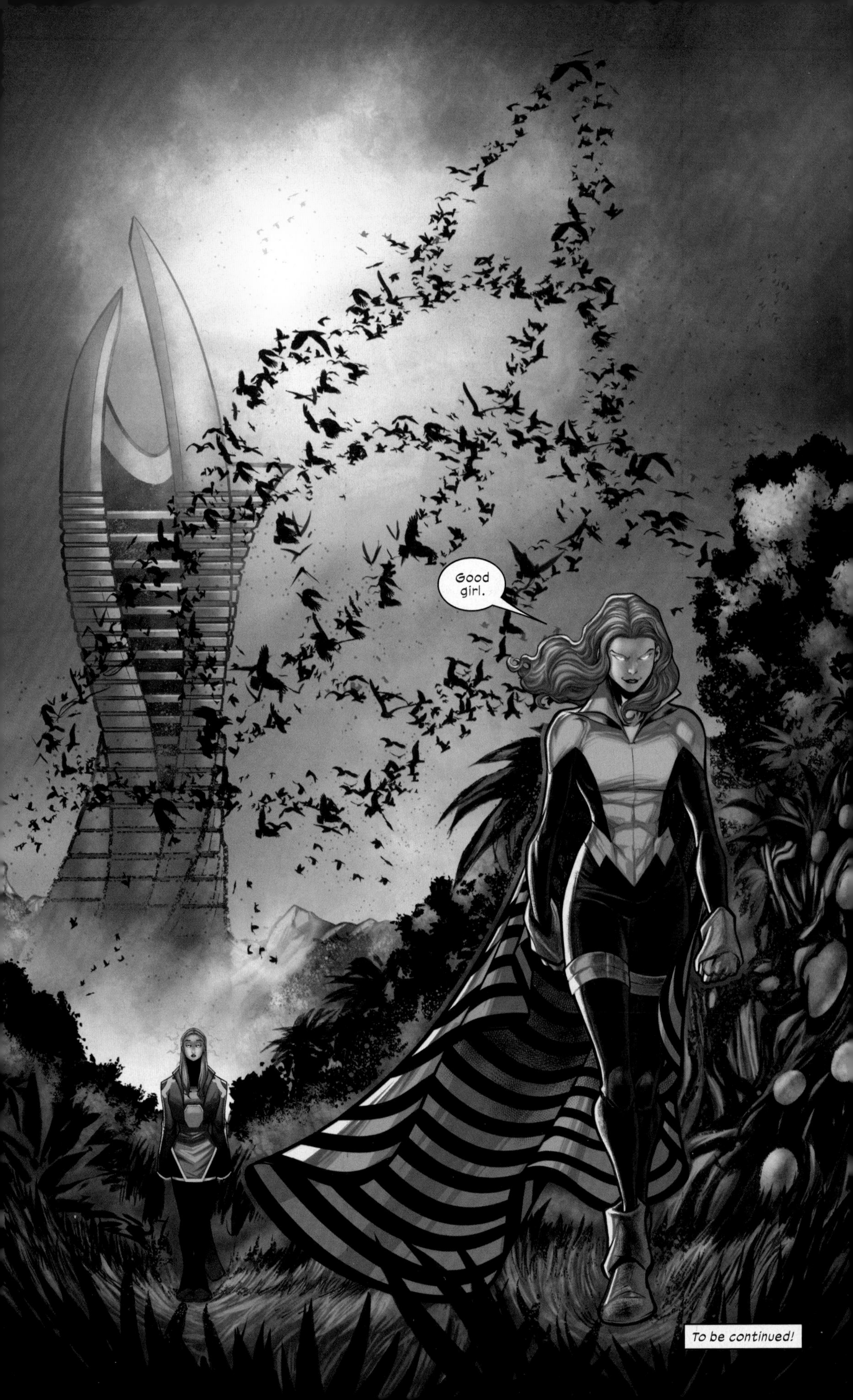
Good girl.
To be continued!

FROM THE PHONE OF DAVID ALLEYNE

SM We have to talk about this, David

You can't just drop a bombshell about your dying recently and then act like I don't know

But you ALREADY know everything I know. **DA**

I told you, I died around the same time as Loa and Rahne.

Our deaths were presumably related.

SM Why would you go get yourself involved in all that, you were depowered

Gee, I dunno, Sofia. Why would you go to the MOJOVERSE while depowered? **DA**

SM ...

point lol

-_- **DA**

Wait...

Why am I suddenly getting a million calls from Tommy?

SOFIA

SM Told Tommy, not sorry

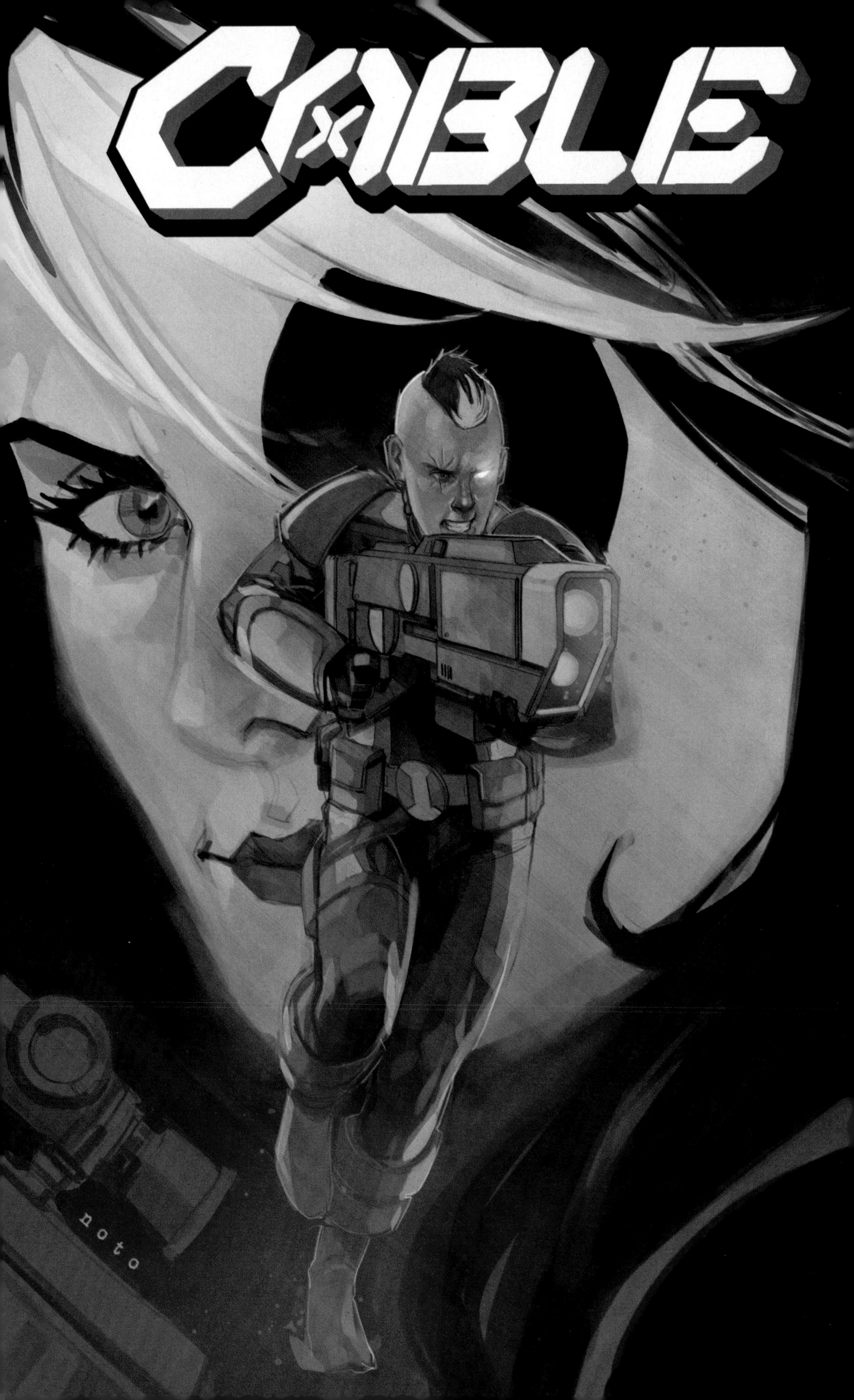
CABLE
noto

⌐ca__[0.8]
 [ble_[0.8]

There is only hate in Stryfe's heart, and I hate that he looks like me. It puts me off my game. Causes me to make mistakes.

-- NATE SUMMERS

⌐ca__[0.X]
 [ble_[0.X]

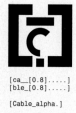

[ca__[0.8].....]
[ble_[0.8].....]

[Cable_alpha.]

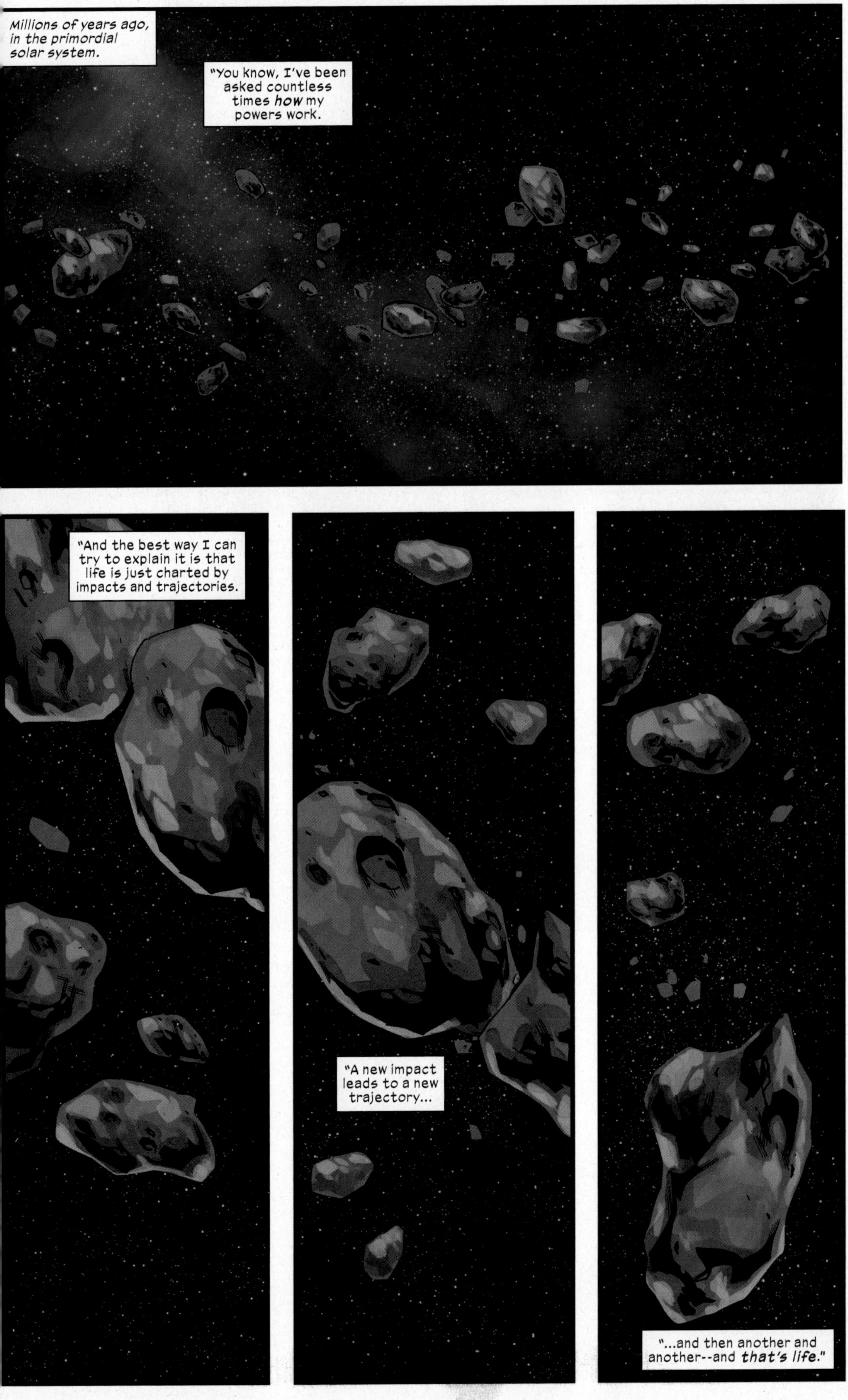
Millions of years ago, in the primordial solar system.
"You know, I've been asked countless times *how* my powers work.
"And the best way I can try to explain it is that life is just charted by impacts and trajectories.
"A new impact leads to a new trajectory...
"...and then another and another--and *that's life.*"

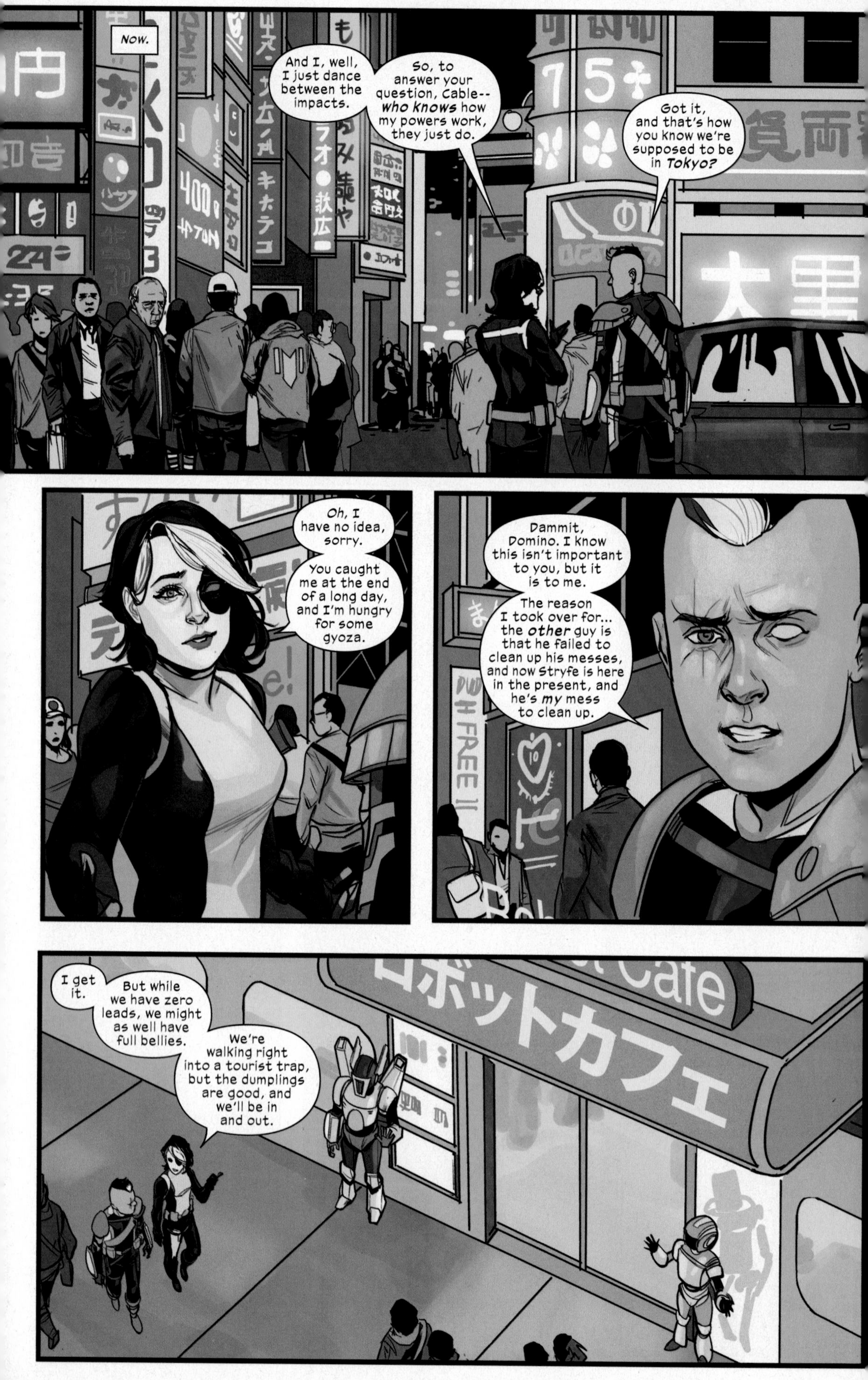
NOW.
And I, well, I just dance between the impacts.
So, to answer your question, Cable-- *who knows* how my powers work, they just do.
Got it, and that's how you know we're supposed to be in *Tokyo?*
Oh, I have no idea, sorry.
You caught me at the end of a long day, and I'm hungry for some gyoza.
Dammit, Domino. I know this isn't important to you, but it is to me.
The reason I took over for... the *other* guy is that he failed to clean up his messes, and now Stryfe is here in the present, and he's *my* mess to clean up.
I get it.
But while we have zero leads, we might as well have full bellies.
We're walking right into a tourist trap, but the dumplings are good, and we'll be in and out.
ロボットカフェ

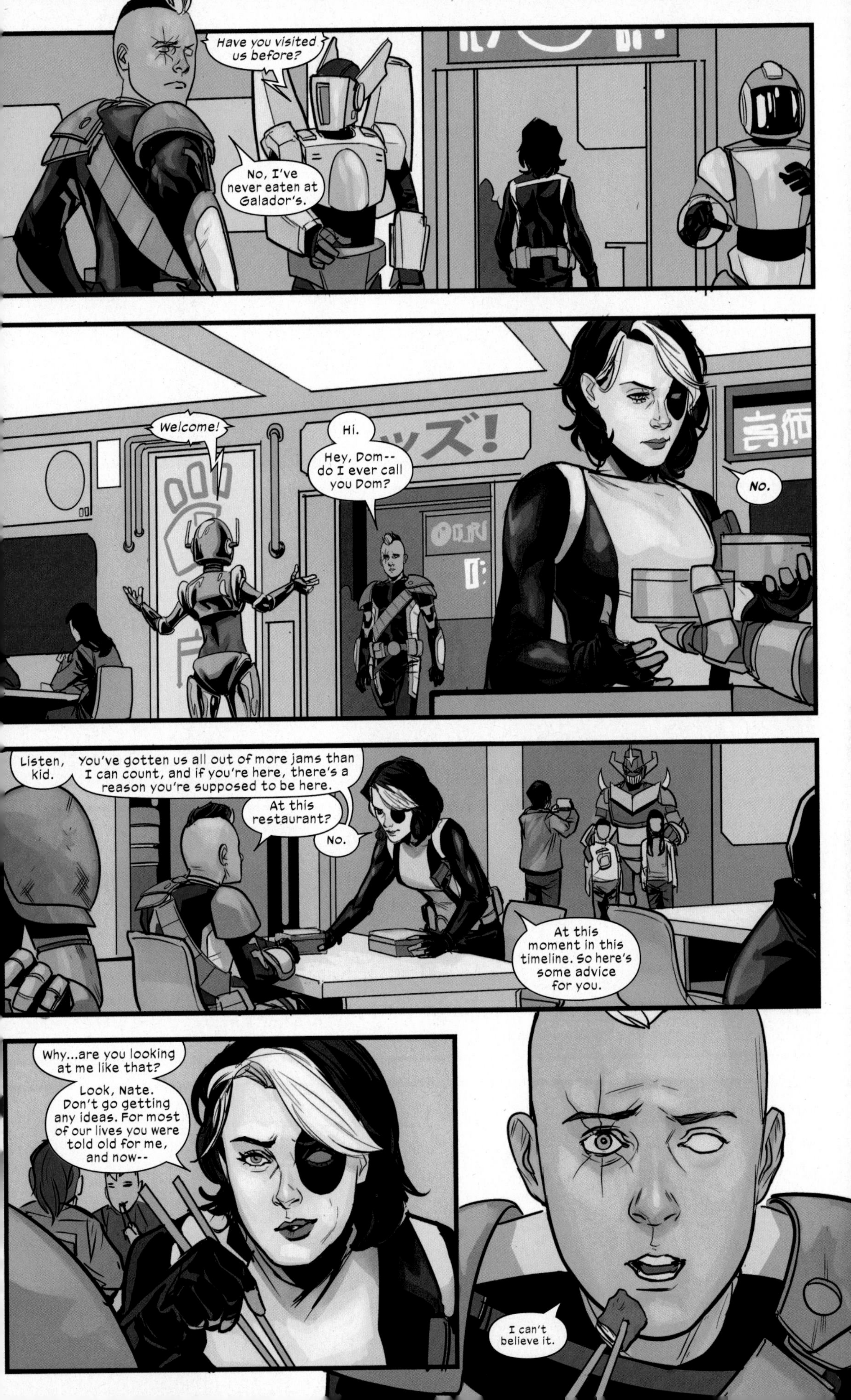
Have you visited us before?
No, I've never eaten at Galador's.
Welcome!
Hi.
Hey, Dom-- do I ever call you Dom?
No.
Listen, kid.
You've gotten us all out of more jams than I can count, and if you're here, there's a reason you're supposed to be here.
At this restaurant?
No.
At this moment in this timeline. So here's some advice for you.
Why...are you looking at me like that?
Look, Nate. Don't go getting any ideas. For most of our lives you were told old for me, and now--
I can't believe it.

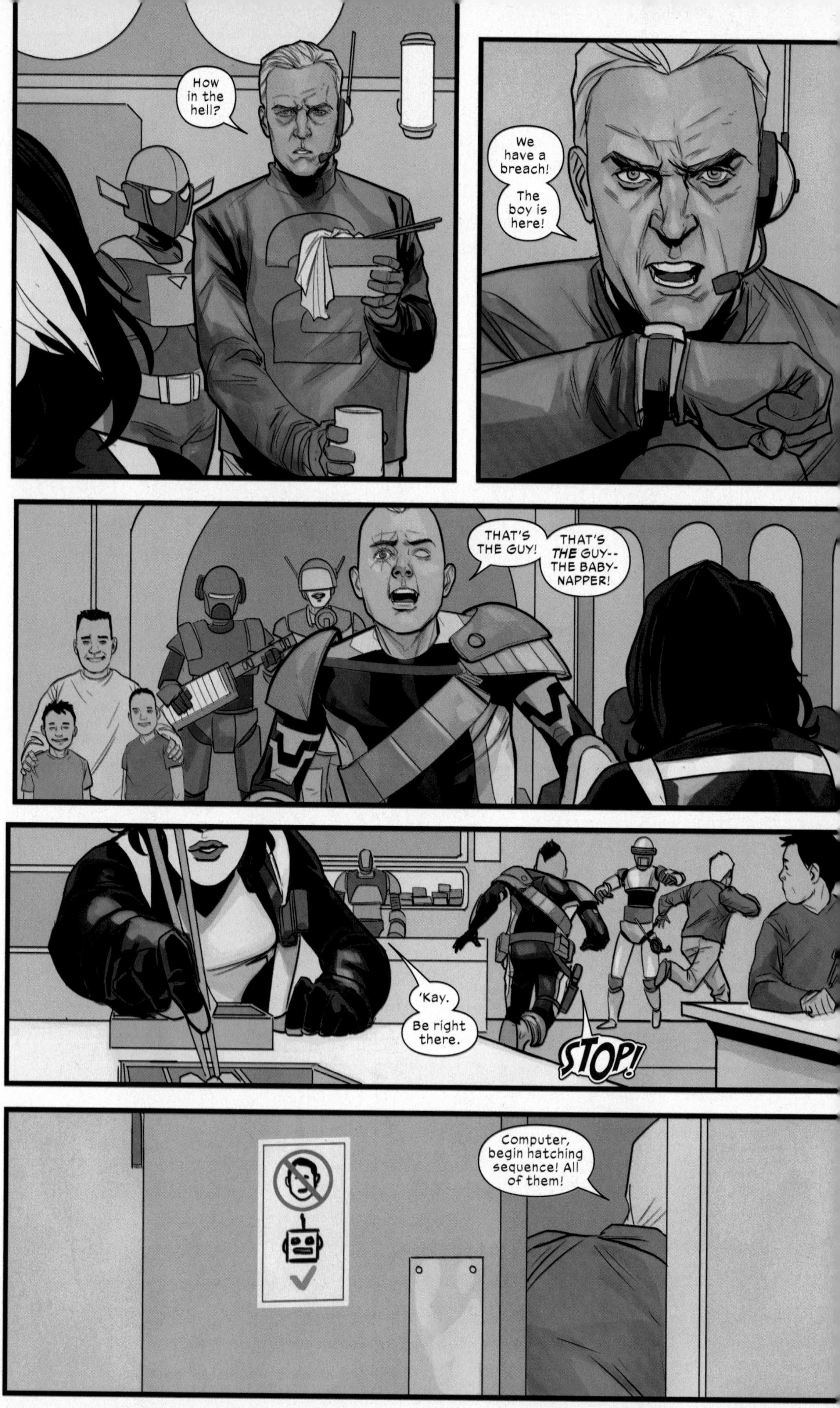
How in the hell?
We have a breach!
The boy is here!
THAT'S THE GUY!
THAT'S THE GUY-- THE BABY-NAPPER!
'Kay.
Be right there.
STOP!
Computer, begin hatching sequence! All of them!

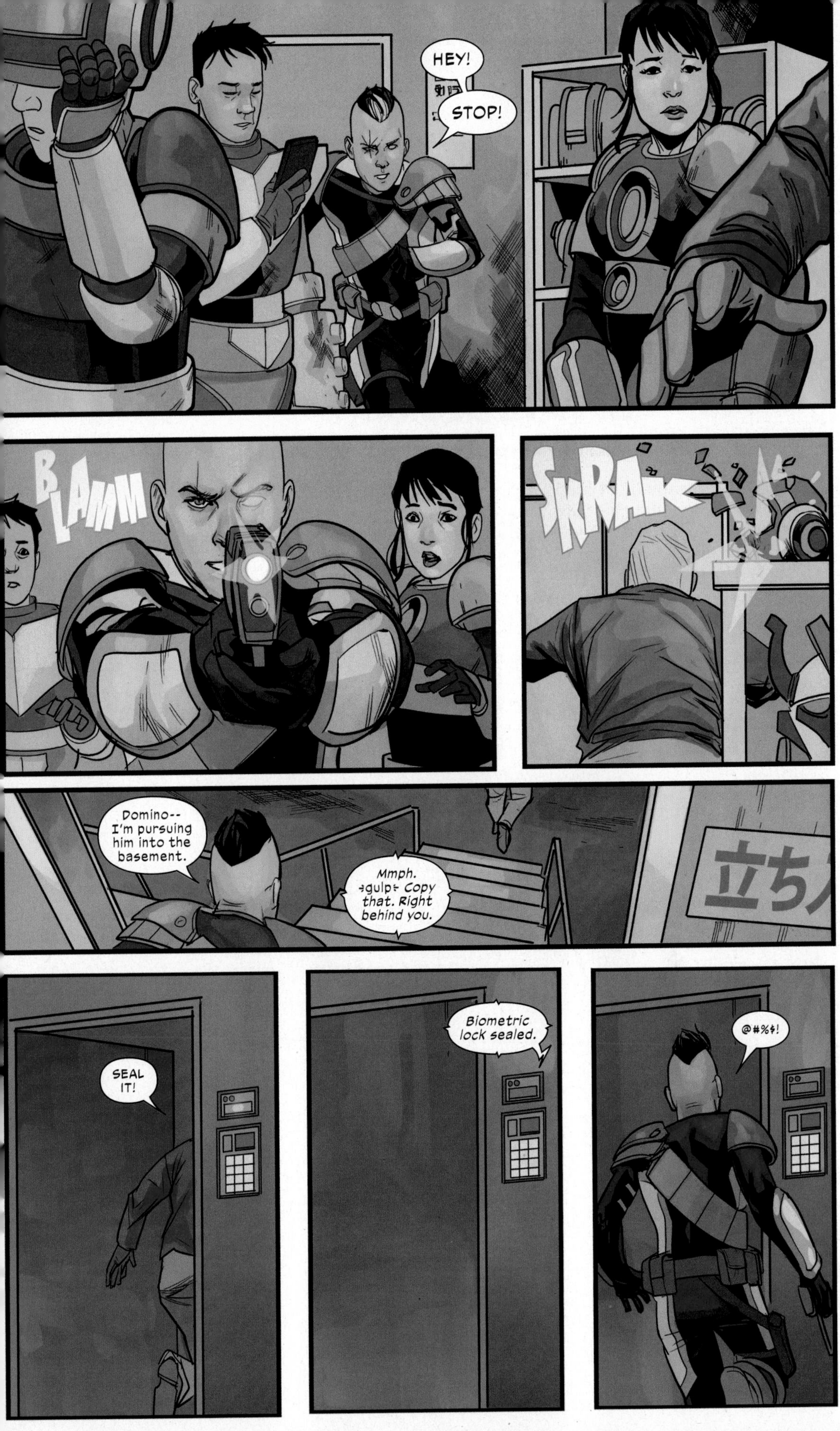
HEY!
STOP!
BLAMM
SKRAK
Domino-- I'm pursuing him into the basement.
Mmph. ‡gulp‡ Copy that. Right behind you.
立ち
SEAL IT!
Biometric lock sealed.
@#%‡!

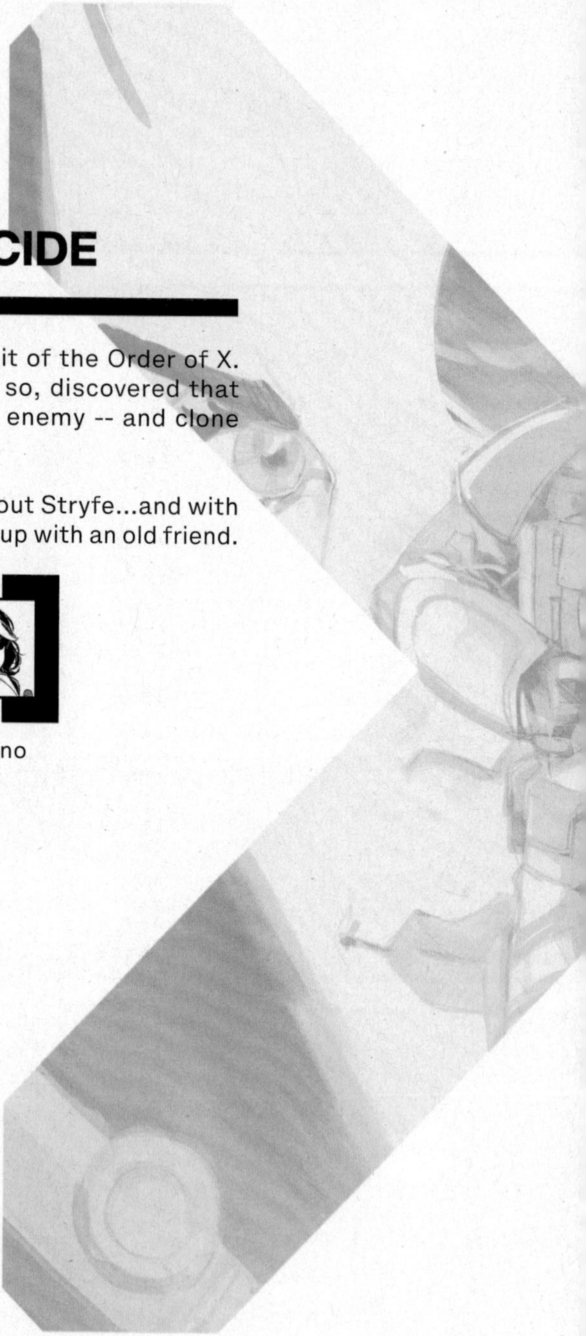

LET FATE DECIDE

CABLE was out of leads in his pursuit of the Order of X. He took down the cult, but in doing so, discovered that they'd been co-opted by Stryfe, the enemy -- and clone -- of his older self.

Now he's on the hunt for the truth about Stryfe...and with no clue where to go next, he's teamed up with an old friend.

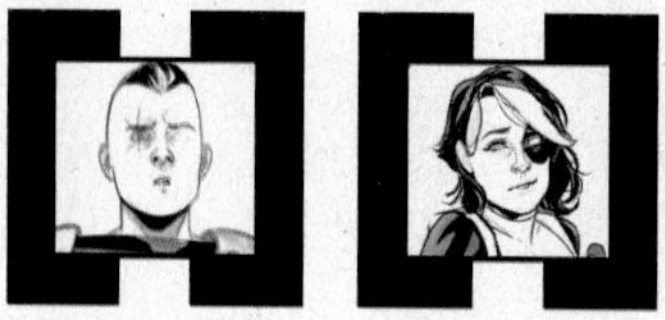

Cable Domino

[00_Reign]
[00___ofX]

CABLE
[X_08]

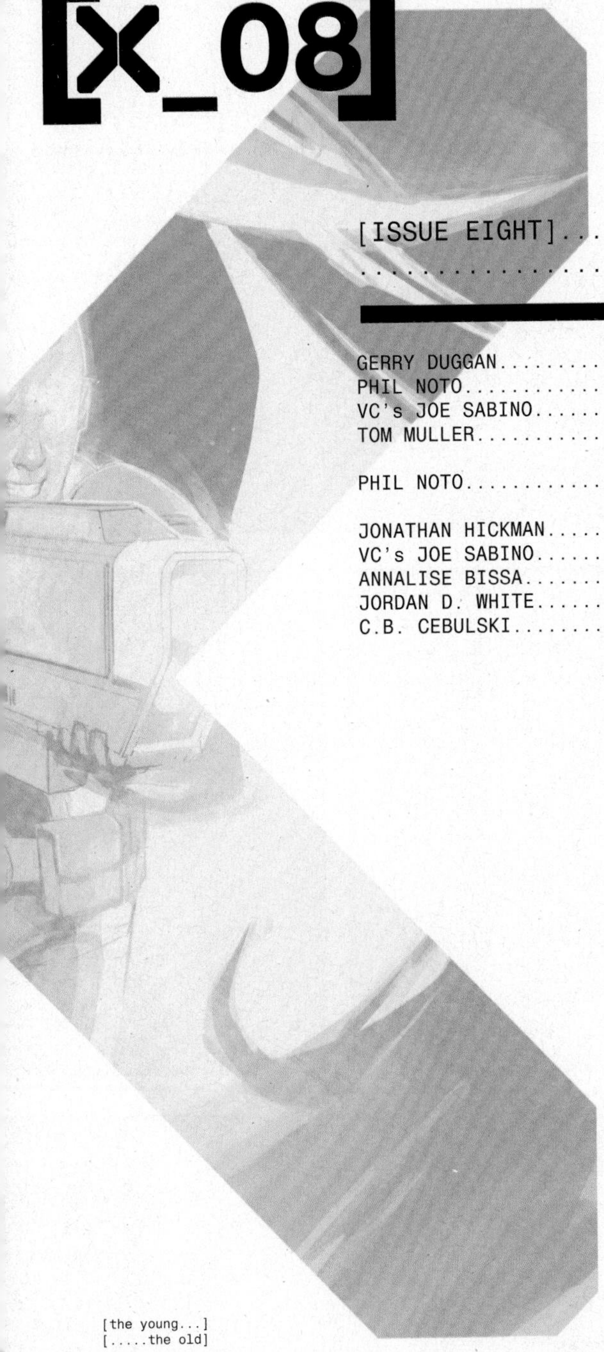

[ISSUE EIGHT]..................................
..........................MY DINNER WITH DOMINO

GERRY DUGGAN..[WRITER]
PHIL NOTO...[ARTIST]
VC's JOE SABINO....................................[LETTERER]
TOM MULLER..[DESIGN]

PHIL NOTO.....................................[COVER ARTIST]

JONATHAN HICKMAN..............................[HEAD OF X]
VC's JOE SABINO..............................[PRODUCTION]
ANNALISE BISSA.........................[ASSOCIATE EDITOR]
JORDAN D. WHITE...................................[EDITOR]
C.B. CEBULSKI............................[EDITOR IN CHIEF]

[the young...]
[.....the old]

[00_00....0]
[00_00....8]

[XX___past]
[00_______]

[00_______]

[future_XX]

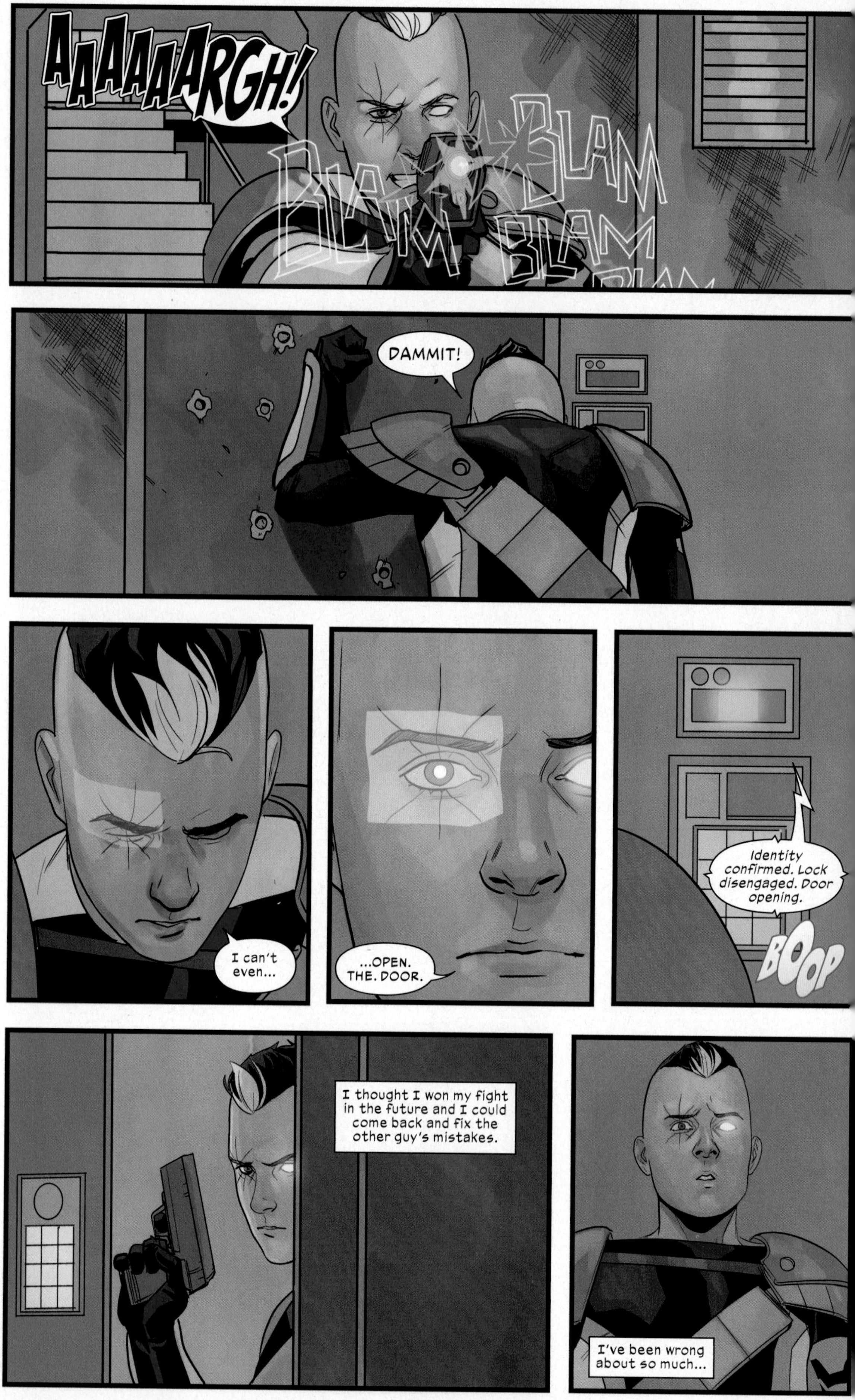
AAAAAARGH!
BLAM BLAM BLAM BLAM
DAMMIT!
I can't even...
...OPEN. THE. DOOR.
Identity confirmed. Lock disengaged. Door opening.
BOOP
I thought I won my fight in the future and I could come back and fix the other guy's mistakes.
I've been wrong about so much...

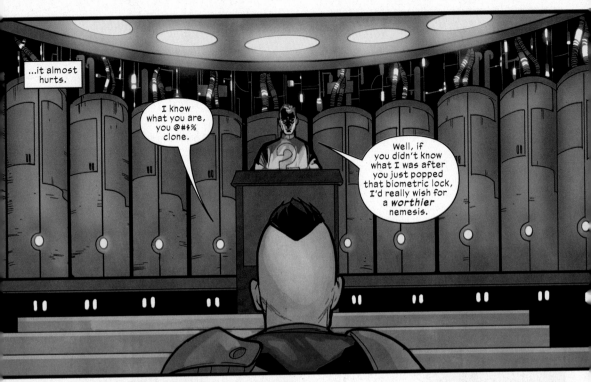

...it almost hurts.

I know what you are, you @#$% clone.

Well, if you didn't know what I was after you just popped that biometric lock, I'd really wish for a *worthier* nemesis.

Step away from the console.

Or *I will kill you.*

I lost contact with the clone in the United States. I assume you killed him?

It's funny. At first, Stryfe was flummoxed. He couldn't understand why you abandoned your war and why you went back in time and took your older self off the board. He assumed it was a trap.

It turns out you just enjoy South Pacific vacations, and for someone who says they don't like clones...well, you sure date enough of them.

I thought I killed Stryfe before I traveled back in time.

Now you're going to step away from that console and tell me where--and *when*--he is--or I swear I'll turn your head into a canoe.

I know. But he'll do *worse.*

There are moments when you can feel the future bum-rushing straight at you--

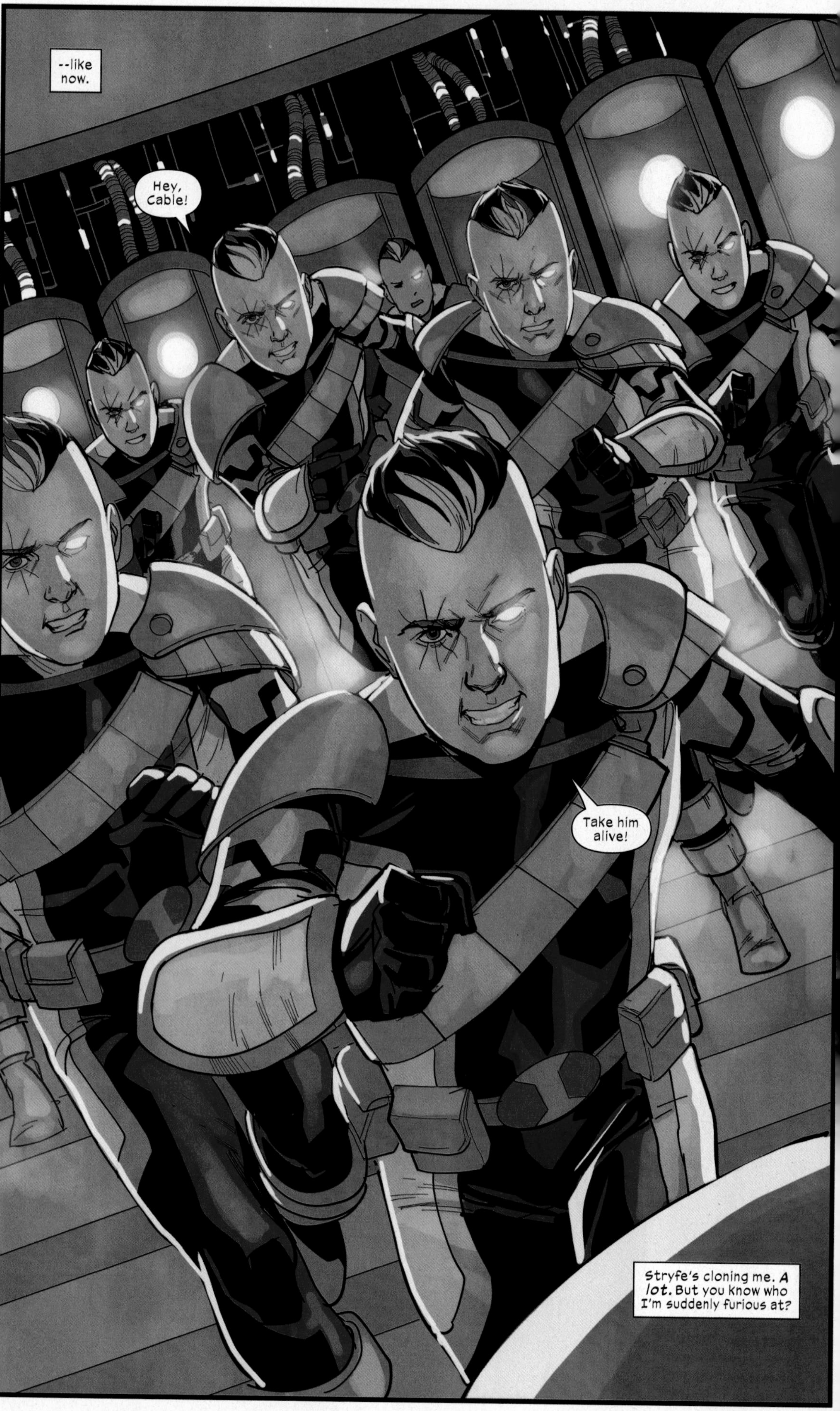
--like now.
Hey, Cable!
Take him alive!
Stryfe's cloning me. *A lot.* But you know who I'm suddenly furious at?

Apocalypse.

He raised the first Stryfe clone--*why?*

Was he trying to sharpen me to do some awful thing that would save us all?

The Big A is gone, and I got other problems-- something Domino said back there--about there being a *reason* I'm here.

gaAAK!

Is this it? Am I here because Stryfe is here, or is the opposite true?

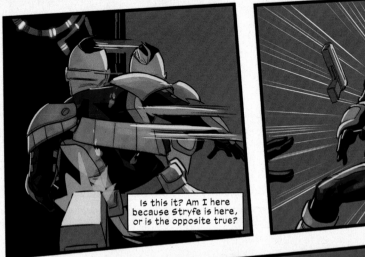

Maybe it doesn't matter--I can't fight the future.

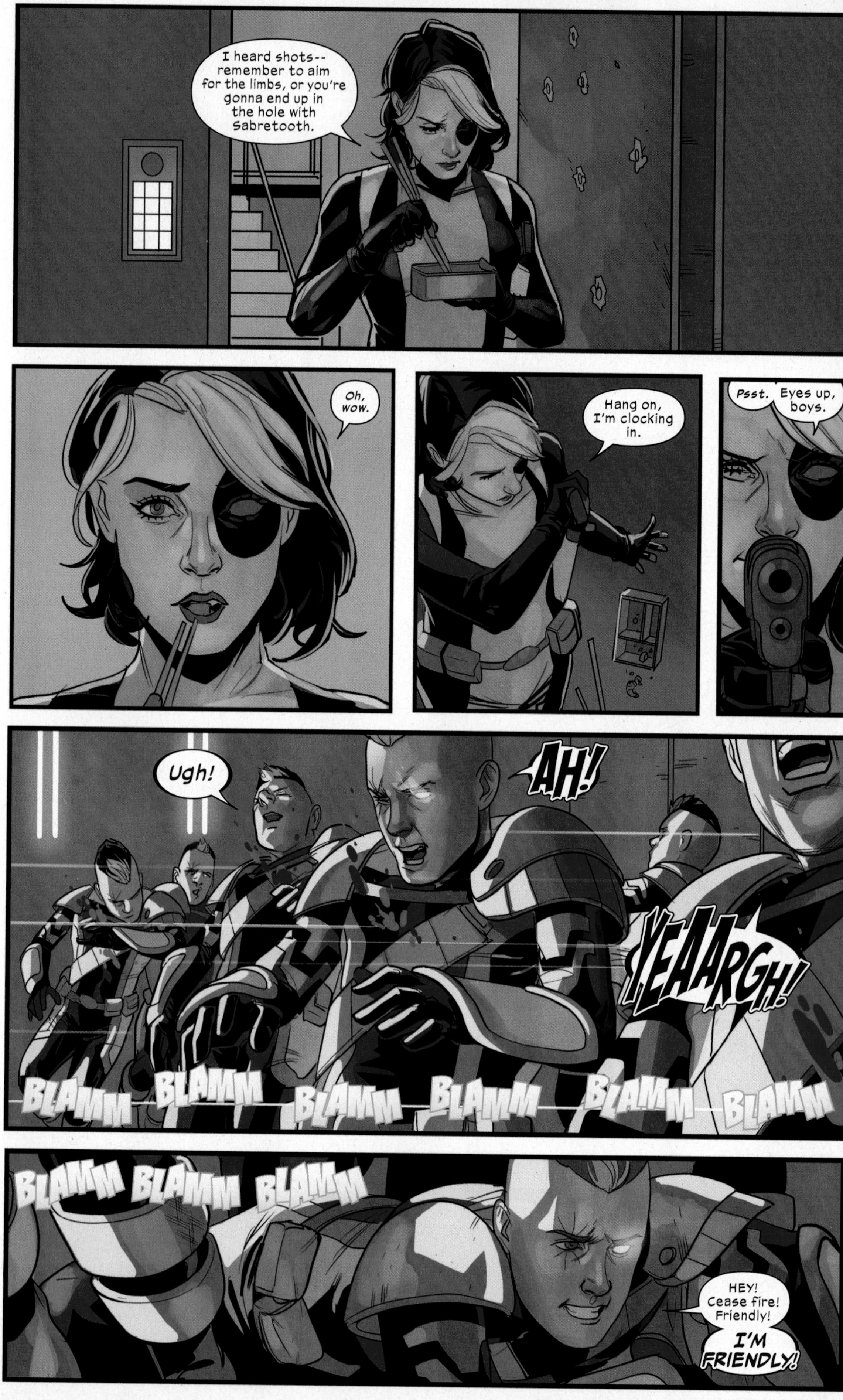

I heard shots--remember to aim for the limbs, or you're gonna end up in the hole with Sabretooth.
Oh, wow.
Hang on, I'm clocking in.
Psst.
Eyes up, boys.
Ugh!
AH!
YEAARGH!
BLAMM BLAMM BLAMM BLAMM BLAMM BLAMM
BLAMM BLAMM BLAMM
HEY! Cease fire! Friendly!
I'M FRIENDLY!

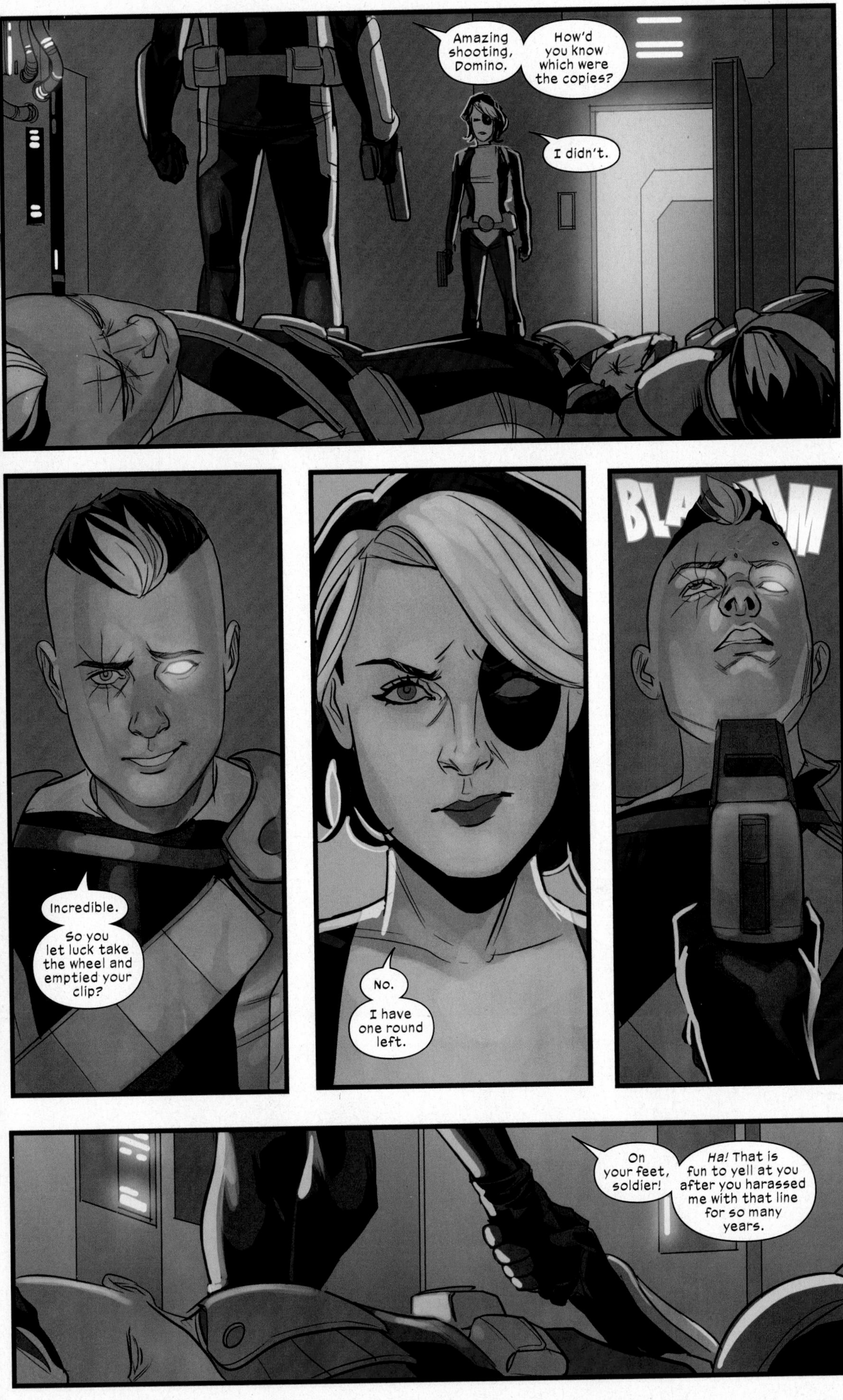
Amazing shooting, Domino.
How'd you know which were the copies?
I didn't.
Incredible.
So you let luck take the wheel and emptied your clip?
No.
I have one round left.
On your feet, soldier!
Ha! That is fun to yell at you after you harassed me with that line for so many years.

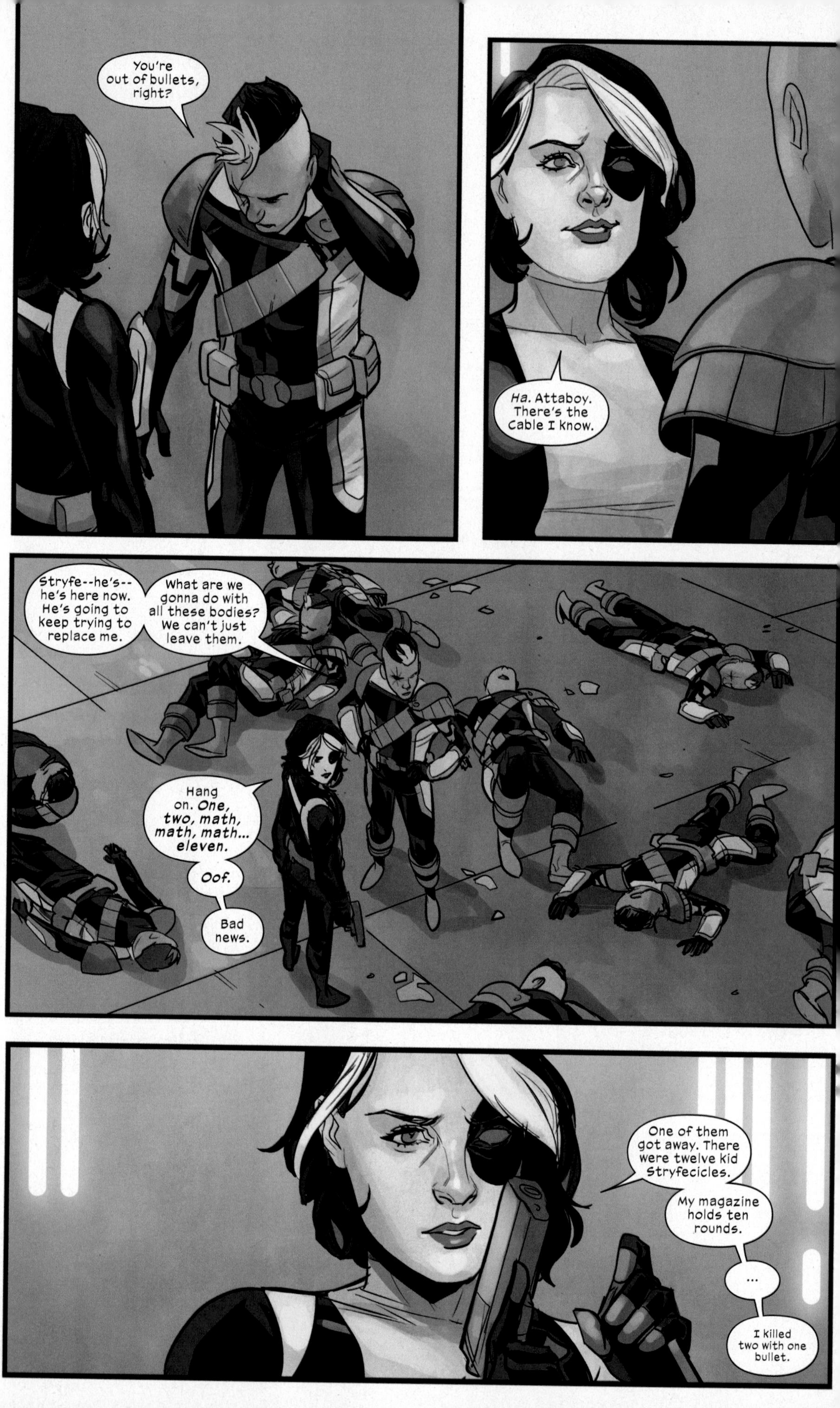

You're out of bullets, right?
Ha. Attaboy. There's the Cable I know.
Stryfe--he's--he's here now. He's going to keep trying to replace me.
What are we gonna do with all these bodies? We can't just leave them.
Hang on. One, two, math, math, math... eleven.
Oof.
Bad news.
One of them got away. There were twelve kid Stryfecicles.
My magazine holds ten rounds.
...
I killed two with one bullet.

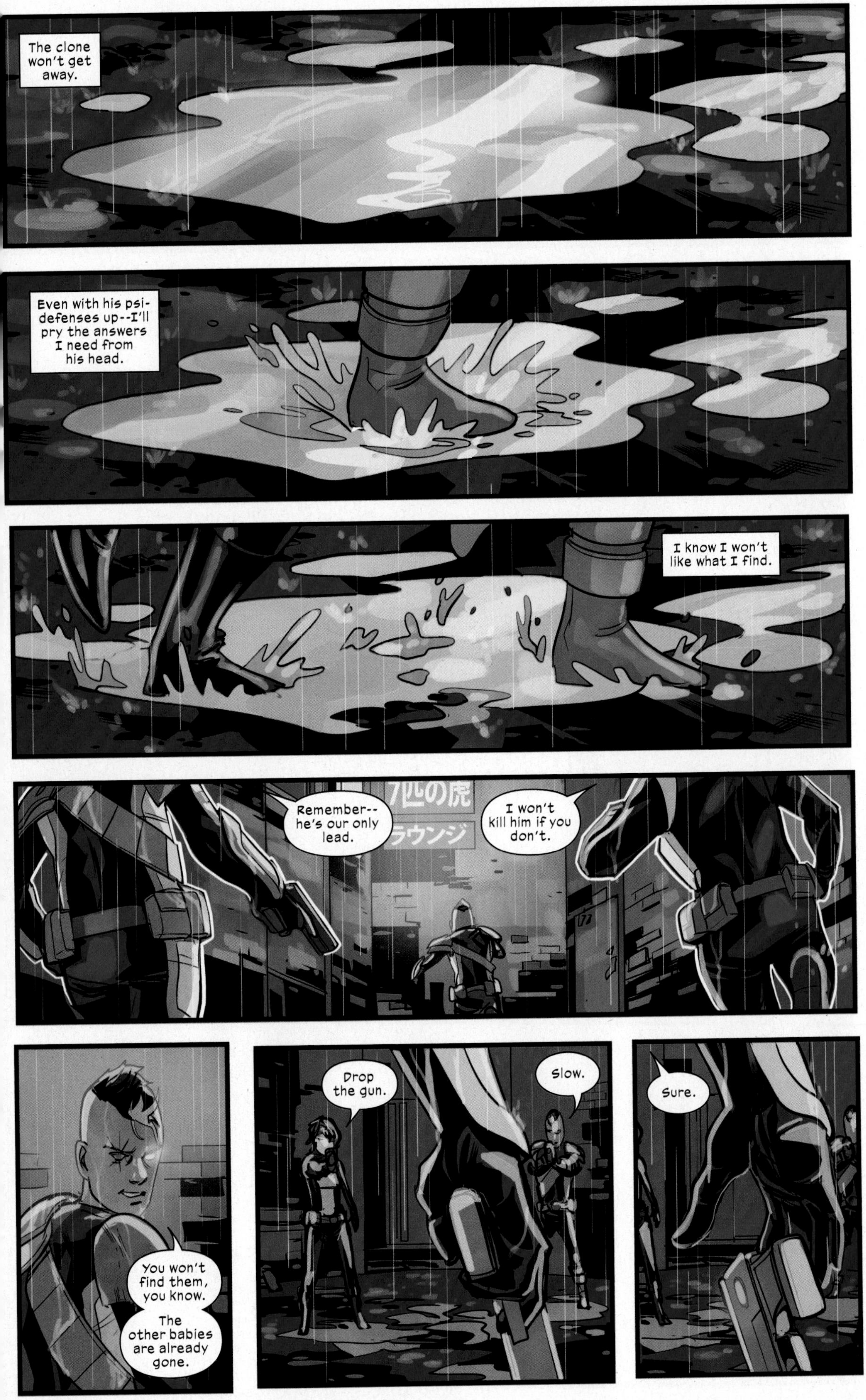

The clone won't get away.
Even with his psi-defenses up--I'll pry the answers I need from his head.
I know I won't like what I find.
7匹の虎
ラウンジ
Remember--he's our only lead.
I won't kill him if you don't.
You won't find them, you know.
The other babies are already gone.
Drop the gun.
Slow.
Sure.

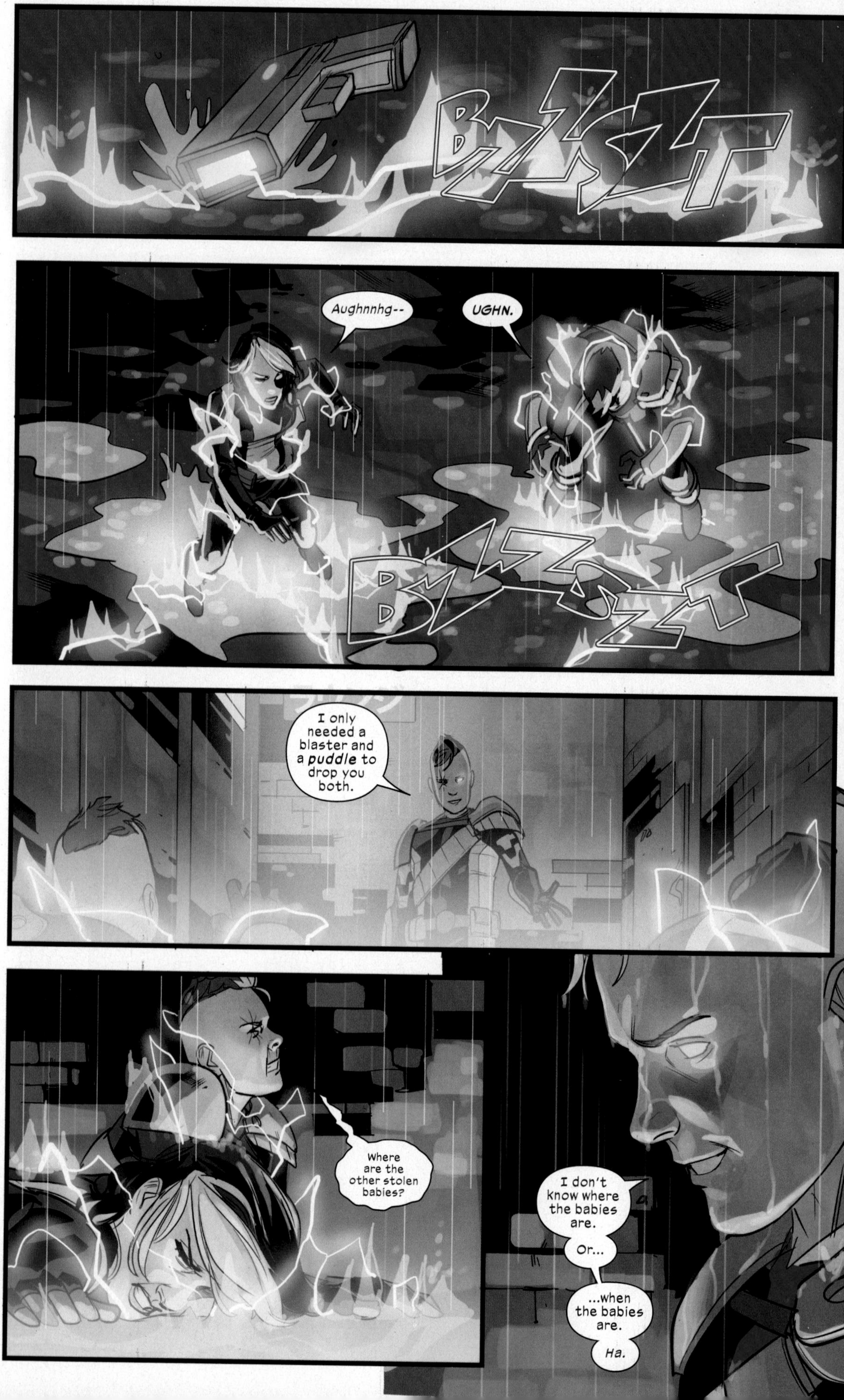
BZZZT
Aughnnhg--
UGHN.
BZZZT
I only needed a blaster and a *puddle* to drop you both.
Where are the other stolen babies?
I don't know where the babies are.
Or...
...when the babies are.
Ha.

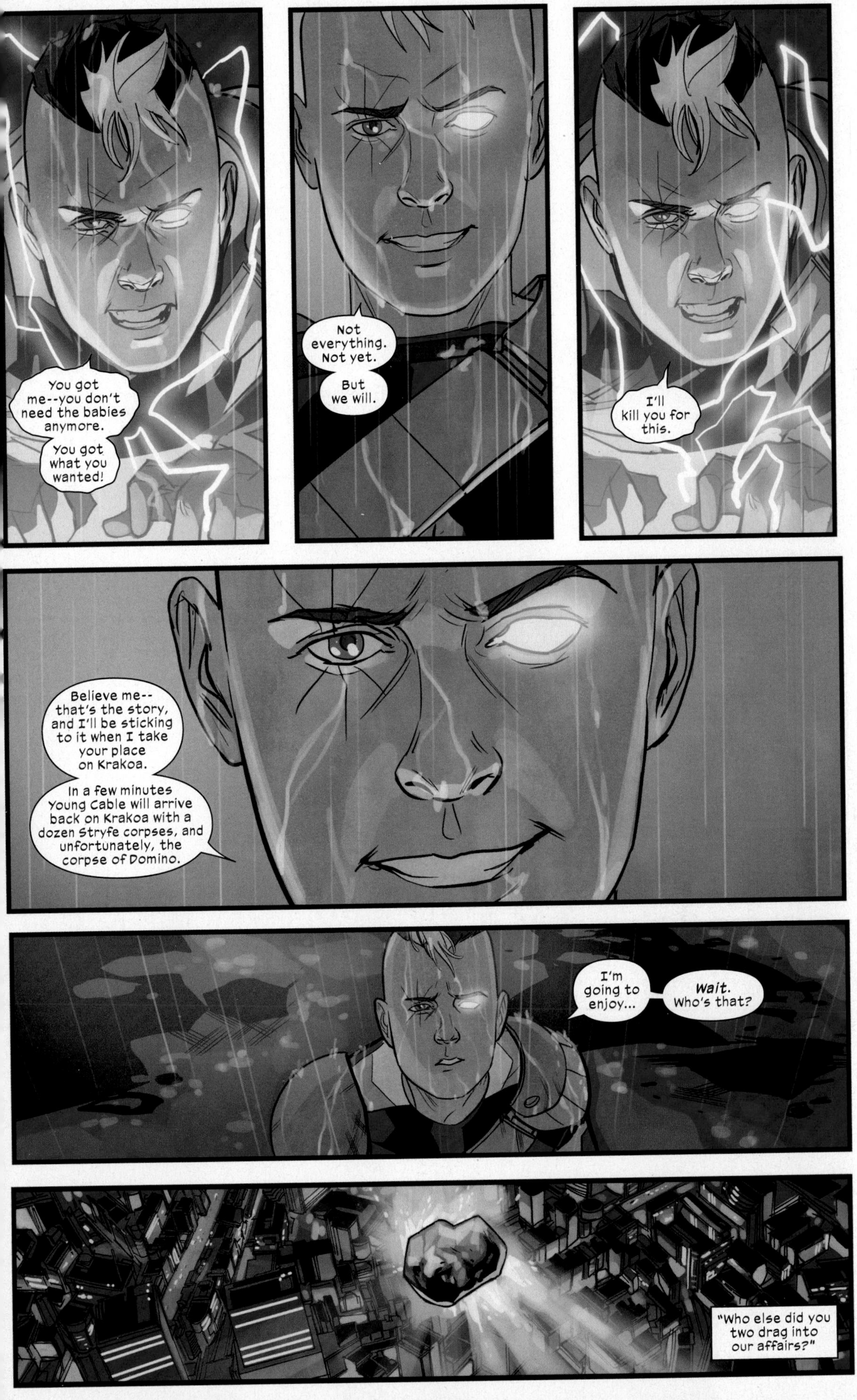
You got me--you don't need the babies anymore.
You got what you wanted!
Not everything. Not yet.
But we will.
I'll kill you for this.
Believe me-- that's the story, and I'll be sticking to it when I take your place on Krakoa.
In a few minutes Young Cable will arrive back on Krakoa with a dozen Stryfe corpses, and unfortunately, the corpse of Domino.
I'm going to enjoy...
Wait. Who's that?
"Who else did you two drag into our affairs?"

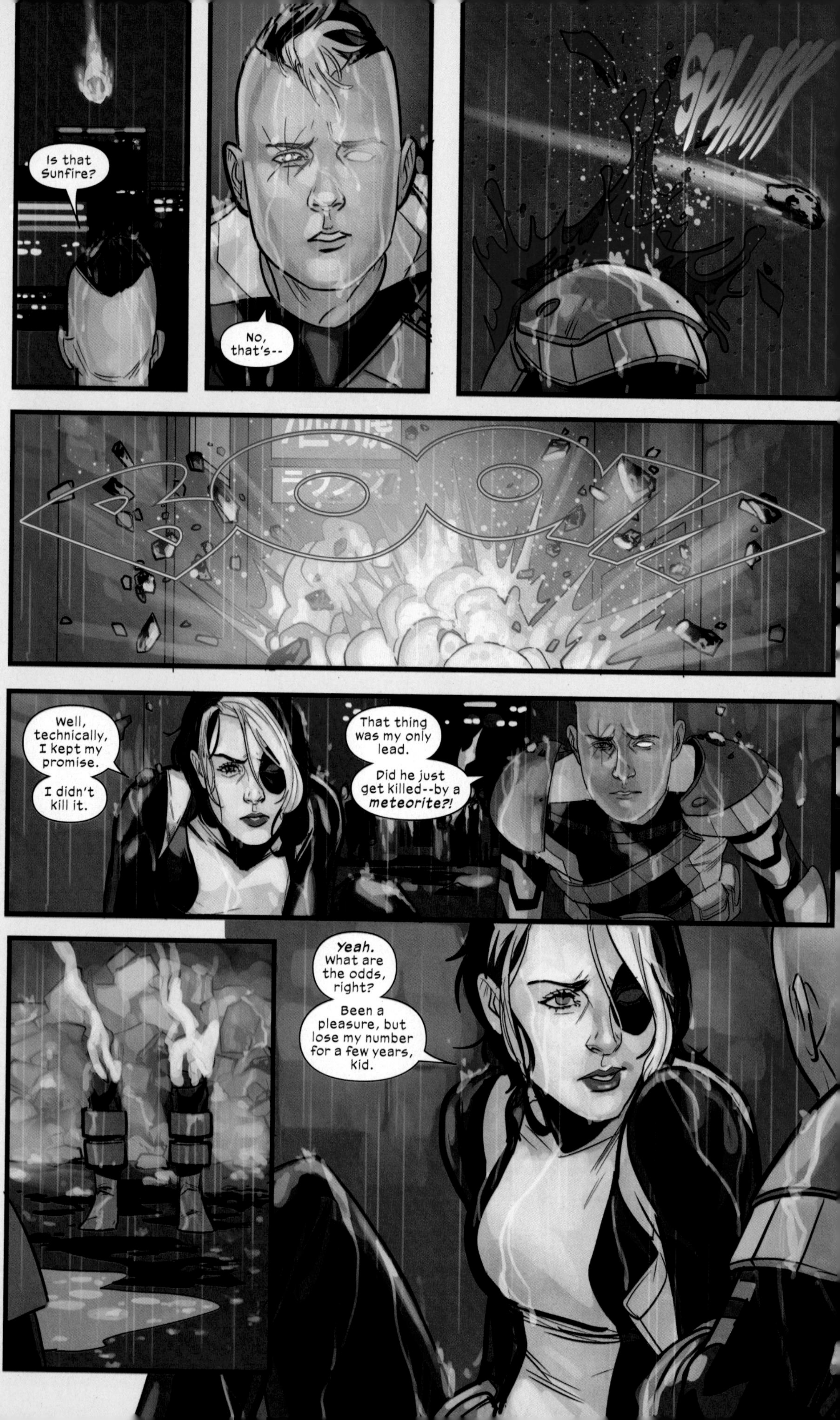
Is that Sunfire?
No, that's--
SPLAKK
BOOM
Well, technically, I kept my promise.
I didn't kill it.
That thing was my only lead.
Did he just get killed--by a *meteorite?!*
Yeah. What are the odds, right?
Been a pleasure, but lose my number for a few years, kid.

Beast — Good news/bad news: Cable and I went to Tokyo for gyoza and ended up causing a mess. Decent size. A Logan-sized mess. Need a cleaning crew. — Domino

That's not the business we're in. Will any of the "mess" be missed?

No. It's 12 Stryfe clones -- well, 11 and change. They're in the body of young Nate. Send someone to puke some acid onto them? Tempest?

Oh, there is one clone of middle-aged Nate -- another copy of the one that was stealing babies in Philly. Nobody will miss him, though. Is Sunfire around? He could just wiggle his fingers and sort this,

Hello?

Stand by.

What's the hold-up? Will Maggot's worm guys eat clones? Do you have Deadpool's number? Maybe he'll want them?

X-Factor is inbound.

Thank you.

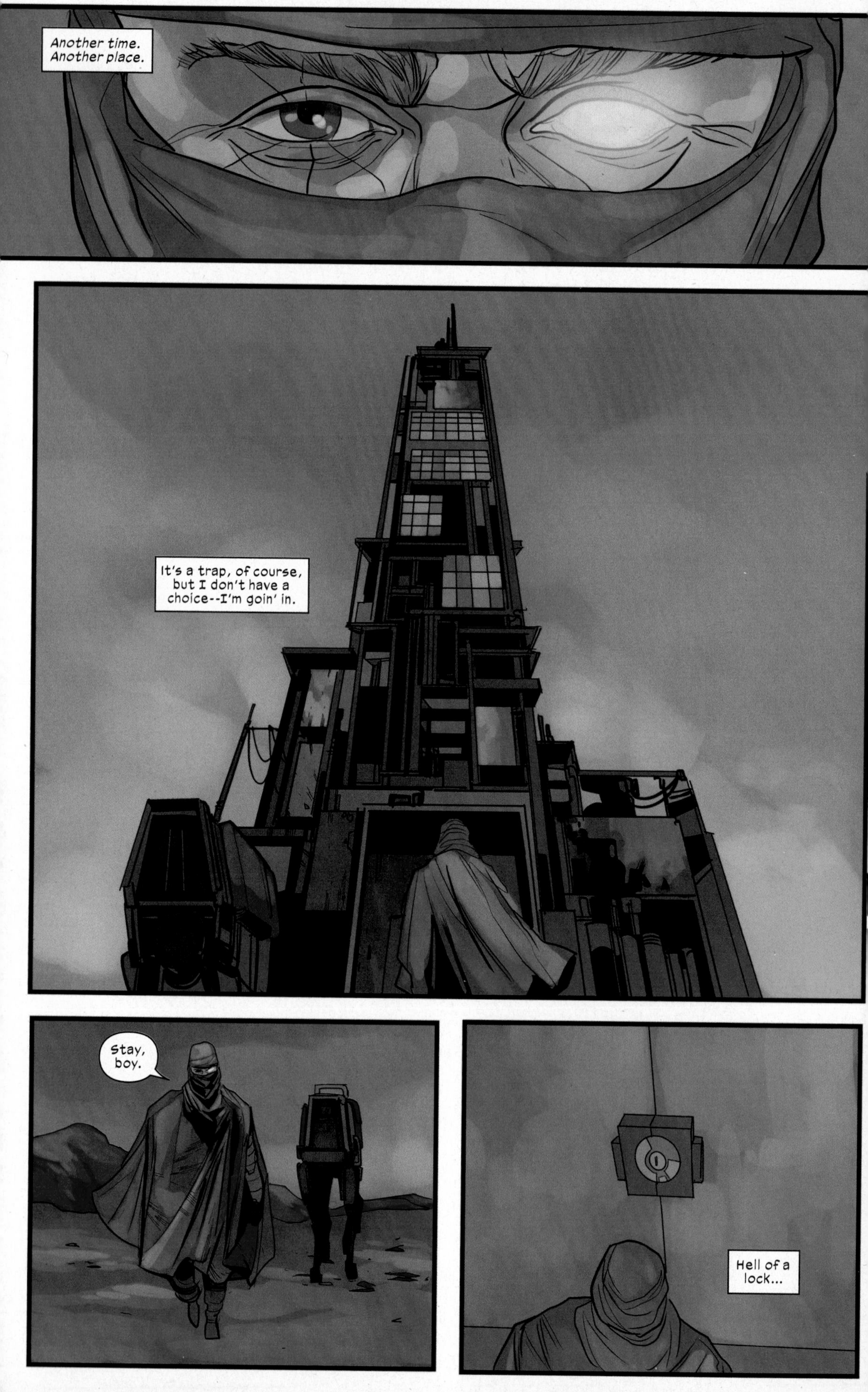
Another time.
Another place.
It's a trap, of course, but I don't have a choice--I'm goin' in.
Stay, boy.
Hell of a lock...

...I can do it the loud way or the quiet way.

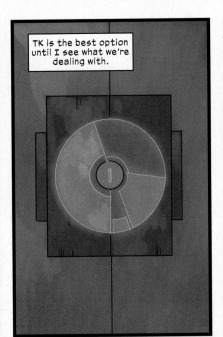

TK is the best option until I see what we're dealing with.

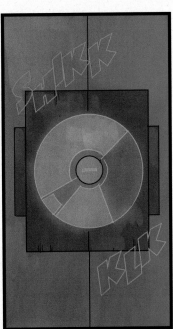

SHIKK

KLK

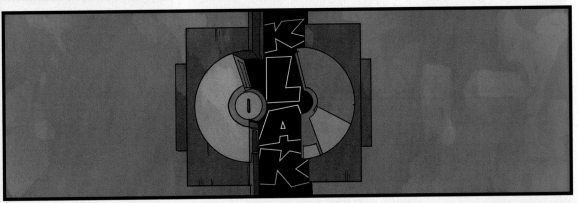

KLAK

No alarms. Stale air. Bad air. Decomp. I'd better not be too late.

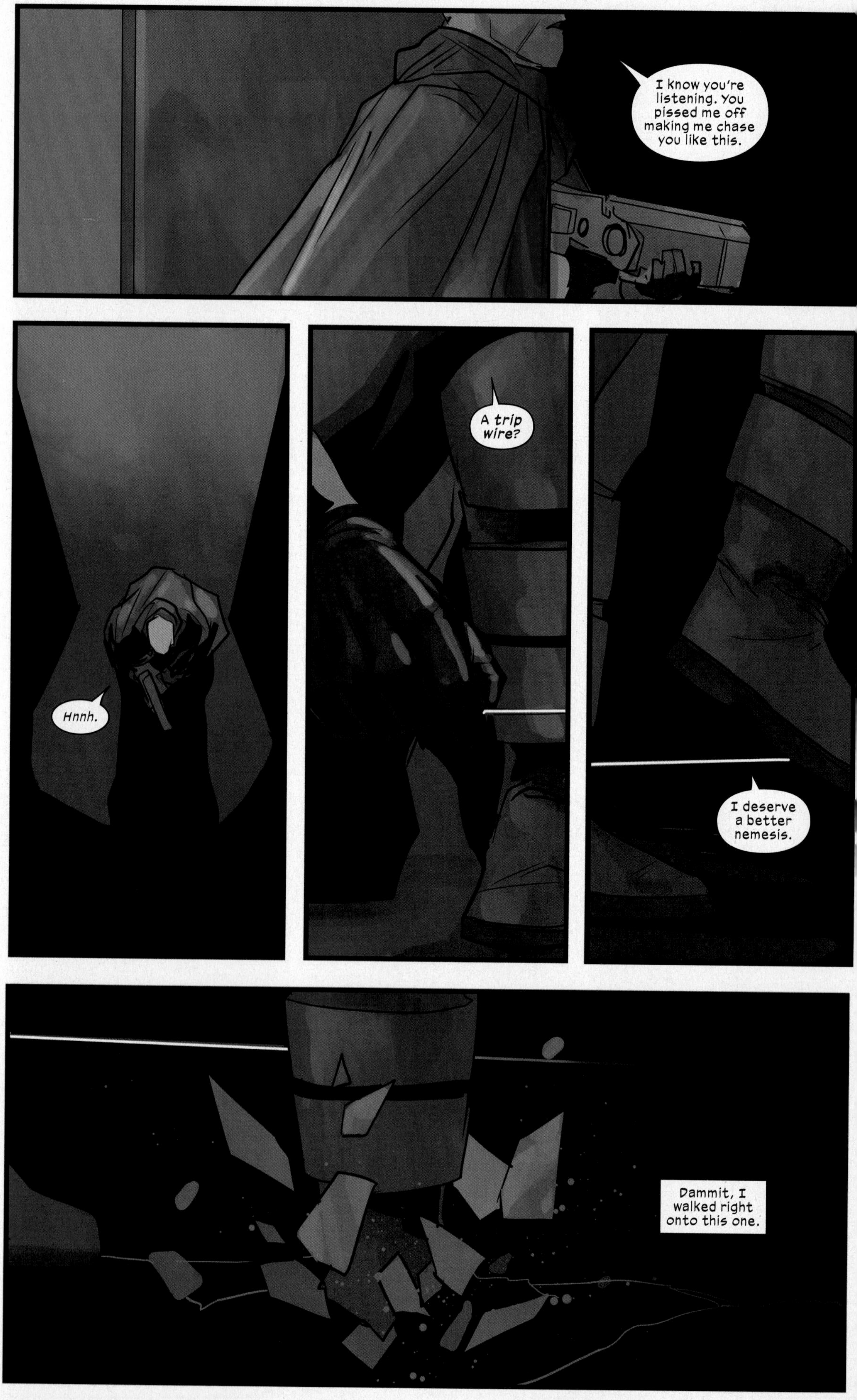
I know you're listening. You pissed me off making me chase you like this.
Hnnh.
A *trip* wire?
I deserve a better nemesis.
Dammit, I walked right onto this one.

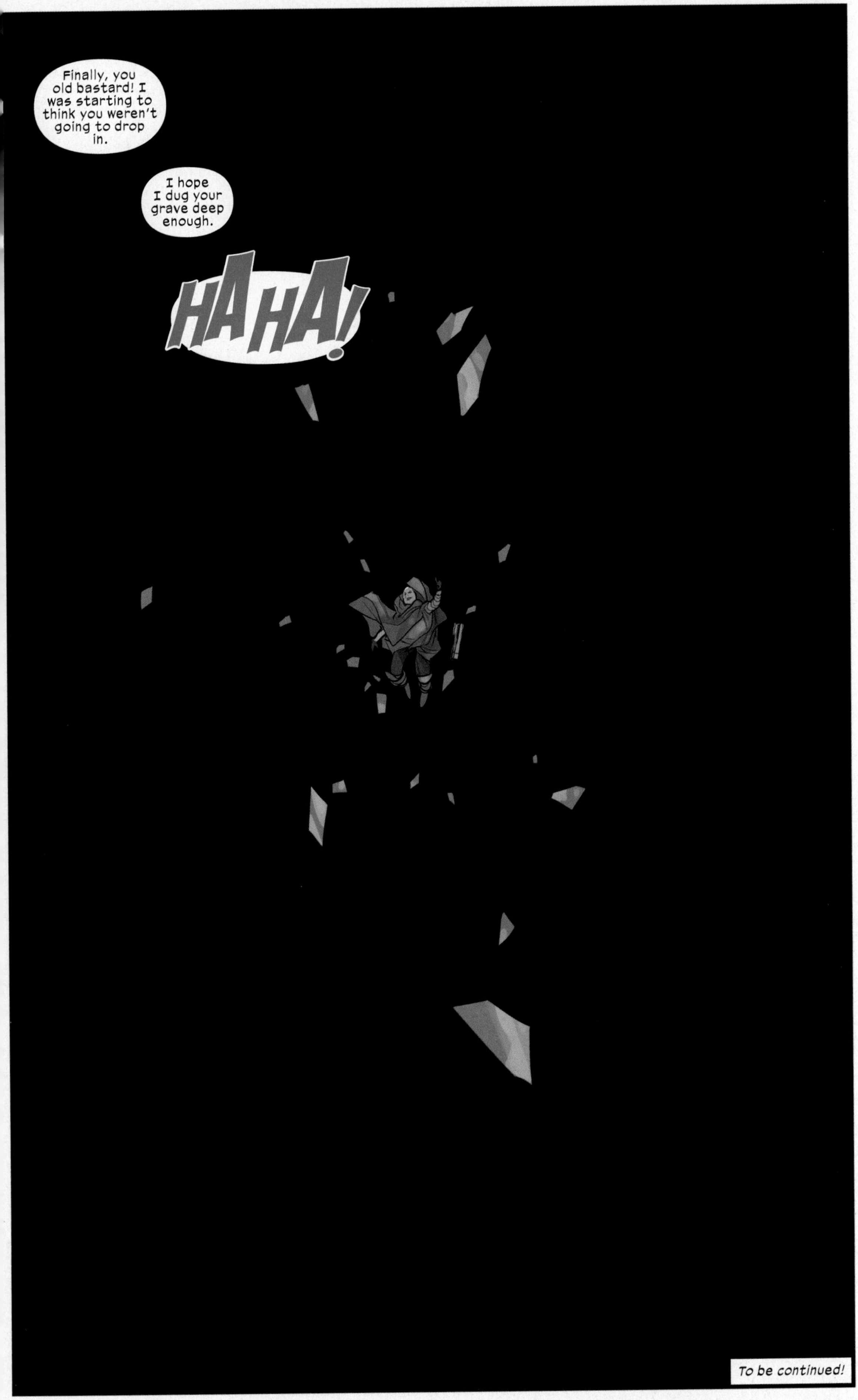
Finally, you old bastard! I was starting to think you weren't going to drop in.
I hope I dug your grave deep enough.
HAHA!
To be continued!

[reign_of_x]

[kra_]
[koa_]

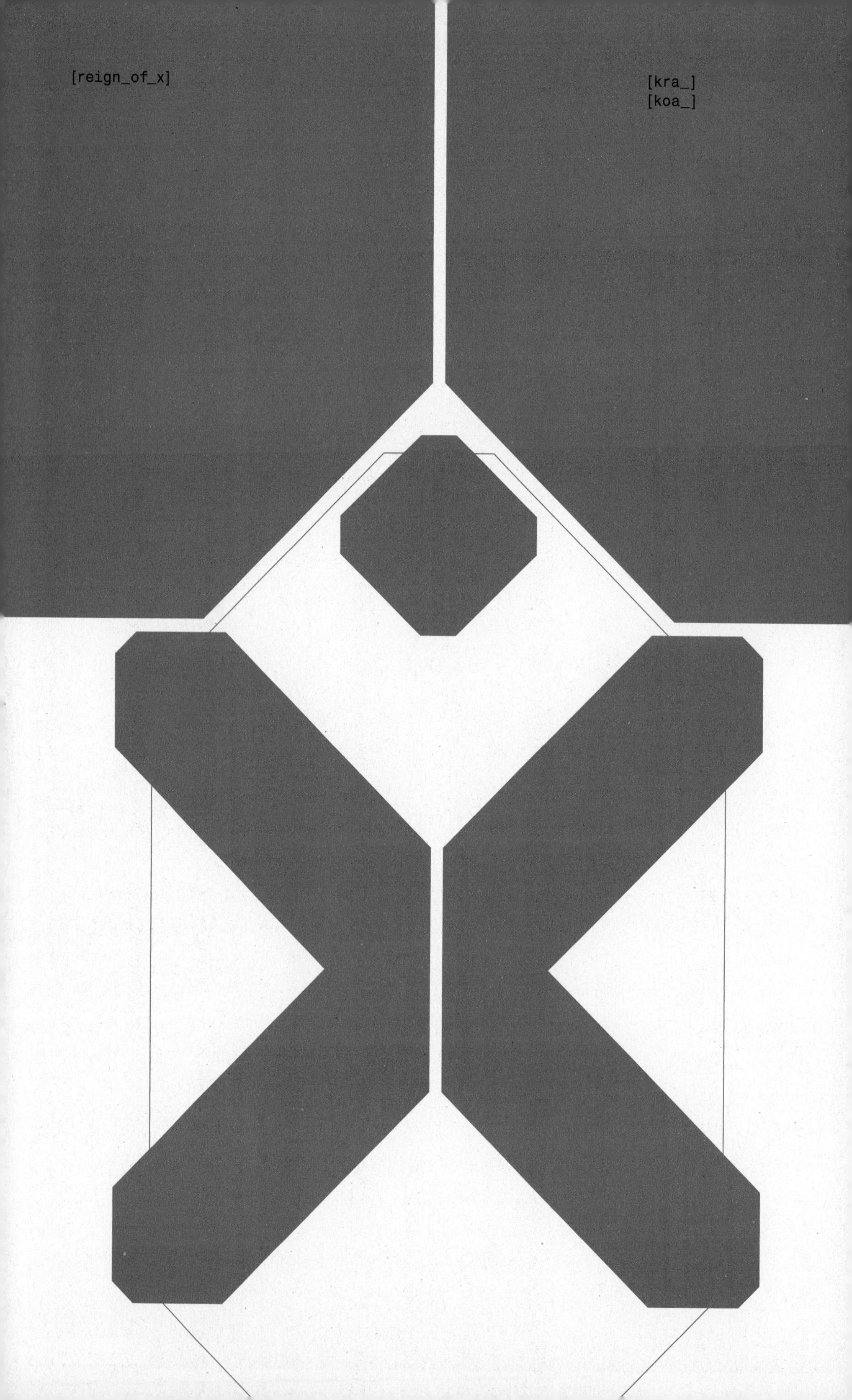

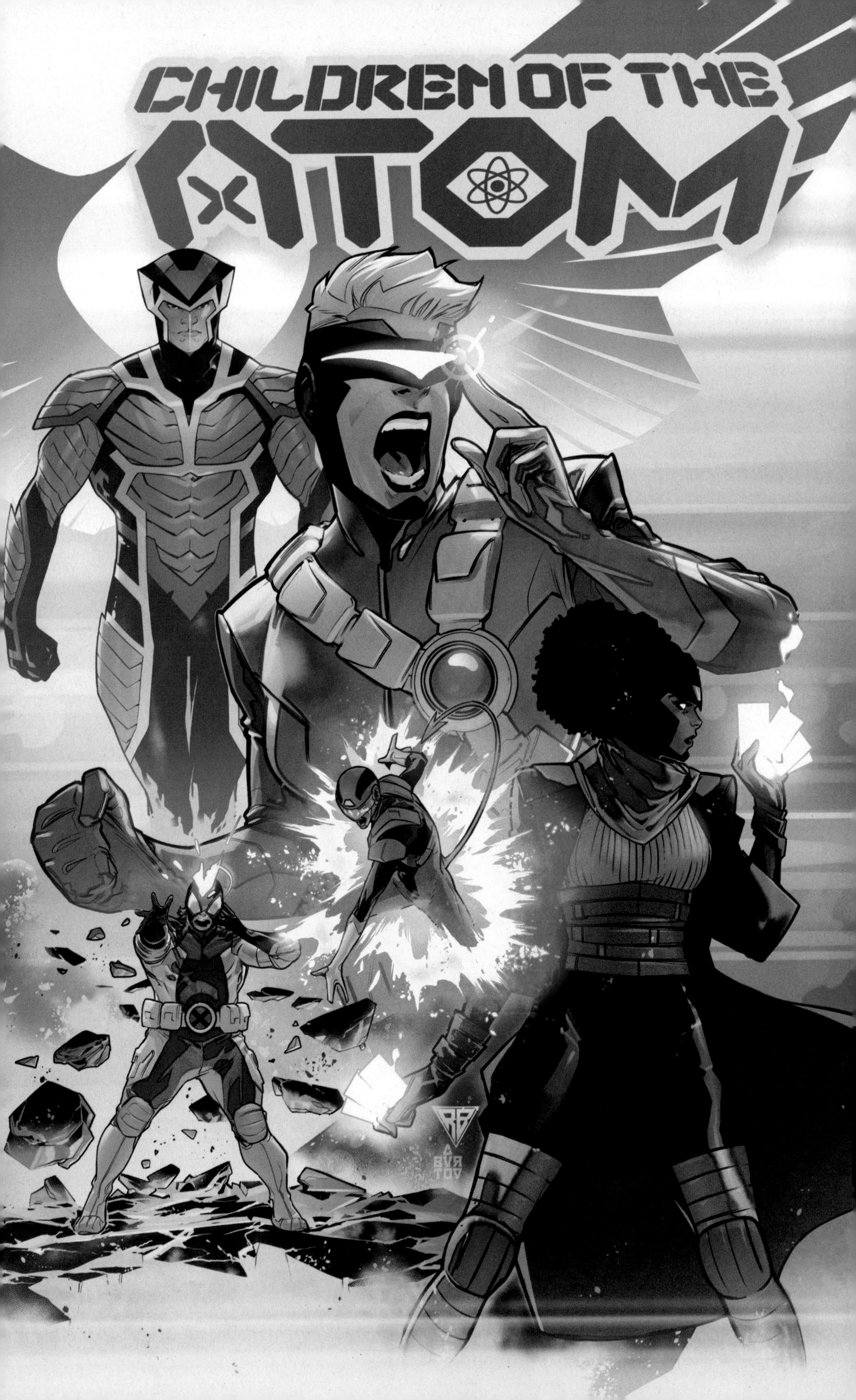
CHILDREN OF THE ATOM

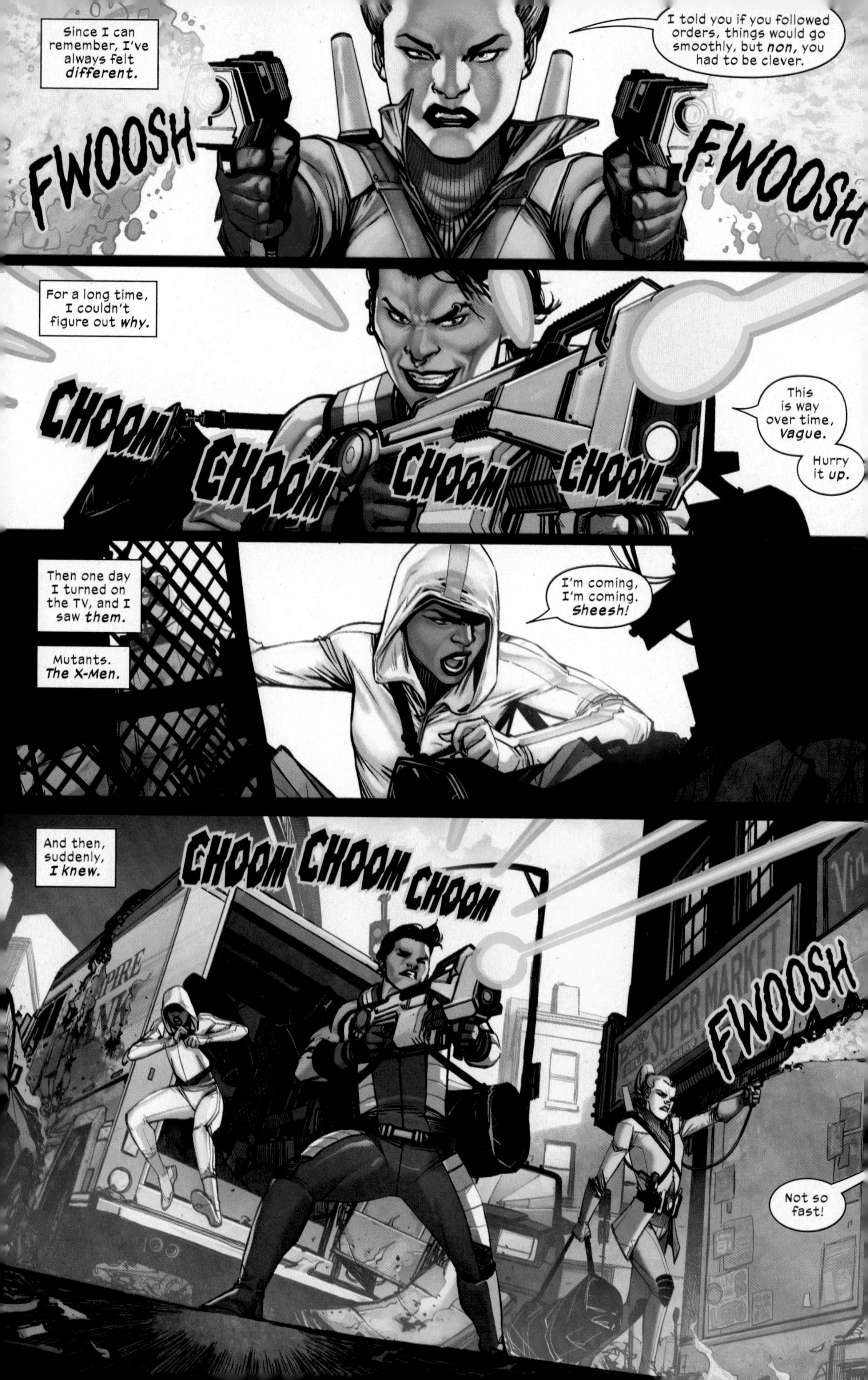
Since I can remember, I've always felt *different*.
I told you if you followed orders, things would go smoothly, but *non*, you had to be clever.
FWOOSH
FWOOSH
For a long time, I couldn't figure out *why*.
CHOOM CHOOM CHOOM CHOOM
This is way over time, *Vague*.
Hurry it *up*.
Then one day I turned on the TV, and I saw *them*.
Mutants. *The X-Men*.
I'm coming, I'm coming. *Sheesh!*
And then, suddenly, *I knew*.
CHOOM CHOOM CHOOM
FWOOSH
SUPER MARKET
Not so fast!

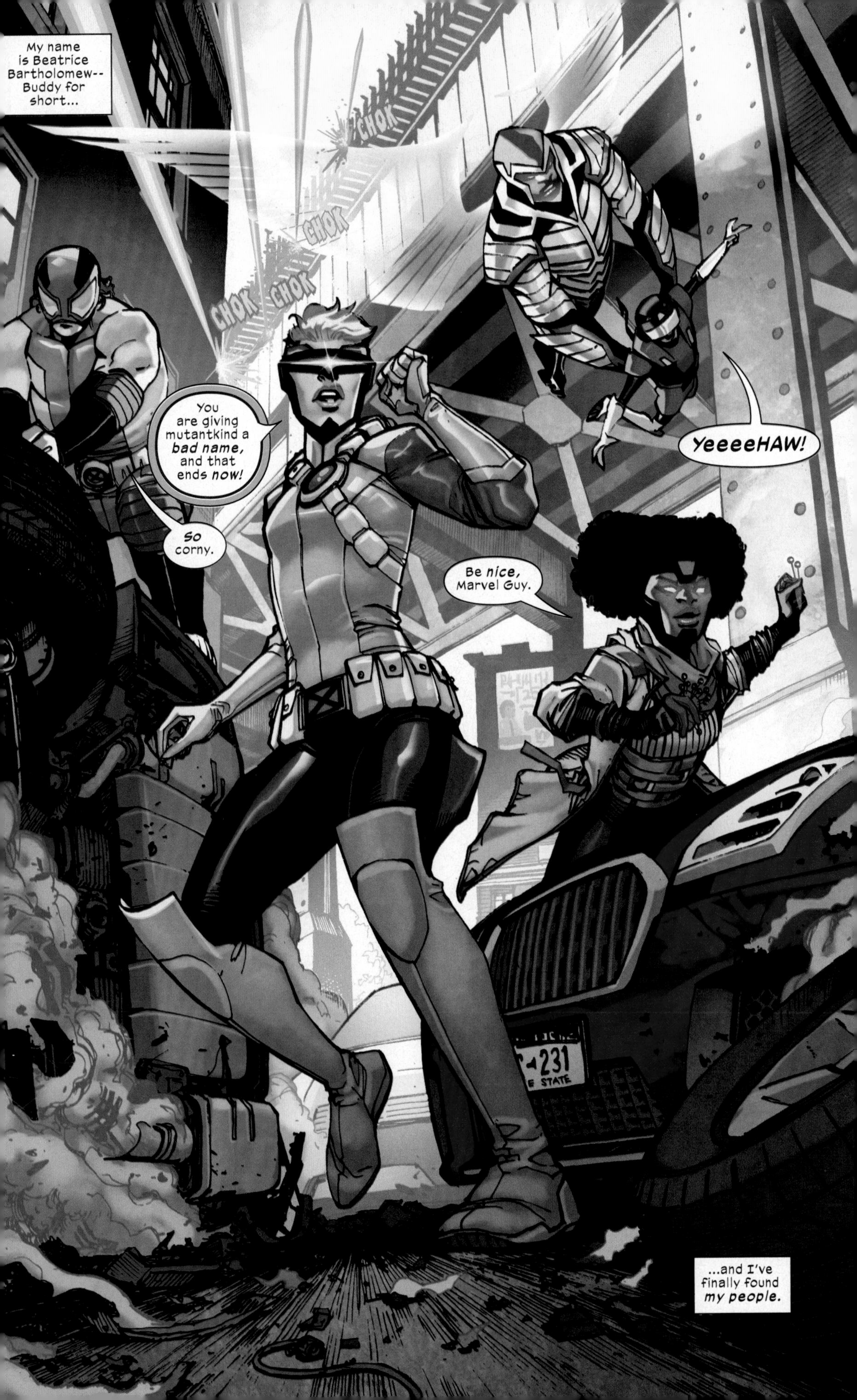
My name is Beatrice Bartholomew--Buddy for short...
CHOK
CHOK
CHOK
CHOK
You are giving mutantkind a *bad name*, and that ends *now!*
So corny.
YeeeeHAW!
Be *nice*, Marvel Guy.
...and I've finally found *my people*.

OLD ENOUGH TO KNOW BETTER

Mutants around the world have flocked to the island-nation of Krakoa for safety, security and to be part of the first mutant society.

But not all mutants have made that journey...

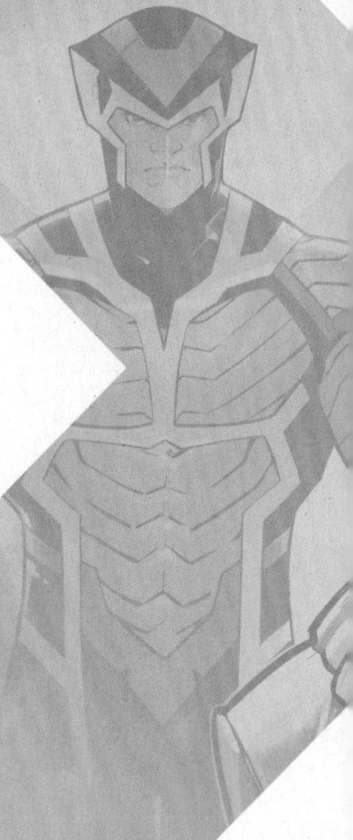

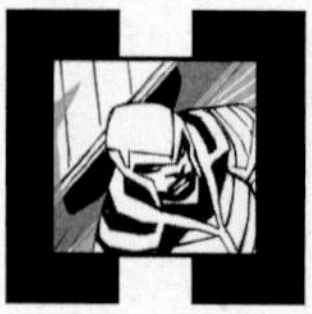

Cherub

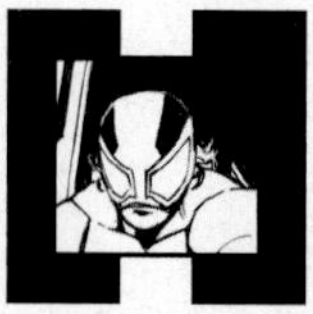

Marvel Guy

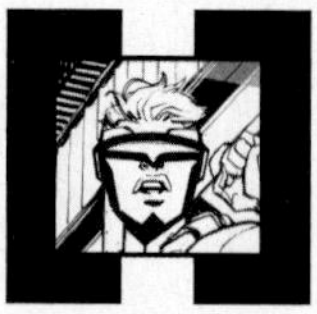

Cyclops-Lass

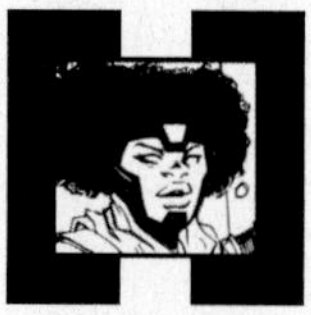

Gimmick

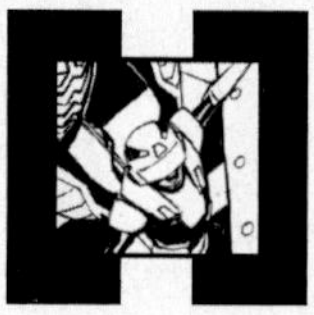

Daycrawler

CHILDREN OF THE ATOM

[X_01]

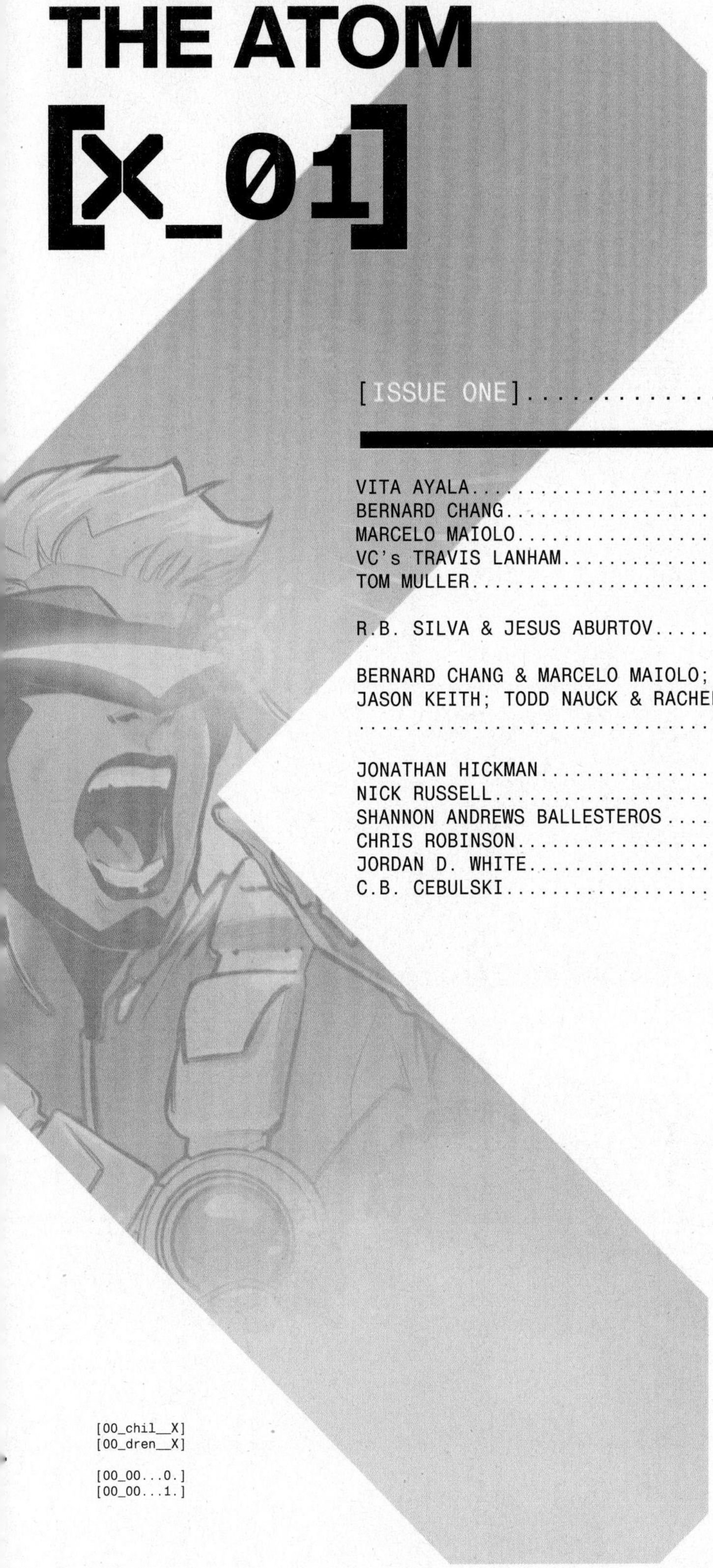

[ISSUE ONE].............................UNCANNY

VITA AYALA...[WRITER]
BERNARD CHANG.......................................[ARTIST]
MARCELO MAIOLO..............................[COLOR ARTIST]
VC's TRAVIS LANHAM.............................[LETTERER]
TOM MULLER..[DESIGN]

R.B. SILVA & JESUS ABURTOV.................[COVER ARTISTS]

BERNARD CHANG & MARCELO MAIOLO; JIM LEE & SCOTT WILLIAMS &
JASON KEITH; TODD NAUCK & RACHELLE ROSENBERG; TOM MULLER...
...................................[VARIANT COVER ARTISTS]

JONATHAN HICKMAN................................[HEAD OF X]
NICK RUSSELL....................................[PRODUCTION]
SHANNON ANDREWS BALLESTEROS.............[ASSISTANT EDITOR]
CHRIS ROBINSON......................................[EDITOR]
JORDAN D. WHITE..............................[SENIOR EDITOR]
C.B. CEBULSKI...............................[EDITOR IN CHIEF]

[00_chil__X]
[00_dren__X]

[00_00...0.]
[00_00...1.]

[00_______]
[00_of____]

[00_the___]

[00__atom__]

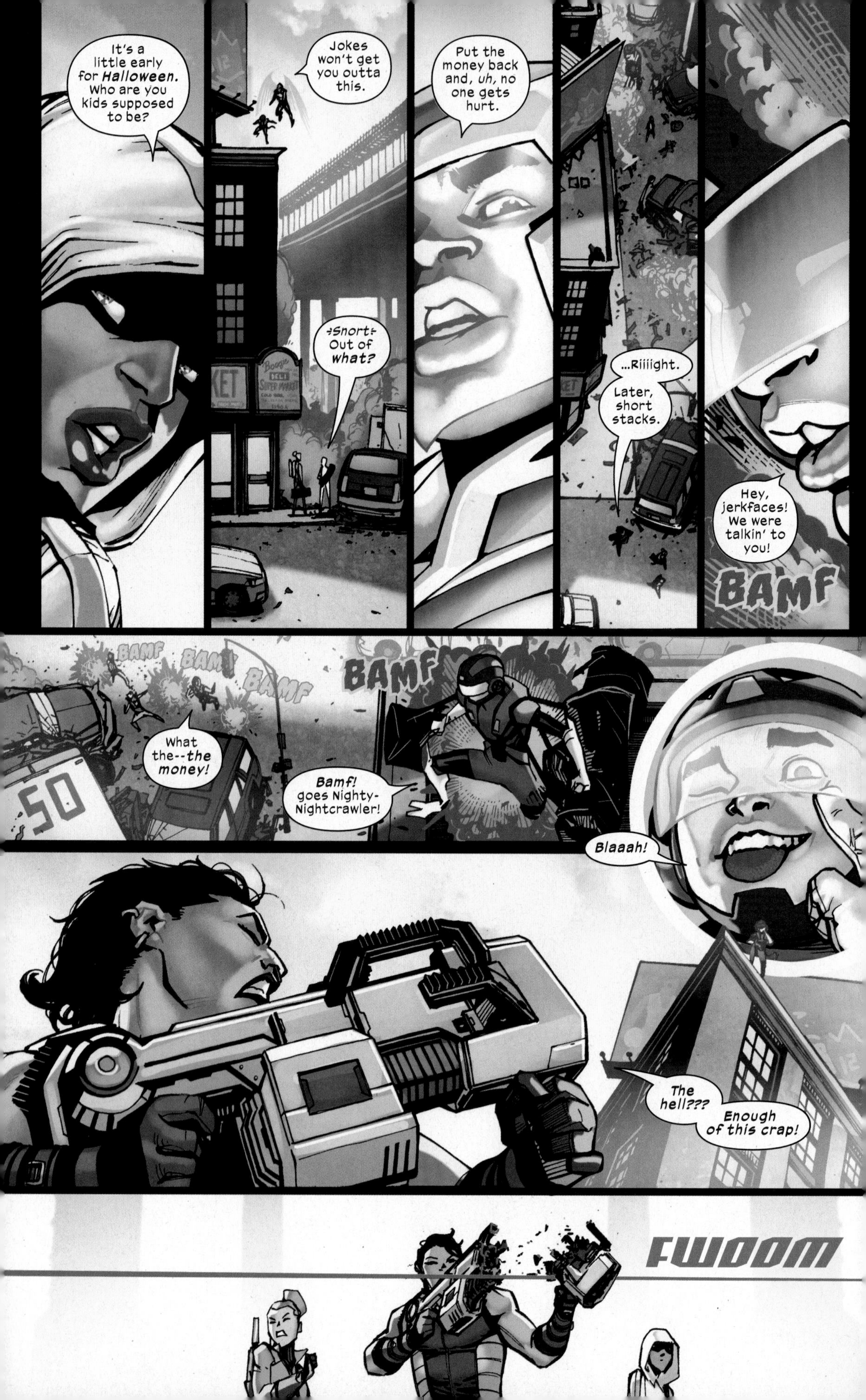
It's a little early for Halloween. Who are you kids supposed to be?
Jokes won't get you outta this.
-Snort- Out of what?
Put the money back and, uh, no one gets hurt.
...Riiiight.
Later, short stacks.
Hey, jerkfaces! We were talkin' to you!
BAMF
BAMF
BAMF
BAMF
BAMF
What the--the money!
Bamf! goes Nighty-Nightcrawler!
Blaaah!
The hell???
Enough of this crap!
FWOOM

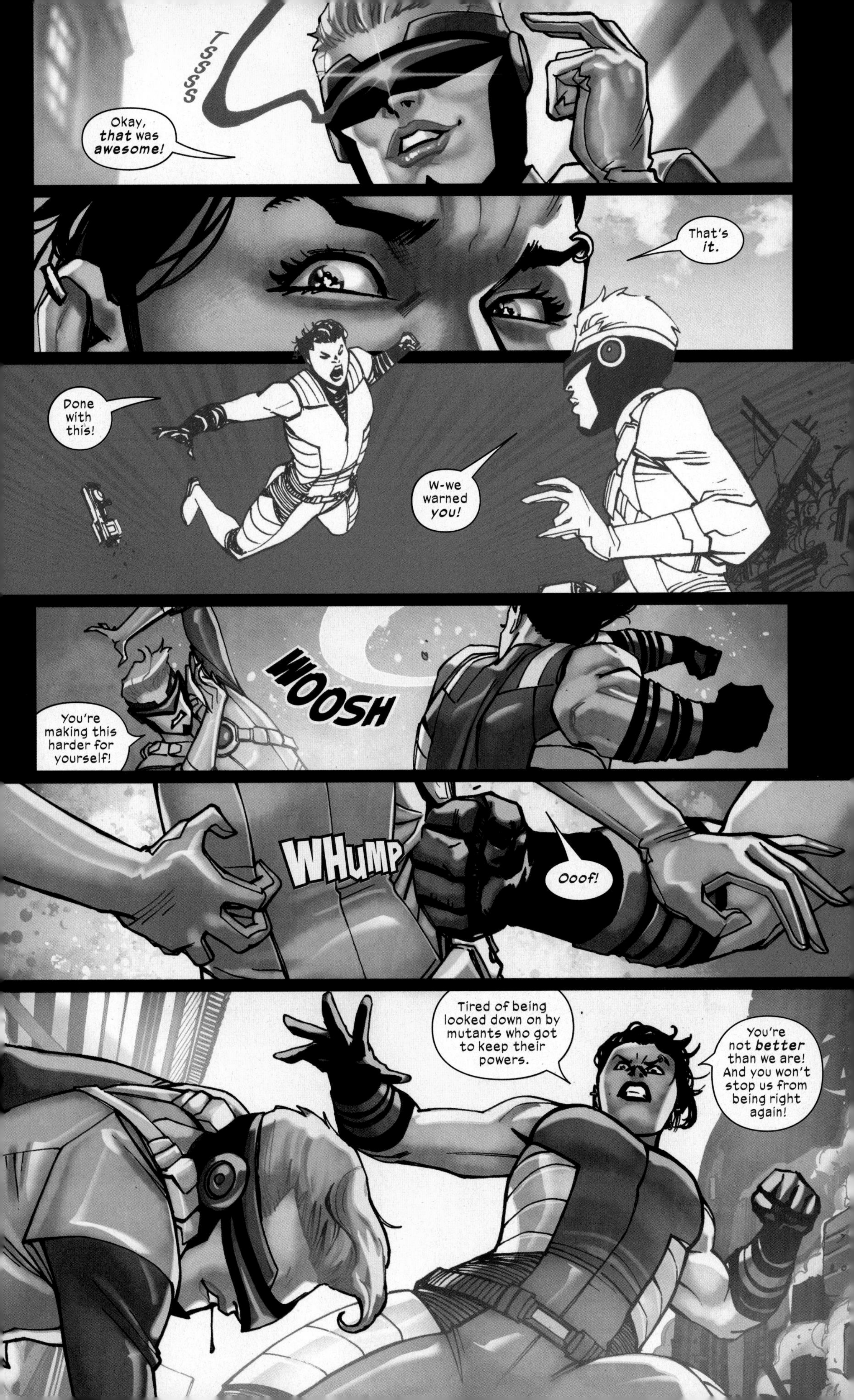
TSSSS
Okay, that was awesome!
That's it.
Done with this!
W-we warned you!
WOOSH
You're making this harder for yourself!
WHUMP
Ooof!
Tired of being looked down on by mutants who got to keep their powers.
You're not better than we are! And you won't stop us from being right again!

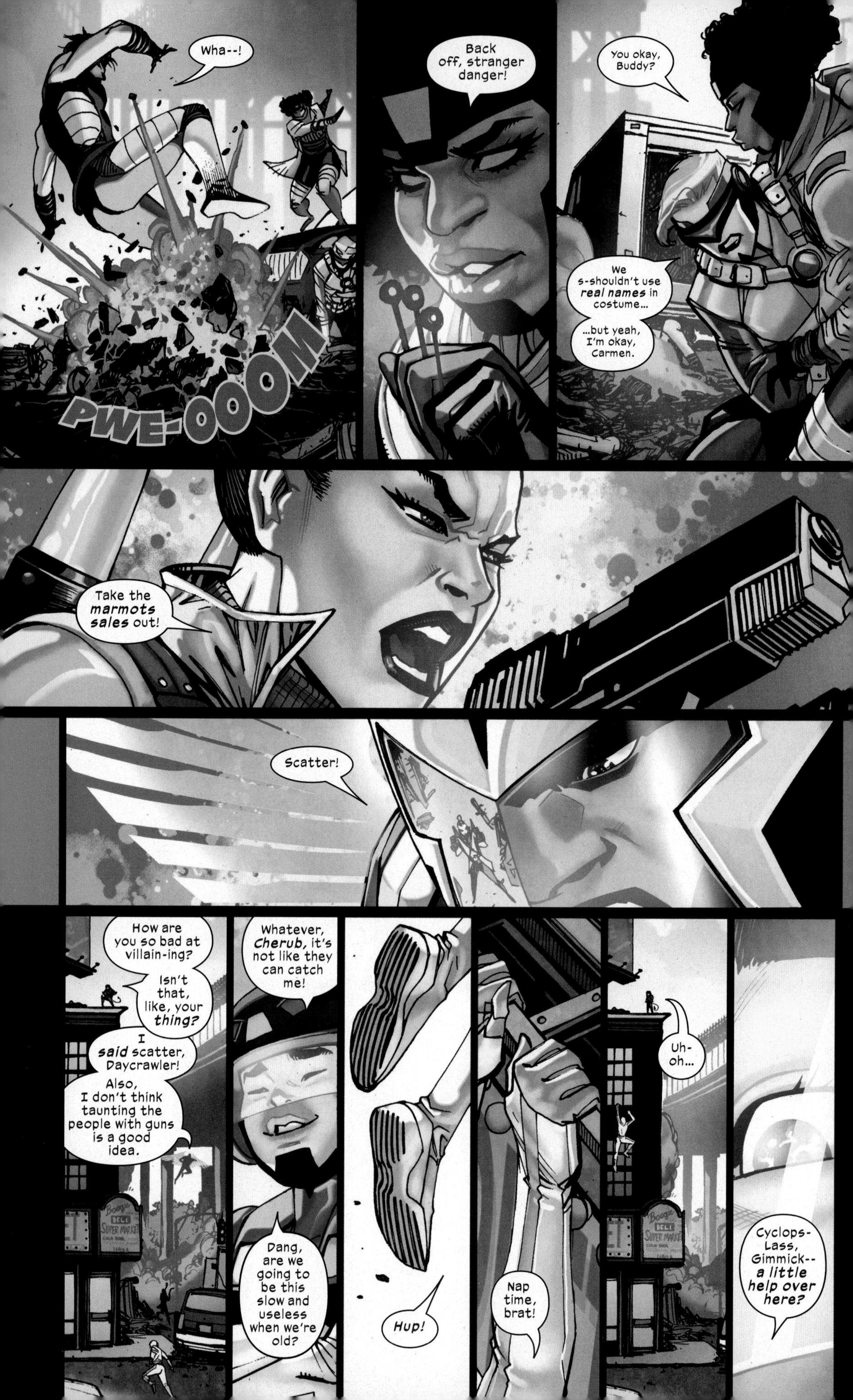

Wha--!
PWE-OOOM
Back off, stranger danger!
You okay, Buddy?
We s-shouldn't use *real names* in costume...
...but yeah, I'm okay, Carmen.
Take the *marmots sales* out!
Scatter!
How are you so bad at villain-ing?
Isn't that, like, your *thing?*
I *said* scatter, Daycrawler!
Also, I don't think taunting the people with guns is a good idea.
Whatever, *Cherub,* it's not like they can catch me!
Dang, are we going to be this slow and useless when we're old?
Hup!
Nap time, brat!
Uh-oh...
Cyclops-Lass, Gimmick-- a little help over here?

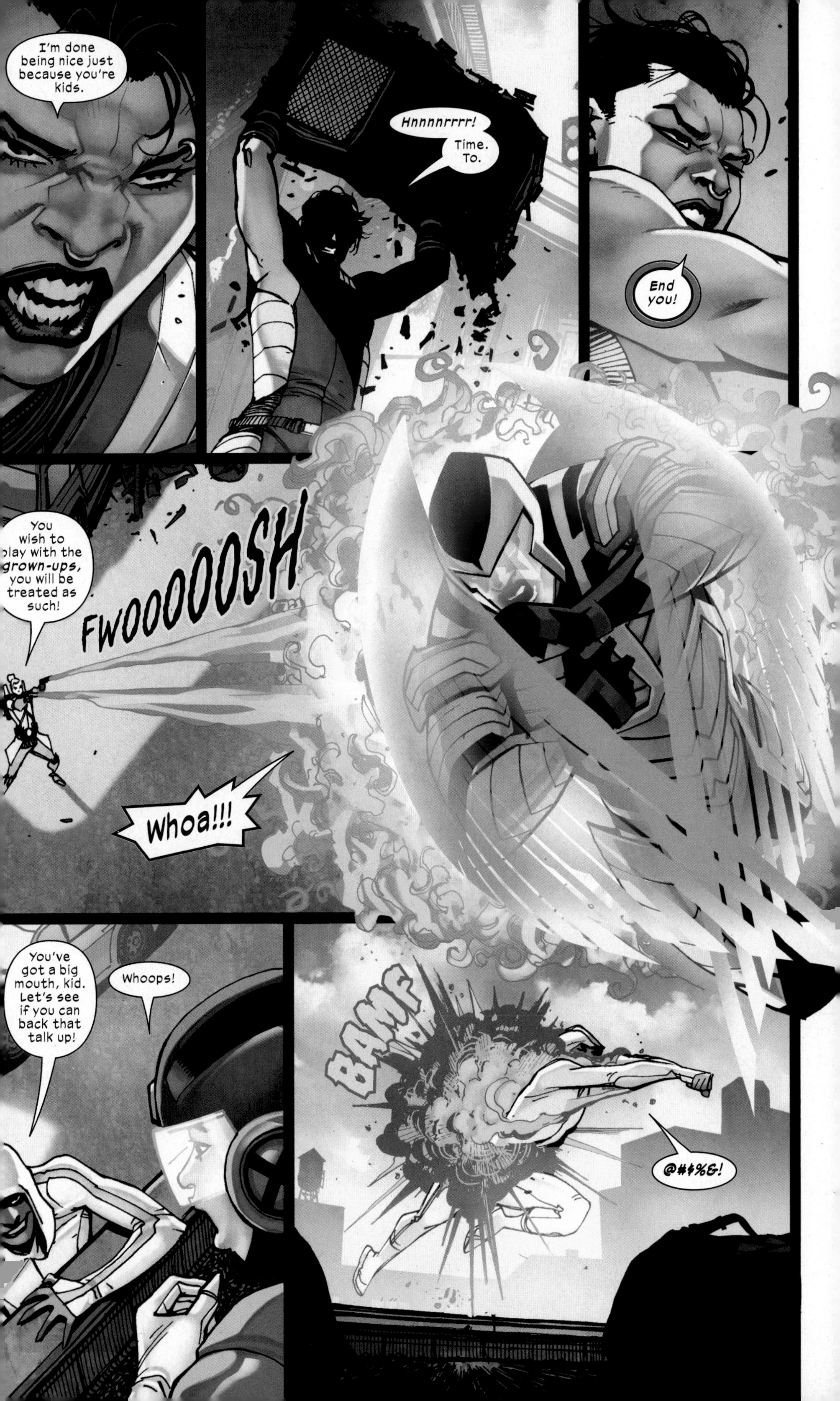
I'm done being nice just because you're kids.
Hnnnnrrrr!
Time. To.
End you!
You wish to play with the grown-ups, you will be treated as such!
FWOOOOOSH
Whoa!!!
You've got a big mouth, kid. Let's see if you can back that talk up!
Whoops!
BAMF
@#$%&!

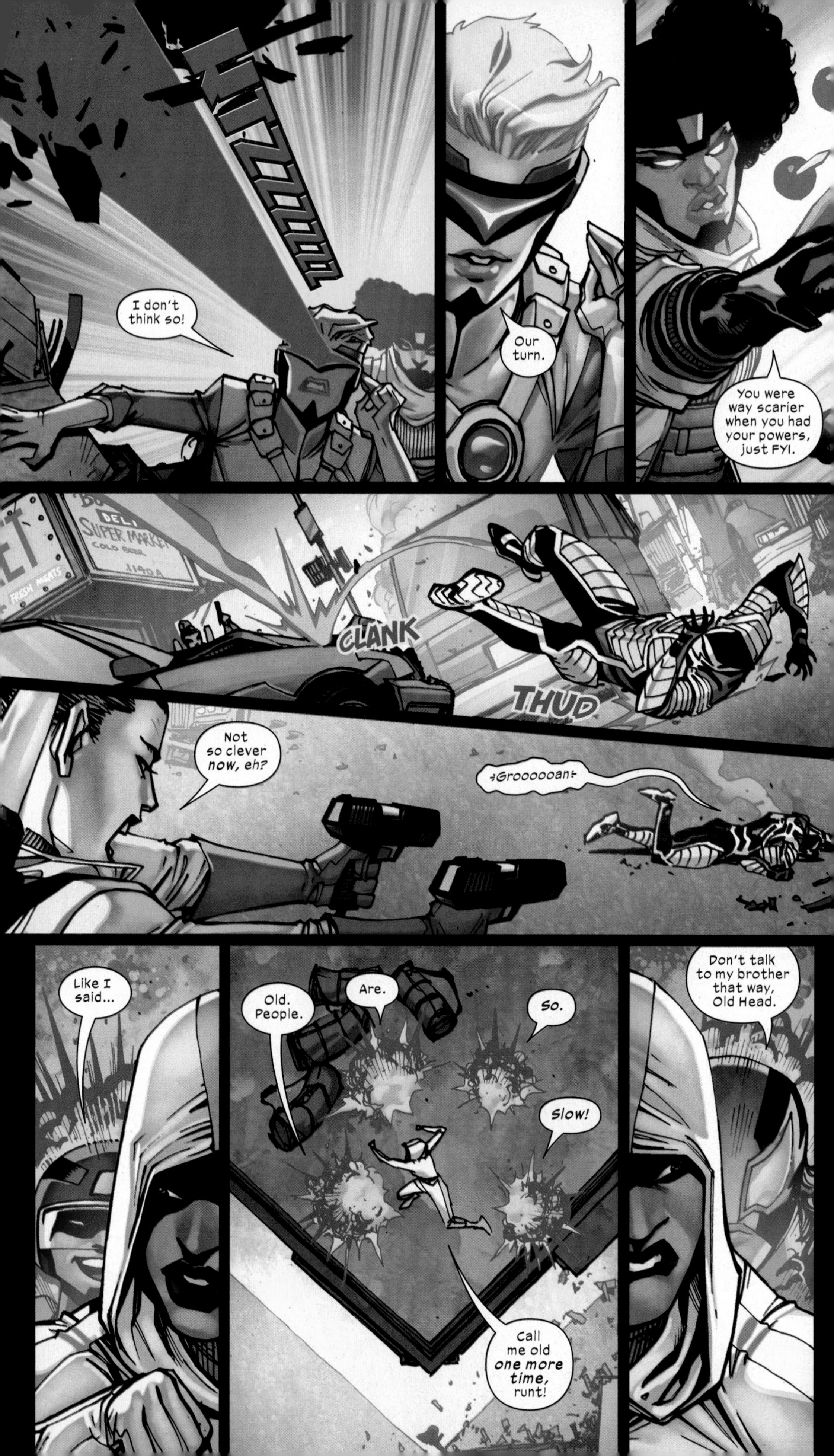

VZZZZZZ
I don't think so!
Our turn.
You were way scarier when you had your powers, just FYI.
DELI
SUPER MARKET
COLD BEER
FRESH MEATS
CLANK
THUD
Not so clever now, eh?
Groooooan
Like I said...
Old. People.
Are.
So.
Slow!
Call me old one more time, runt!
Don't talk to my brother that way, Old Head.

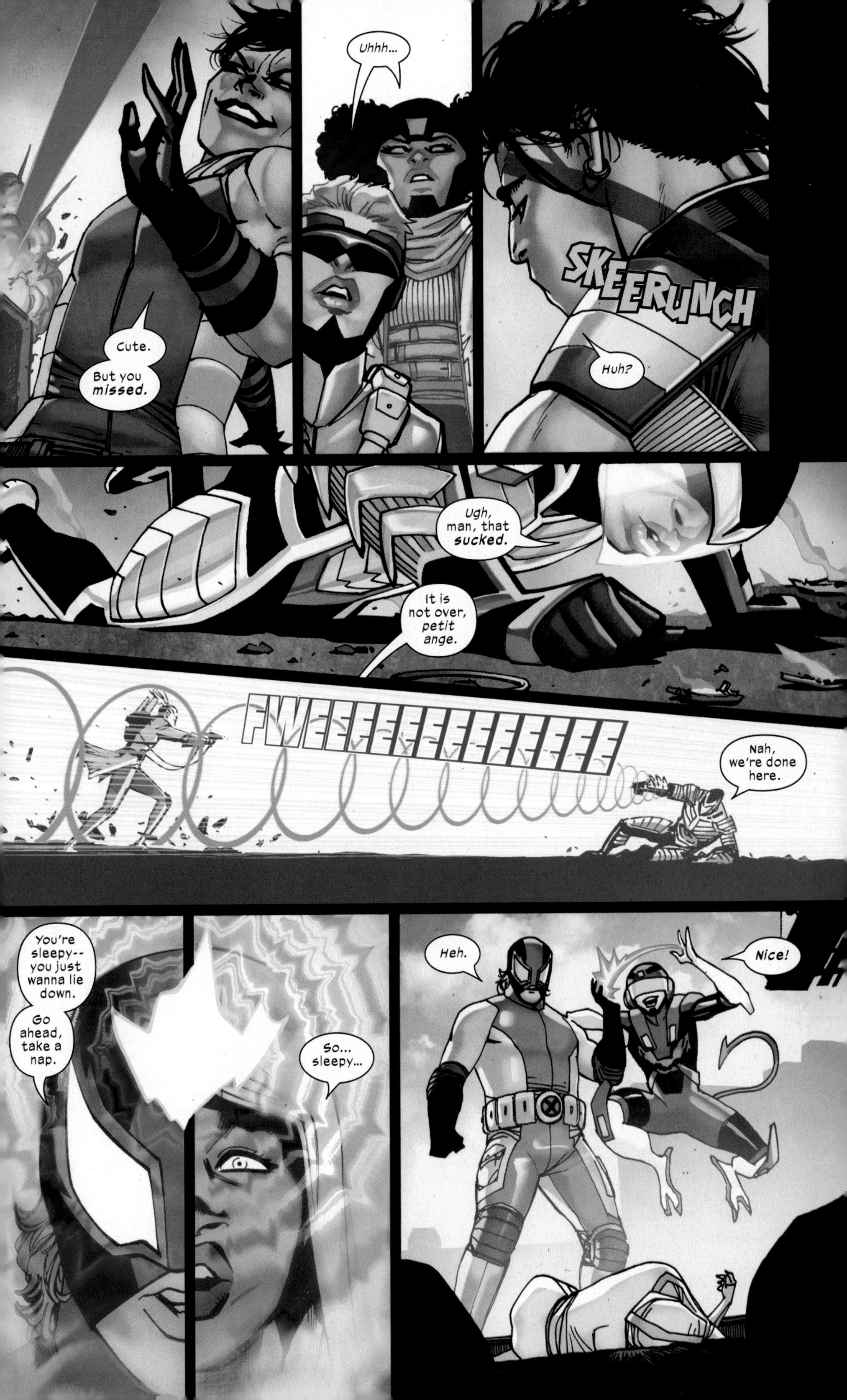
Cute.
But you missed.
Uhhh...
SKEERUNCH
Huh?
Ugh, man, that sucked.
It is not over, petit ange.
FWEEEEEEEEEEEEE
Nah, we're done here.
You're sleepy-- you just wanna lie down.
Go ahead, take a nap.
So... sleepy...
Heh.
Nice!

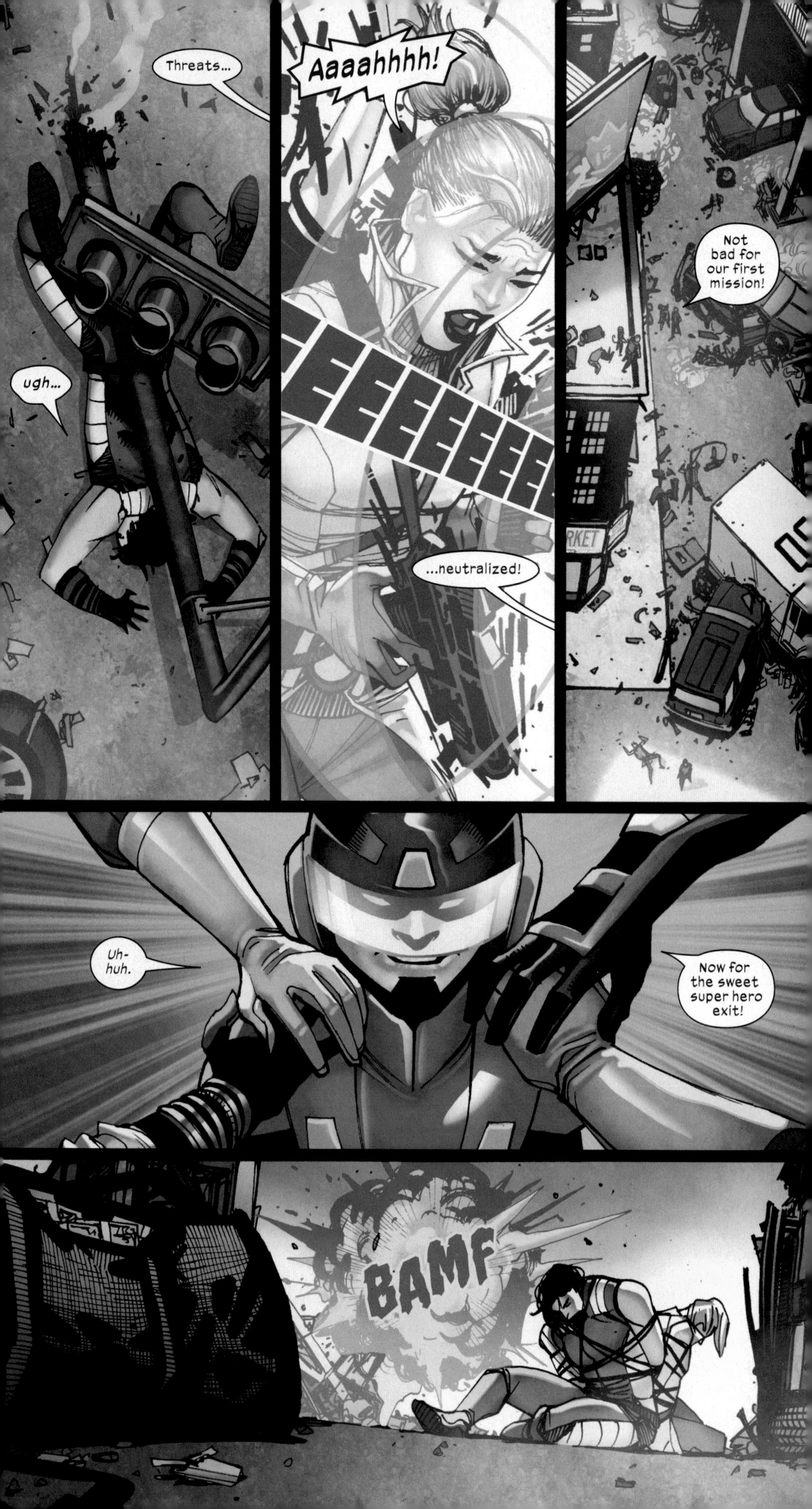

Threats...
ugh...
Aaaahhhh!
EEEEEEEEE
...neutralized!
Not bad for our first mission!
RKET
Uh-huh.
Now for the sweet super hero exit!
BAMF

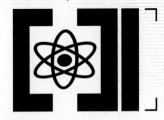

mutantsunmuted.com/unc_uni/groups/hells_belles

THE HELL'S BELLES

original entry by: **ArchivistX**

The Hell's Belles were a group of mercenary mutant women under the direction of ***Cyber**** and often affiliated with a large drug cartel[1].

The group consisted of ***Briquette****, ***Tremolo****, ***Flambé**** and ***Vague****.

The mutant ***Shrew**** was originally part of the crew but quit and later agreed to testify against them in exchange for immunity. The remaining Hell's Belles came into conflict with X-Factor when they attempted to kill Shrew for her betrayal.

POWERS

Briquette – superhuman strength, molten-hot skin (can melt objects on contact), invulnerability, claws.

Tremolo – energy blasts, vibration waves.

Flambé – manipulates fire/flames by controlling oxygen molecules. Cannot produce flames, but once they are lit, can make them hotter and focus them into jets.

Vague – flight and invisibility.

WHERE ARE THEY NOW?

All of the Hell's Belles, with the exception of Briquette, were depowered on M-Day but still operate as career criminals.

* See individual entries on these mutants for more details on their histories and origins!
[1] Citation needed

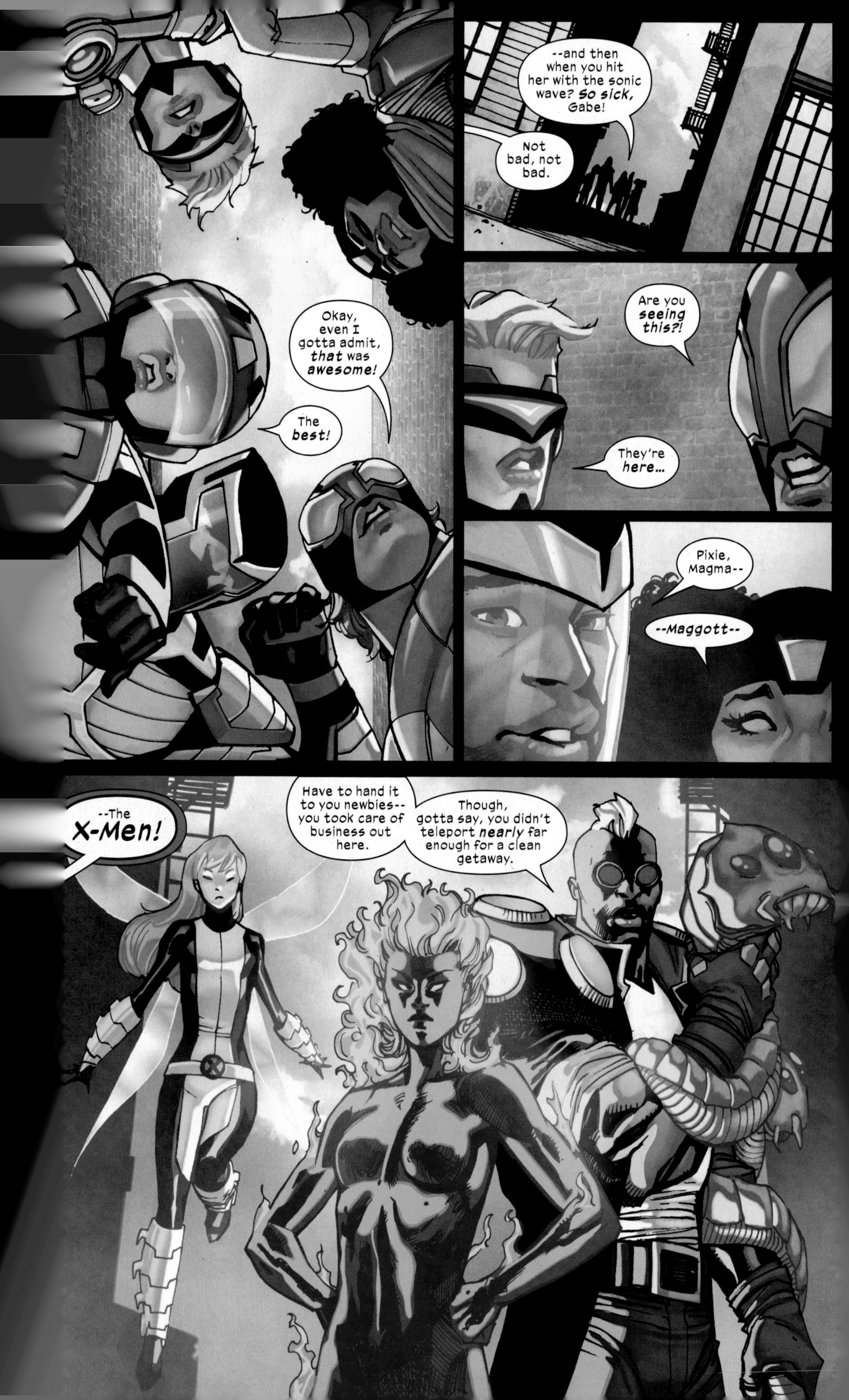

Okay, even I gotta admit, that was awesome!
The best!
--and then when you hit her with the sonic wave? So sick, Gabe!
Not bad, not bad.
Are you seeing this?!
They're here...
Pixie, Magma--
--Maggott--
--The X-Men!
Have to hand it to you newbies--you took care of business out here.
Though, gotta say, you didn't teleport nearly far enough for a clean getaway.

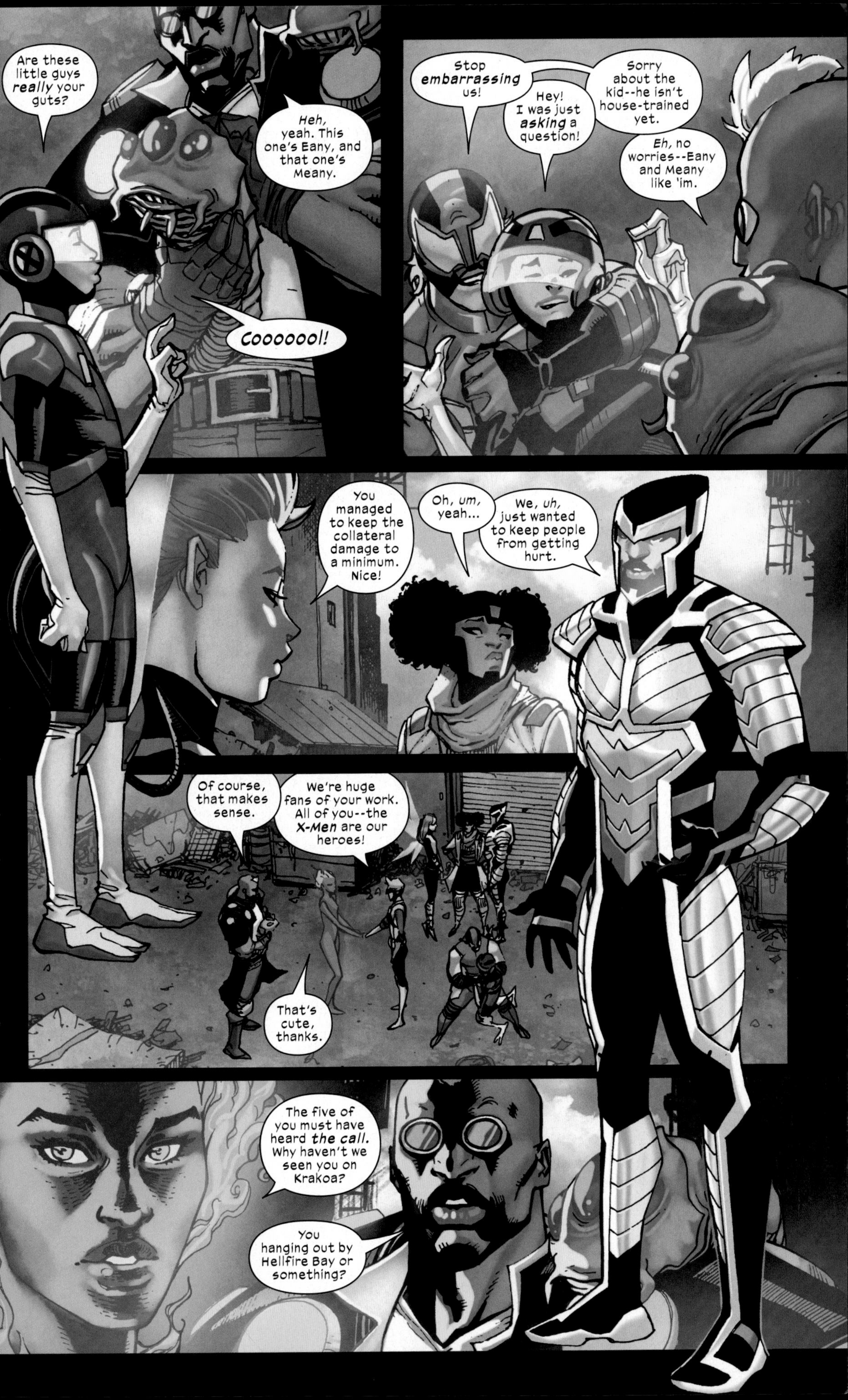

Are these little guys *really* your guts?
Heh, yeah. This one's Eany, and that one's Meany.
Cooooool!
Stop *embarrassing* us!
Hey! I was just *asking* a question!
Sorry about the kid--he isn't house-trained yet.
Eh, no worries--Eany and Meany like 'im.
You managed to keep the collateral damage to a minimum. Nice!
Oh, *um,* yeah...
We, *uh,* just wanted to keep people from getting hurt.
Of course, that makes sense.
We're huge fans of your work. All of you--the *X-Men* are our heroes!
That's cute, thanks.
The five of you must have heard *the call.* Why haven't we seen you on Krakoa?
You hanging out by Hellfire Bay or something?

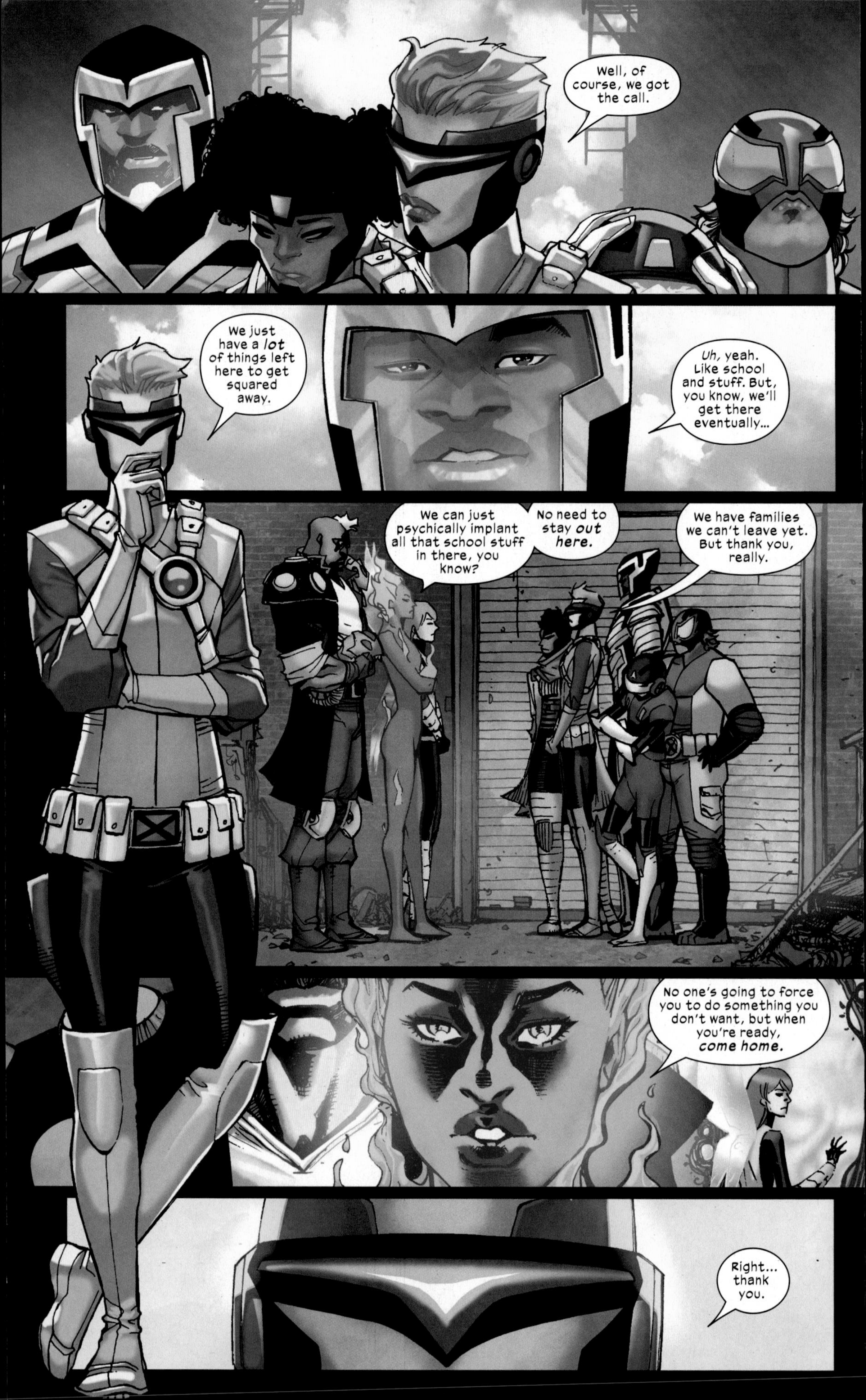
Well, of course, we got the call.
We just have a *lot* of things left here to get squared away.
Uh, yeah. Like school and stuff. But, you know, we'll get there eventually...
We can just psychically implant all that school stuff in there, you know?
No need to stay *out here.*
We have families we can't leave yet. But thank you, really.
No one's going to force you to do something you don't want, but when you're ready, **come home.**
Right... thank you.

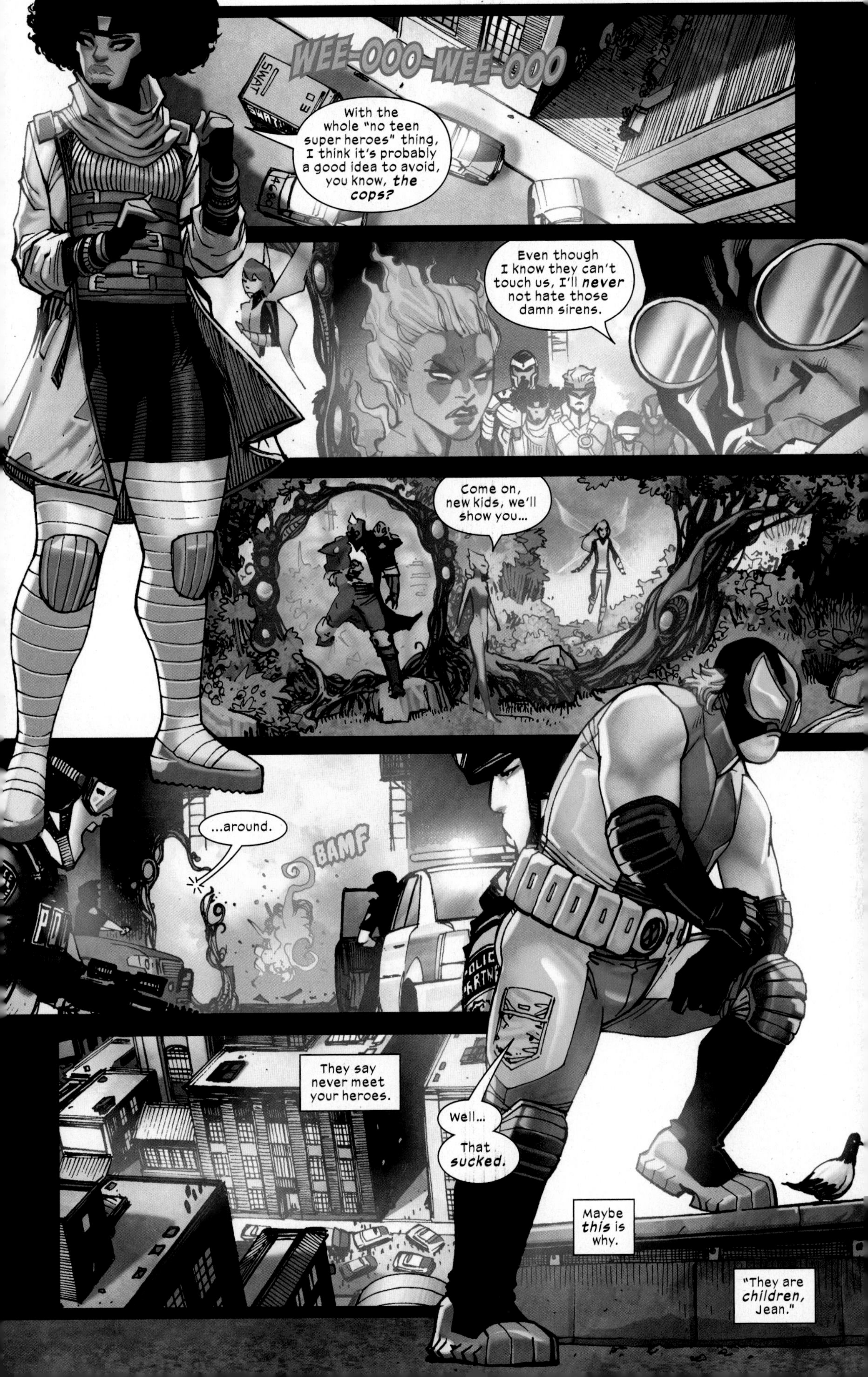
WEE-OOO-WEE-OOO
SWAT
With the whole "no teen super heroes" thing, I think it's probably a good idea to avoid, you know, the cops?
Even though I know they can't touch us, I'll never not hate those damn sirens.
Come on, new kids, we'll show you...
...around.
BAMF
They say never meet your heroes.
Well...
That sucked.
Maybe this is why.
"They are children, Jean."

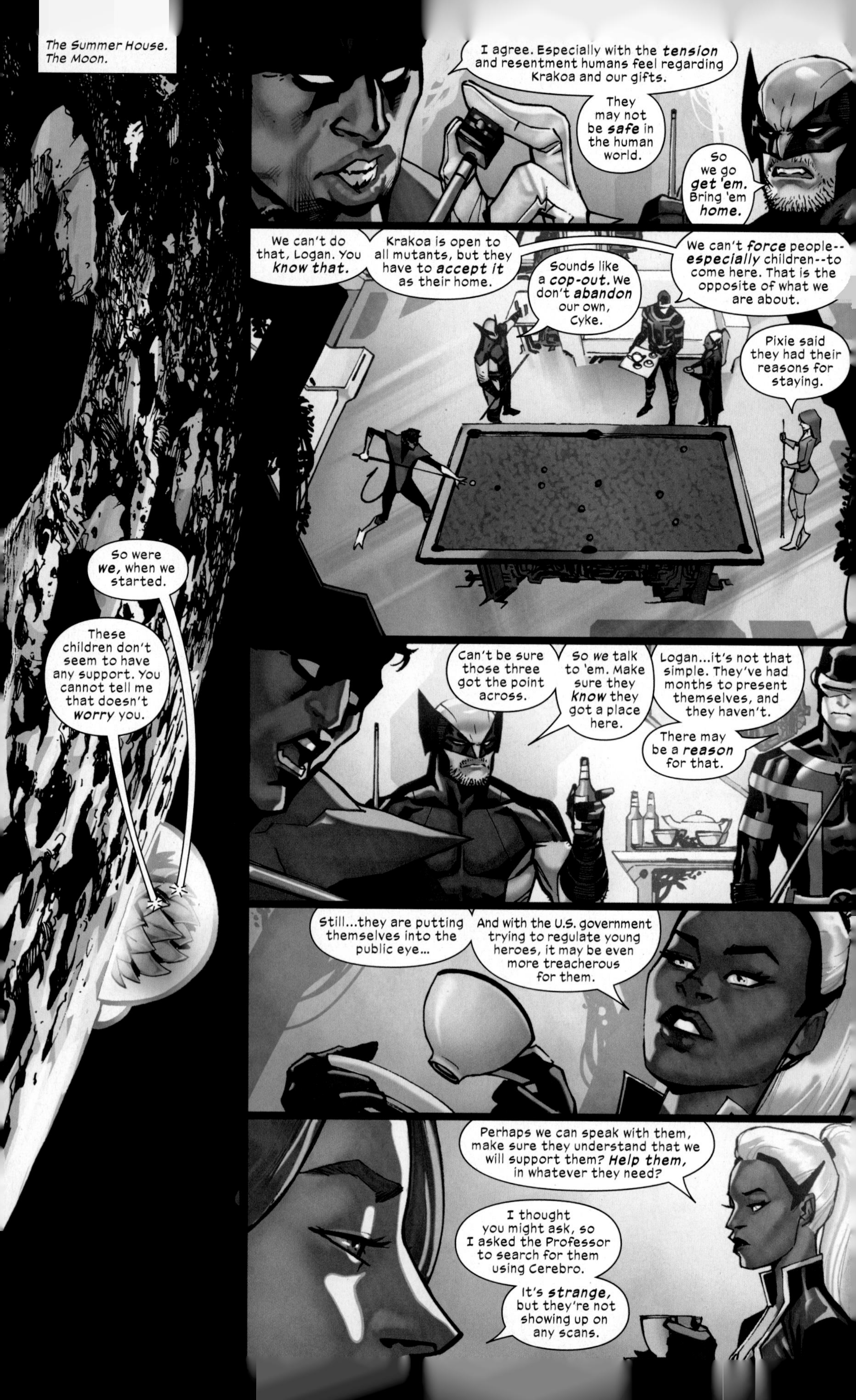
The Summer House. The Moon.
I agree. Especially with the tension and resentment humans feel regarding Krakoa and our gifts.
They may not be safe in the human world.
So we go get 'em. Bring 'em home.
We can't do that, Logan. You know that.
Krakoa is open to all mutants, but they have to accept it as their home.
We can't force people-- especially children--to come here. That is the opposite of what we are about.
Sounds like a cop-out. We don't abandon our own, Cyke.
Pixie said they had their reasons for staying.
So were we, when we started.
These children don't seem to have any support. You cannot tell me that doesn't worry you.
Can't be sure those three got the point across.
So we talk to 'em. Make sure they know they got a place here.
Logan...it's not that simple. They've had months to present themselves, and they haven't.
There may be a reason for that.
Still...they are putting themselves into the public eye...
And with the U.S. government trying to regulate young heroes, it may be even more treacherous for them.
Perhaps we can speak with them, make sure they understand that we will support them? Help them, in whatever they need?
I thought you might ask, so I asked the Professor to search for them using Cerebro.
It's strange, but they're not showing up on any scans.

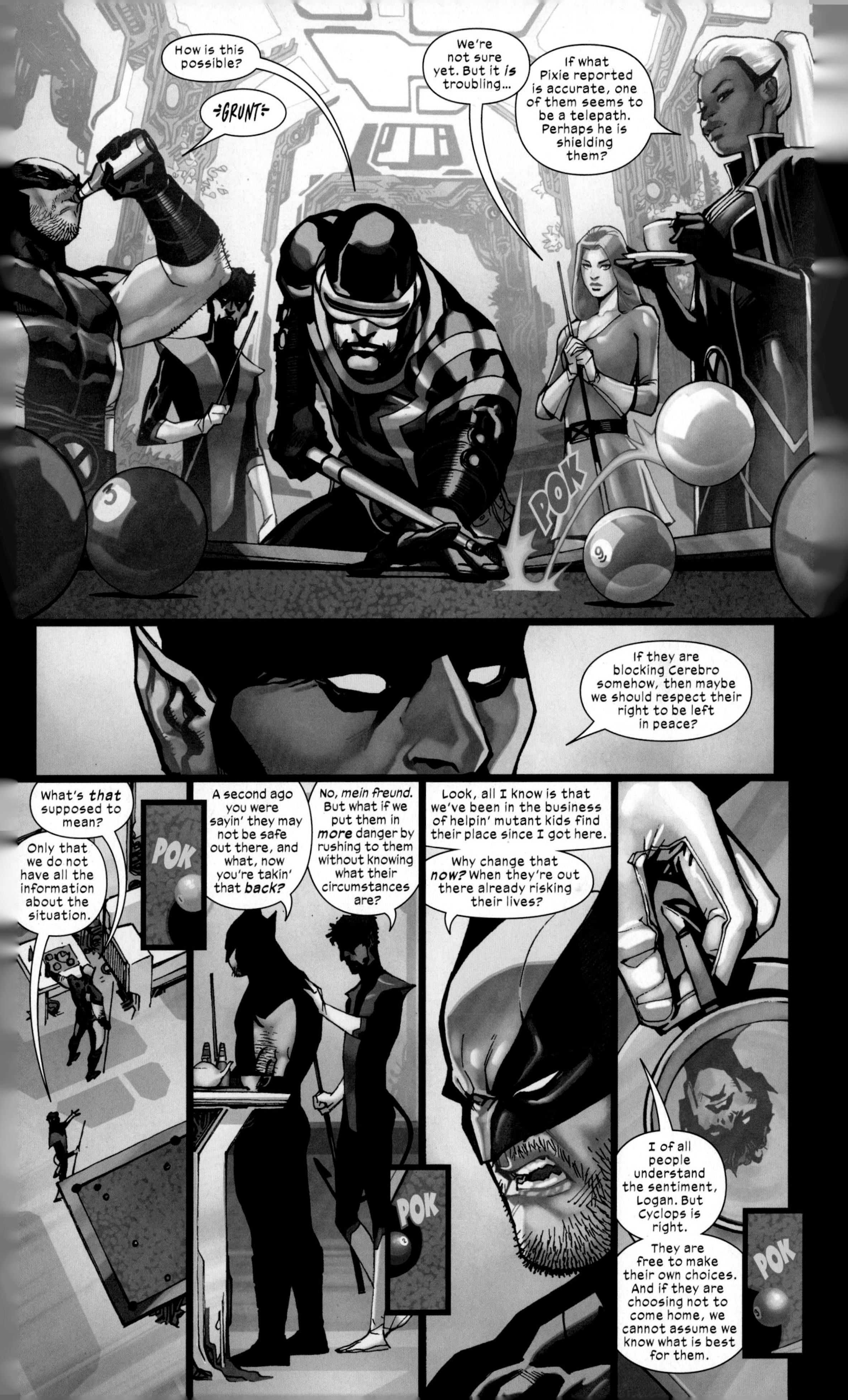
How is this possible?
GRUNT
We're not sure yet. But it is troubling...
If what Pixie reported is accurate, one of them seems to be a telepath. Perhaps he is shielding them?
POK
If they are blocking Cerebro somehow, then maybe we should respect their right to be left in peace?
What's that supposed to mean?
Only that we do not have all the information about the situation.
POK
A second ago you were sayin' they may not be safe out there, and what, now you're takin' that back?
No, mein freund. But what if we put them in more danger by rushing to them without knowing what their circumstances are?
POK
Look, all I know is that we've been in the business of helpin' mutant kids find their place since I got here.
Why change that now? When they're out there already risking their lives?
I of all people understand the sentiment, Logan. But Cyclops is right.
They are free to make their own choices. And if they are choosing not to come home, we cannot assume we know what is best for them.
POK

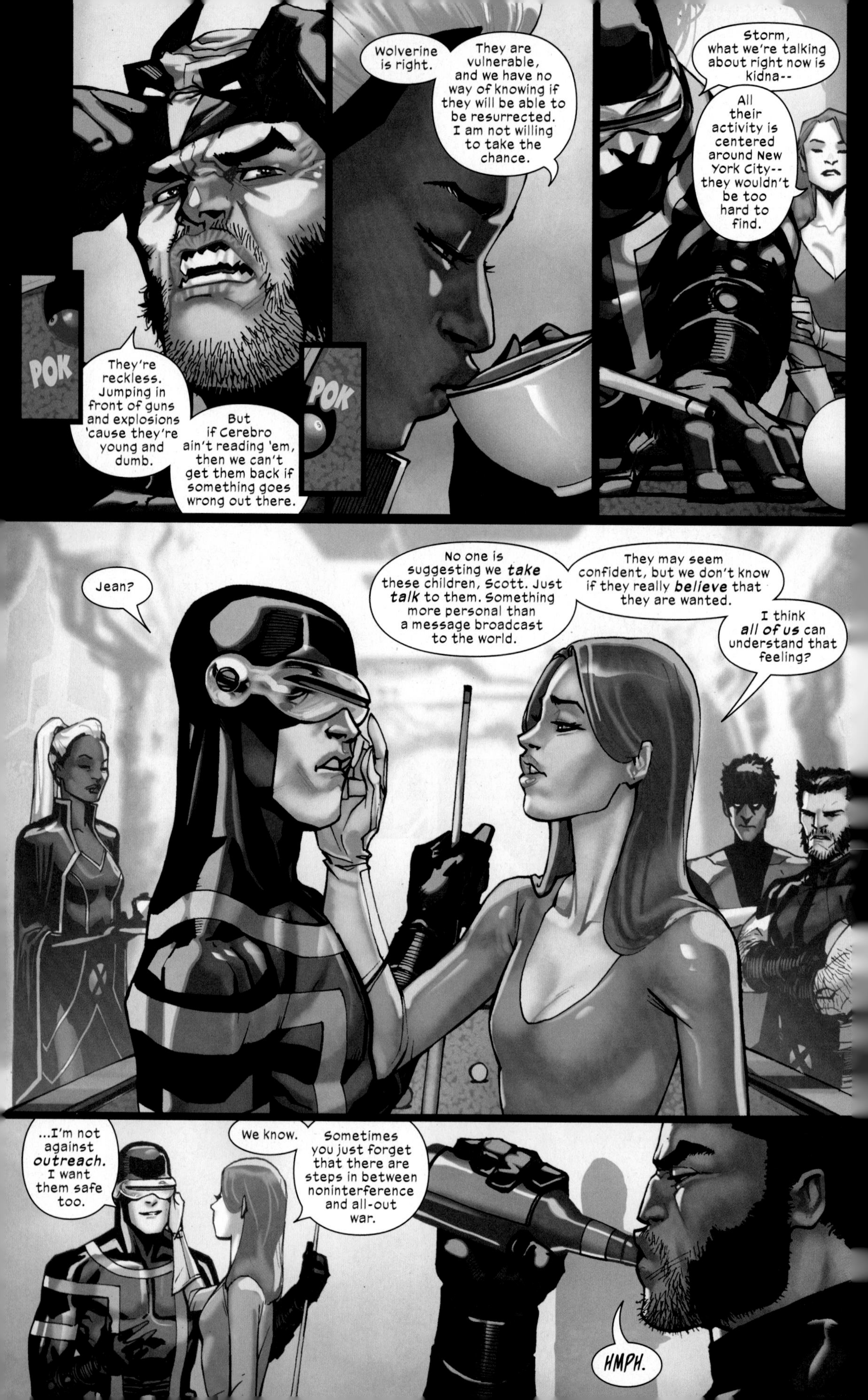

They're reckless. Jumping in front of guns and explosions 'cause they're young and dumb.
POK
But if Cerebro ain't reading 'em, then we can't get them back if something goes wrong out there.
POK
Wolverine is right.
They are vulnerable, and we have no way of knowing if they will be able to be resurrected. I am not willing to take the chance.
Storm, what we're talking about right now is kidna--
All their activity is centered around New York City--they wouldn't be too hard to find.
Jean?
No one is suggesting we *take* these children, Scott. Just *talk* to them. Something more personal than a message broadcast to the world.
They may seem confident, but we don't know if they really *believe* that they are wanted.
I think *all of us* can understand that feeling?
...I'm not against *outreach*. I want them safe too.
We know.
Sometimes you just forget that there are steps in between noninterference and all-out war.
HMPH.

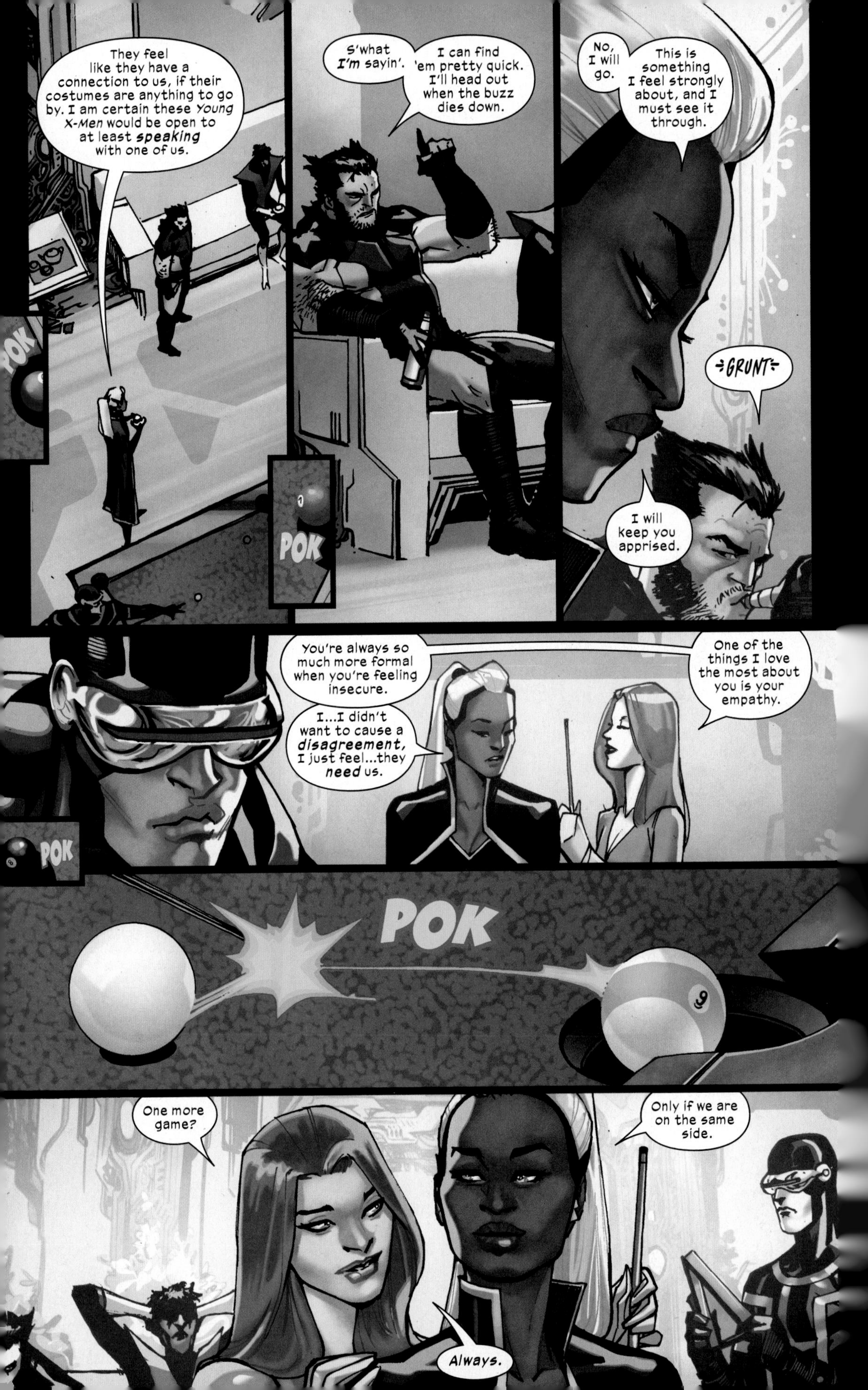
They feel like they have a connection to us, if their costumes are anything to go by. I am certain these *Young X-Men* would be open to at least **speaking** with one of us.
POK
S'what ***I'm*** sayin'.
I can find 'em pretty quick. I'll head out when the buzz dies down.
POK
No, I will go.
This is something I feel strongly about, and I must see it through.
GRUNT
I will keep you apprised.
You're always so much more formal when you're feeling insecure.
One of the things I love the most about you is your empathy.
I...I didn't want to cause a ***disagreement,*** I just feel...they ***need*** us.
POK
POK
One more game?
Only if we are on the same side.
Always.

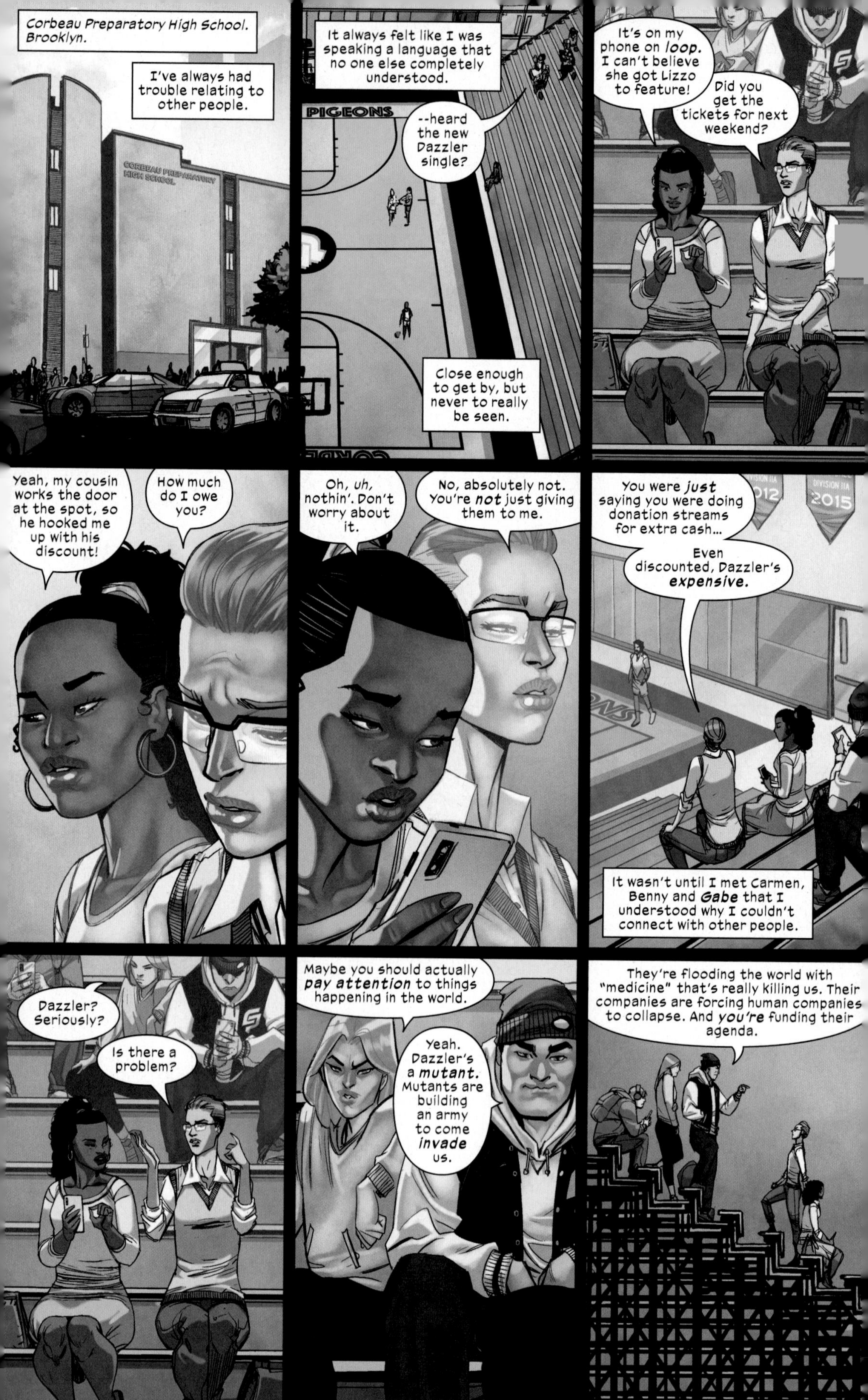
Corbeau Preparatory High School. Brooklyn.
I've always had trouble relating to other people.
CORBEAU PREPARATORY HIGH SCHOOL
It always felt like I was speaking a language that no one else completely understood.
PIGEONS
--heard the new Dazzler single?
Close enough to get by, but never to really be seen.
It's on my phone on loop. I can't believe she got Lizzo to feature!
Did you get the tickets for next weekend?
Yeah, my cousin works the door at the spot, so he hooked me up with his discount!
How much do I owe you?
Oh, uh, nothin'. Don't worry about it.
No, absolutely not. You're not just giving them to me.
You were just saying you were doing donation streams for extra cash...
Even discounted, Dazzler's expensive.
It wasn't until I met Carmen, Benny and Gabe that I understood why I couldn't connect with other people.
Dazzler? Seriously?
Is there a problem?
Maybe you should actually pay attention to things happening in the world.
Yeah. Dazzler's a mutant. Mutants are building an army to come invade us.
They're flooding the world with "medicine" that's really killing us. Their companies are forcing human companies to collapse. And you're funding their agenda.

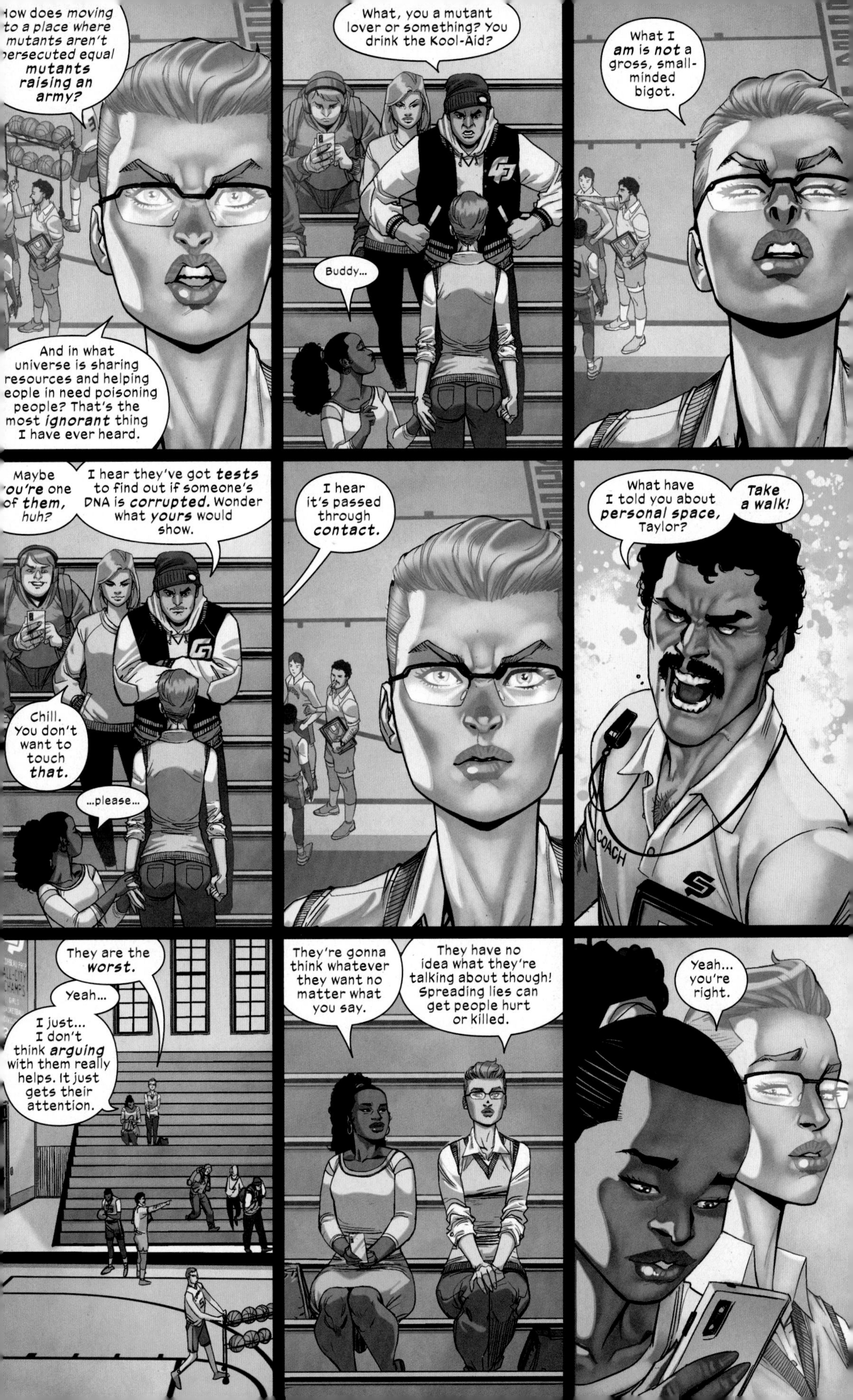
How does moving to a place where mutants aren't persecuted equal mutants raising an army?
And in what universe is sharing resources and helping people in need poisoning people? That's the most ignorant thing I have ever heard.
What, you a mutant lover or something? You drink the Kool-Aid?
Buddy...
What I am is not a gross, small-minded bigot.
Maybe you're one of them, huh?
I hear they've got tests to find out if someone's DNA is corrupted. Wonder what yours would show.
Chill. You don't want to touch that.
...please...
I hear it's passed through contact.
What have I told you about personal space, Taylor?
Take a walk!
COACH
They are the worst.
Yeah...
I just... I don't think arguing with them really helps. It just gets their attention.
They're gonna think whatever they want no matter what you say.
They have no idea what they're talking about though! Spreading lies can get people hurt or killed.
Yeah... you're right.

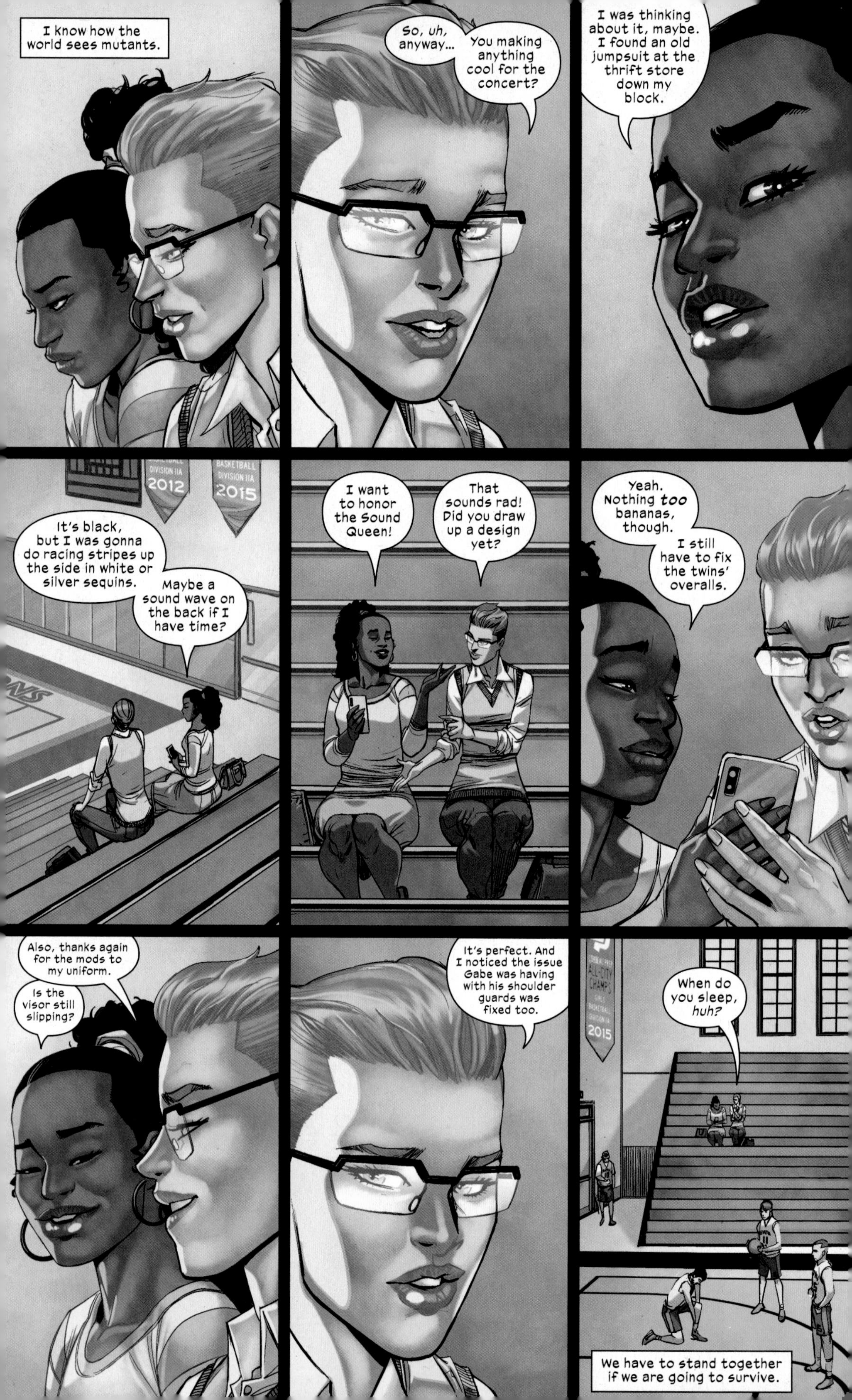
I know how the world sees mutants.
So, uh, anyway...
You making anything cool for the concert?
I was thinking about it, maybe. I found an old jumpsuit at the thrift store down my block.
DIVISION IIA 2012
BASKETBALL DIVISION IIA 2015
It's black, but I was gonna do racing stripes up the side in white or silver sequins.
Maybe a sound wave on the back if I have time?
I want to honor the Sound Queen!
That sounds rad! Did you draw up a design yet?
Yeah. Nothing *too* bananas, though.
I still have to fix the twins' overalls.
Also, thanks again for the mods to my uniform.
Is the visor still slipping?
It's perfect. And I noticed the issue Gabe was having with his shoulder guards was fixed too.
ALL-CITY CHAMPS
2015
When do you sleep, *huh?*
We have to stand together if we are going to survive.

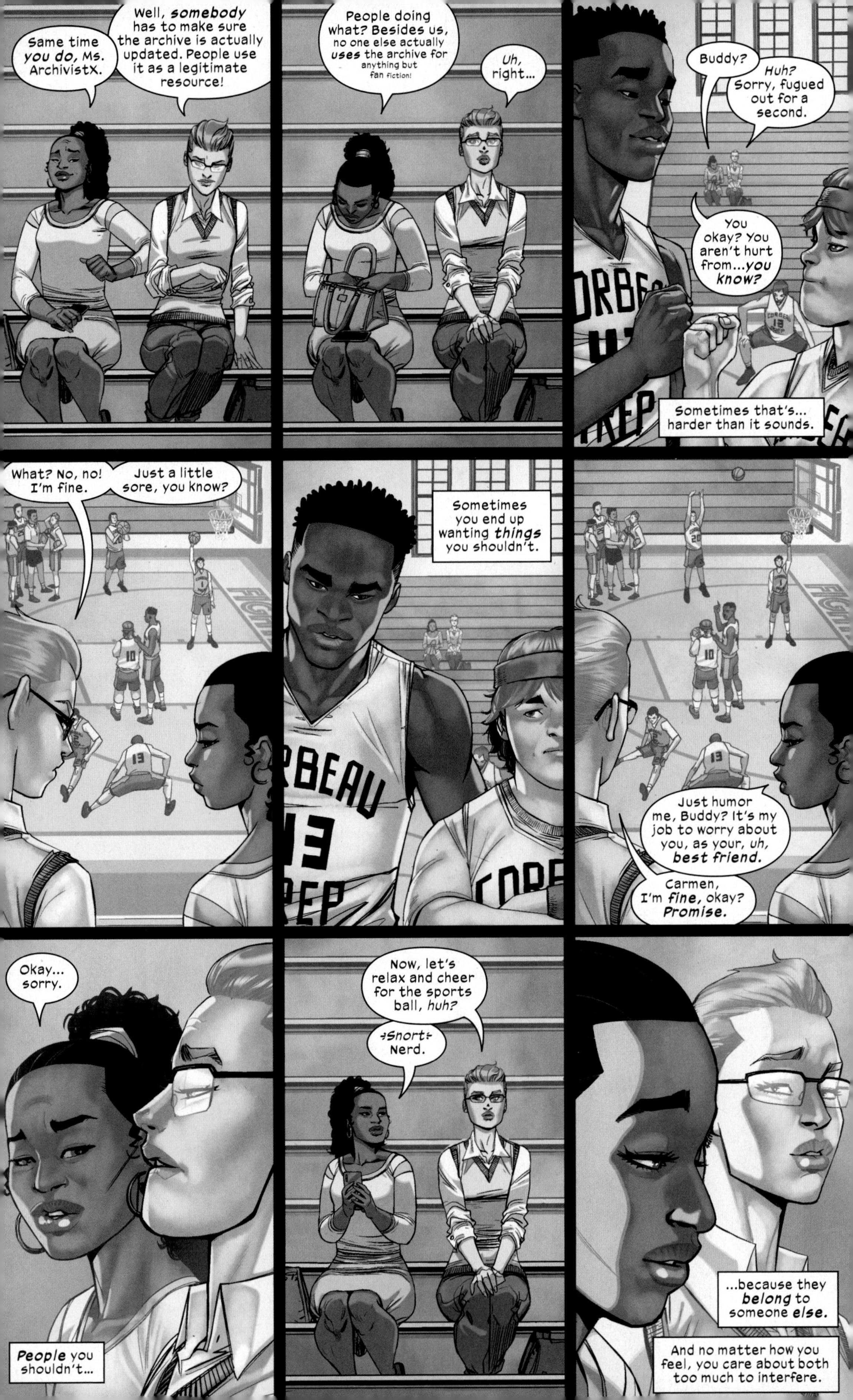
Same time you do, Ms. ArchivistX.
Well, somebody has to make sure the archive is actually updated. People use it as a legitimate resource!
People doing what? Besides us, no one else actually uses the archive for anything but fan fiction!
Uh, right...
Buddy?
Huh? Sorry, fugued out for a second.
You okay? You aren't hurt from...you know?
Sometimes that's... harder than it sounds.
What? No, no! I'm fine.
Just a little sore, you know?
Sometimes you end up wanting things you shouldn't.
Just humor me, Buddy? It's my job to worry about you, as your, uh, best friend.
Carmen, I'm fine, okay? Promise.
Okay... sorry.
People you shouldn't...
Now, let's relax and cheer for the sports ball, huh?
Snort Nerd.
...because they belong to someone else.
And no matter how you feel, you care about both too much to interfere.

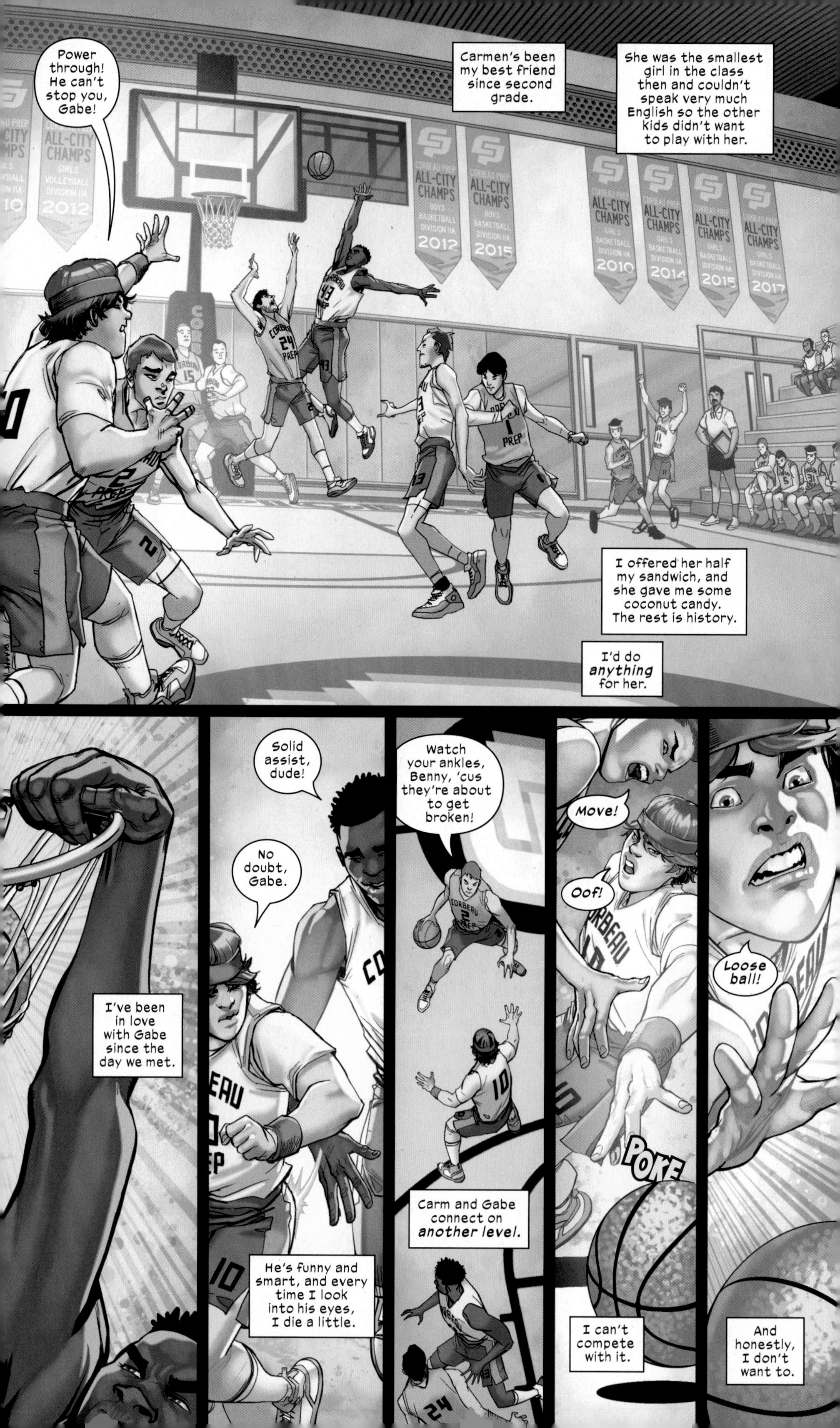
Power through! He can't stop you, Gabe!
Carmen's been my best friend since second grade.
She was the smallest girl in the class then and couldn't speak very much English so the other kids didn't want to play with her.
ALL-CITY CHAMPS GIRLS VOLLEYBALL DIVISION IIA 2012
ALL-CITY CHAMPS BOYS BASKETBALL DIVISION IIA 2012
ALL-CITY CHAMPS BOYS BASKETBALL DIVISION IIA 2015
ALL-CITY CHAMPS GIRLS BASKETBALL DIVISION IIA 2010
ALL-CITY CHAMPS GIRLS BASKETBALL DIVISION IIA 2014
ALL-CITY CHAMPS GIRLS BASKETBALL DIVISION IIA 2015
ALL-CITY CHAMPS GIRLS BASKETBALL DIVISION IIA 2017
I offered her half my sandwich, and she gave me some coconut candy. The rest is history.
I'd do *anything* for her.
I've been in love with Gabe since the day we met.
Solid assist, dude!
No doubt, Gabe.
He's funny and smart, and every time I look into his eyes, I die a little.
Watch your ankles, Benny, 'cus they're about to get broken!
Carm and Gabe connect on ***another level.***
Move!
Oof!
POKE
I can't compete with it.
Loose ball!
And honestly, I don't want to.

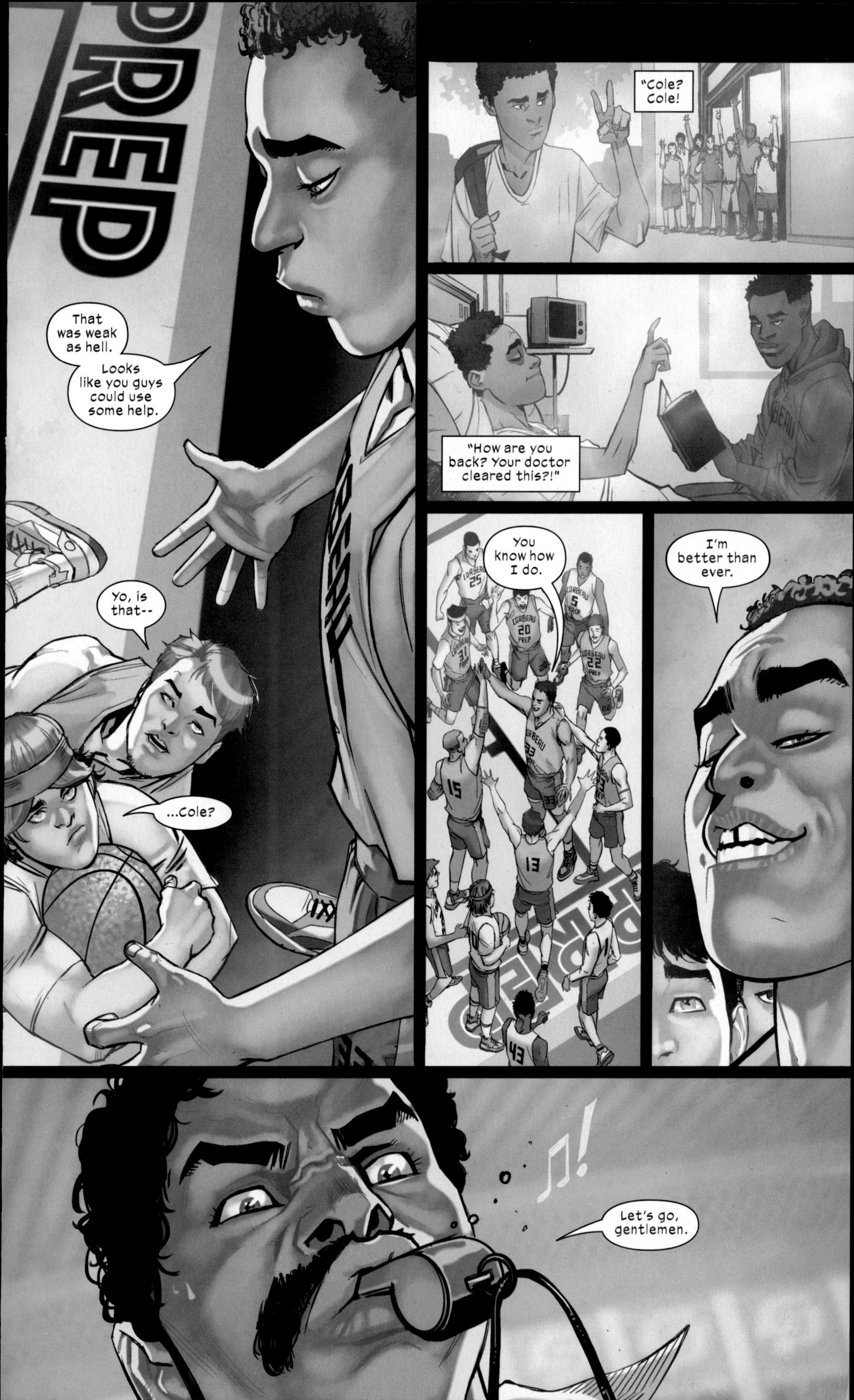
That was weak as hell.
Looks like you guys could use some help.
Yo, is that--
...Cole?
"Cole? Cole!
"How are you back? Your doctor cleared this?!"
You know how I do.
I'm better than ever.
Let's go, gentlemen.

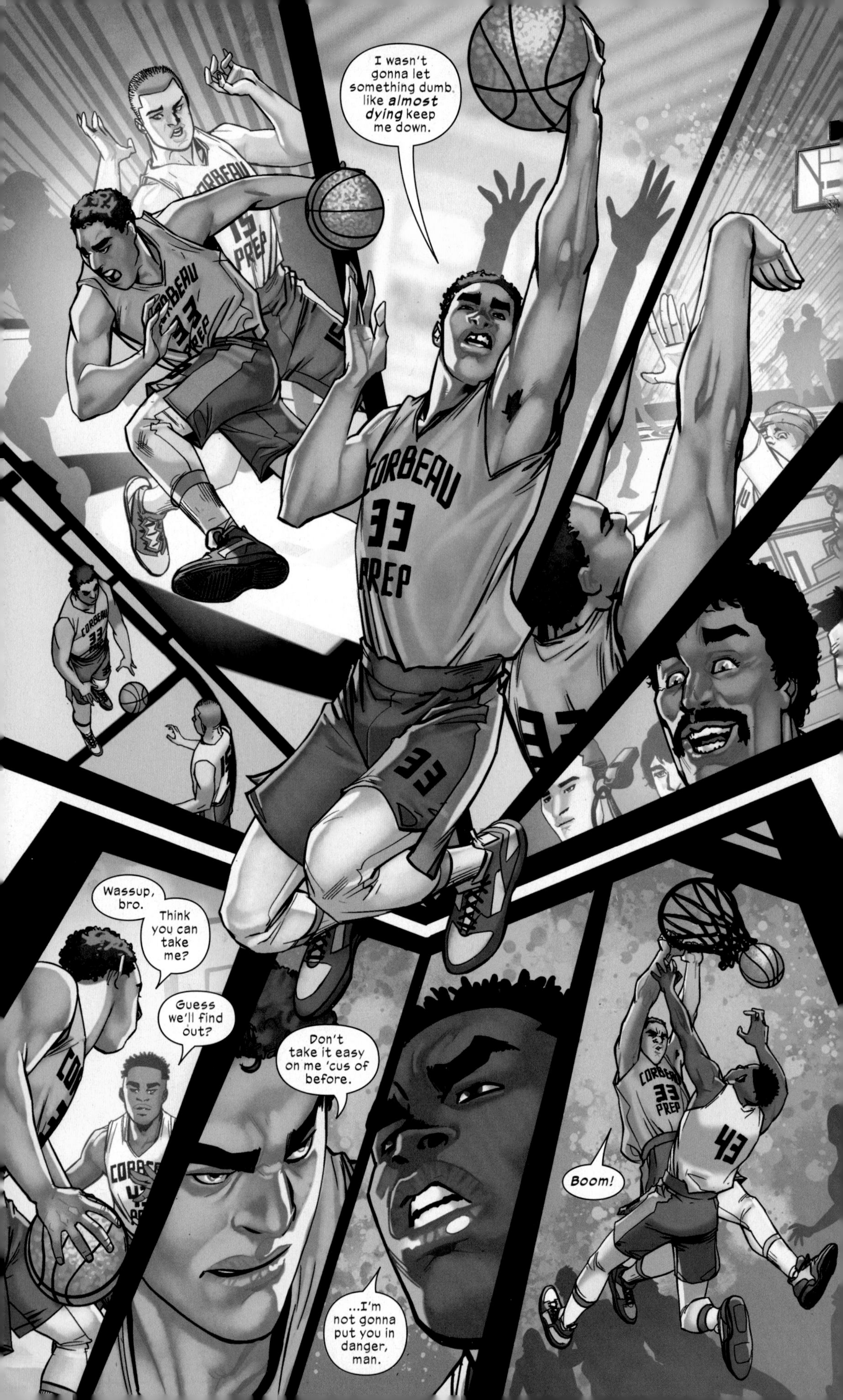

I wasn't gonna let something dumb like *almost dying* keep me down.
CORBEAU 15 PREP
CORBEAU 33 PREP
CORBEAU 33 PREP
Wassup, bro.
Think you can take me?
Guess we'll find out?
Don't take it easy on me 'cus of before.
...I'm not gonna put you in danger, man.
CORBEAU 33 PREP
43
Boom!

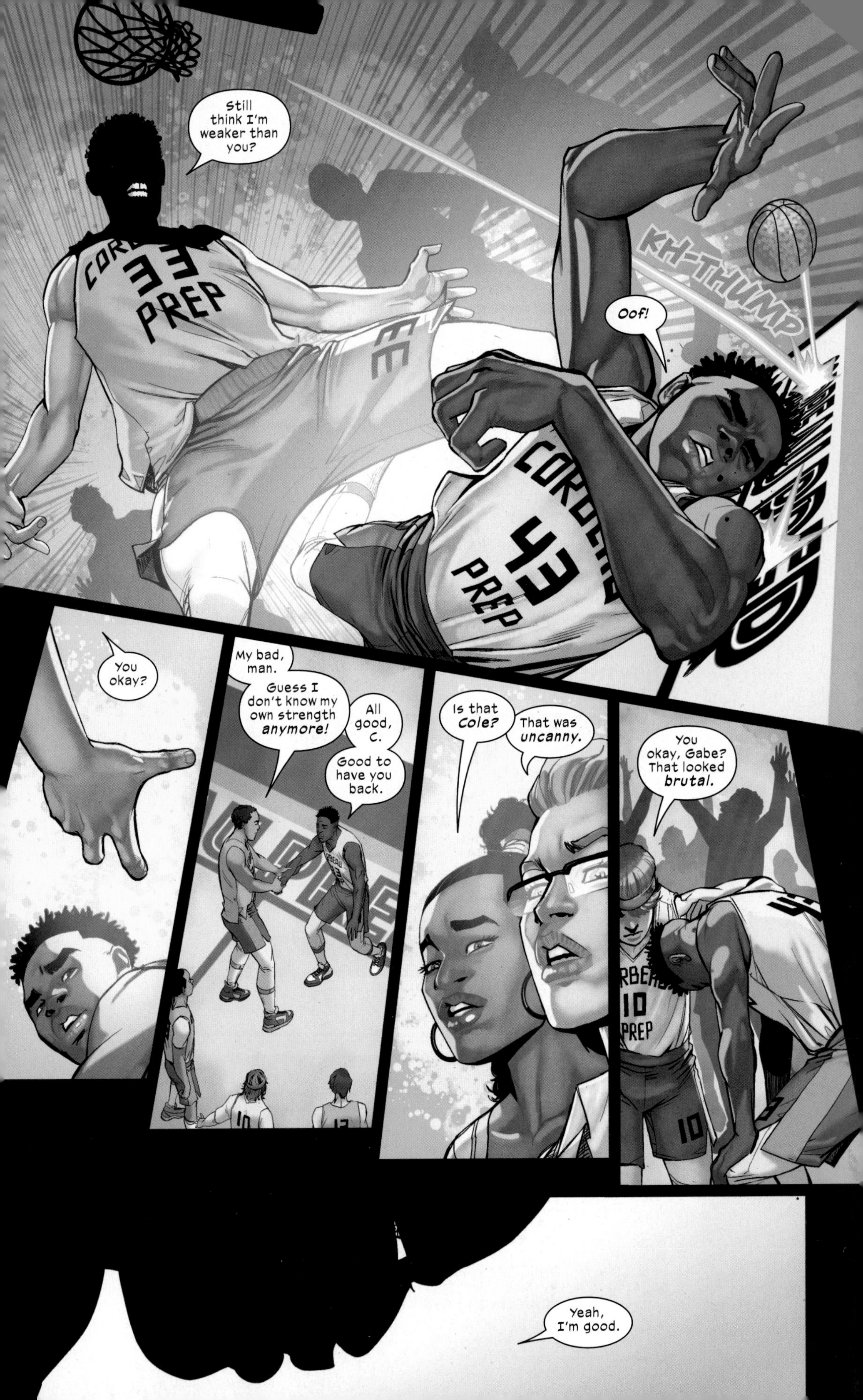

Still think I'm weaker than you?
KH-THUMP
Oof!
You okay?
My bad, man.
Guess I don't know my own strength anymore!
All good, C.
Good to have you back.
Is that Cole?
That was uncanny.
You okay, Gabe? That looked brutal.
Yeah, I'm good.

mutantsunmuted.com/

A site dedicated to archiving all footage involving mutants!

NEWEST VIDEO

 Wolverine Spotted Fighting Ghost Rider Wearing a Cape?

FEATURED VIDEO

 Jumbo Carnation & Dazzler Spotted in Tribeca – New Collab?

IN THE NEWS

Footage from the media.

MUTANT FIGHTS

Your faves wrecking the government, battling each other, and causing general carnage!

SIGHTINGS

Mutant sightings all over the world, uploaded by members!

FAN ENCOUNTERS

Mutants walk among us and apparently love to sign autographs!

FORUM

> But how do the gates work???

> I tried the one in Washington Square Park and nothing happened! I was still in Manhattan.

> They only work for muties. My neighbor walked through one and disappeared.

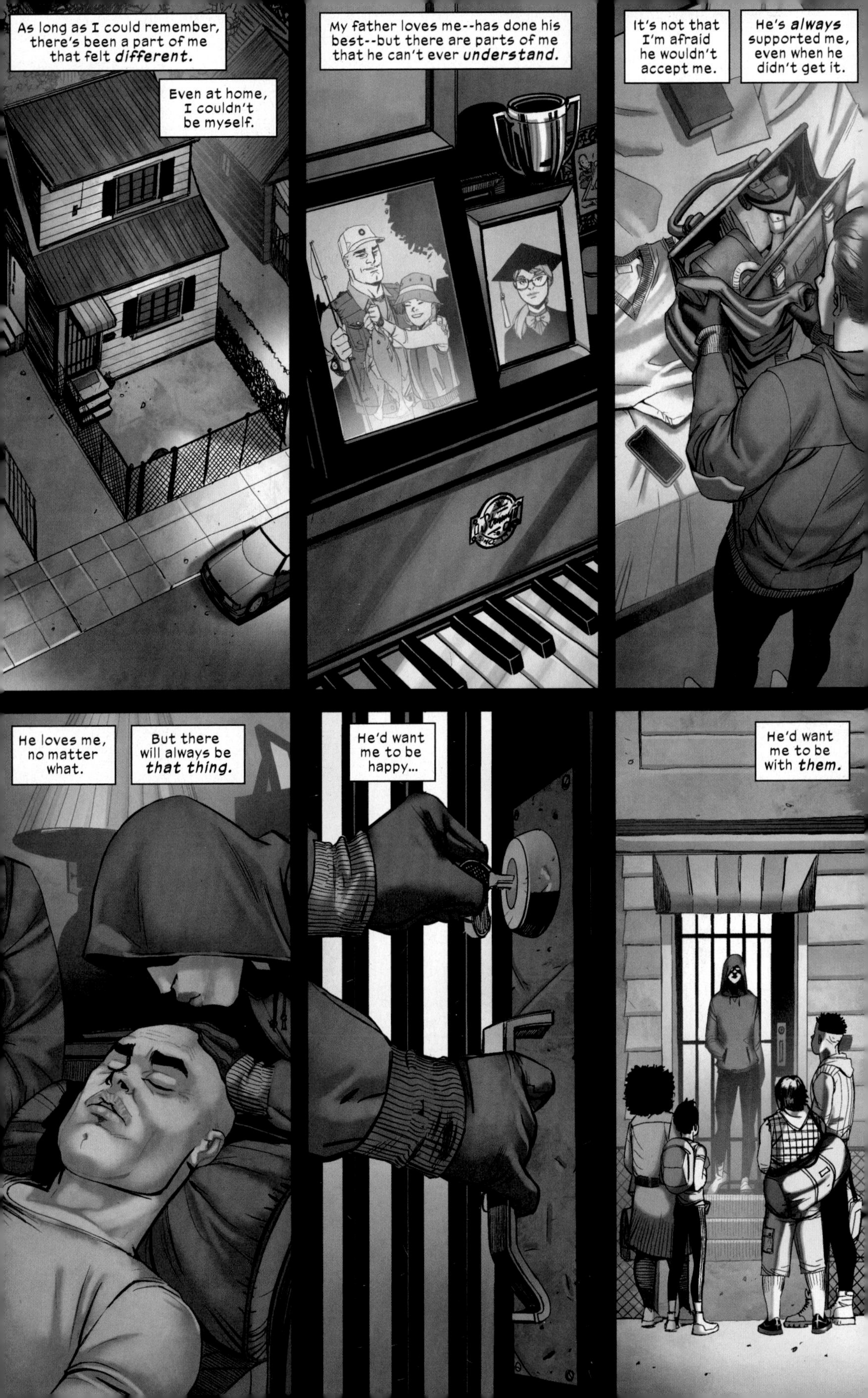
As long as I could remember, there's been a part of me that felt *different.*
Even at home, I couldn't be myself.
My father loves me--has done his best--but there are parts of me that he can't ever *understand.*
It's not that I'm afraid he wouldn't accept me.
He's *always* supported me, even when he didn't get it.
He loves me, no matter what.
But there will always be *that thing.*
He'd want me to be happy...
He'd want me to be with *them.*

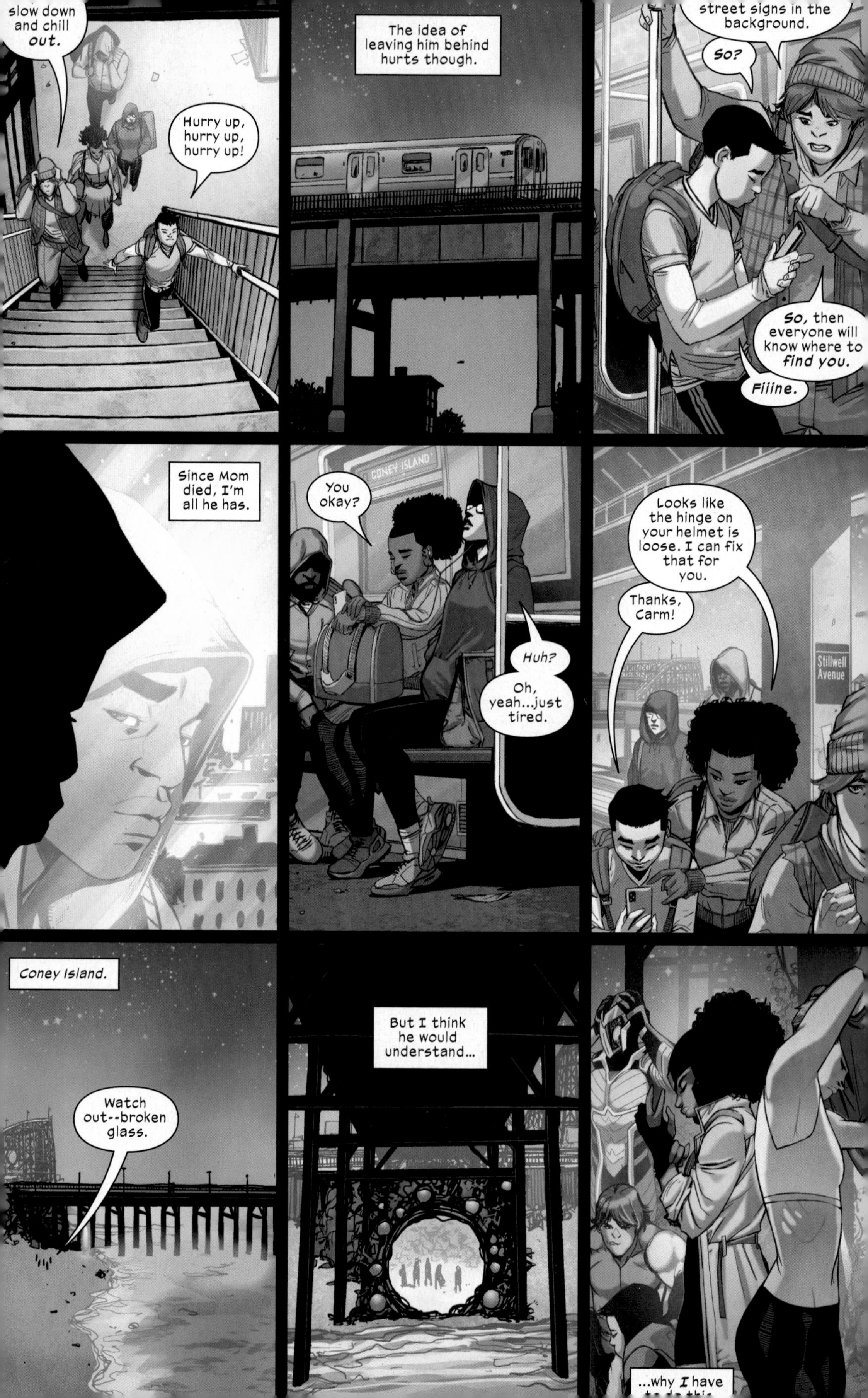
slow down and chill out.
Hurry up, hurry up, hurry up!
The idea of leaving him behind hurts though.
street signs in the background.
So?
So, then everyone will know where to find you.
Fiiine.
Since Mom died, I'm all he has.
CONEY ISLAND
You okay?
Huh?
Oh, yeah...just tired.
Looks like the hinge on your helmet is loose. I can fix that for you.
Thanks, Carm!
Stillwell Avenue
Coney Island.
Watch out--broken glass.
But I think he would understand...
...why I have

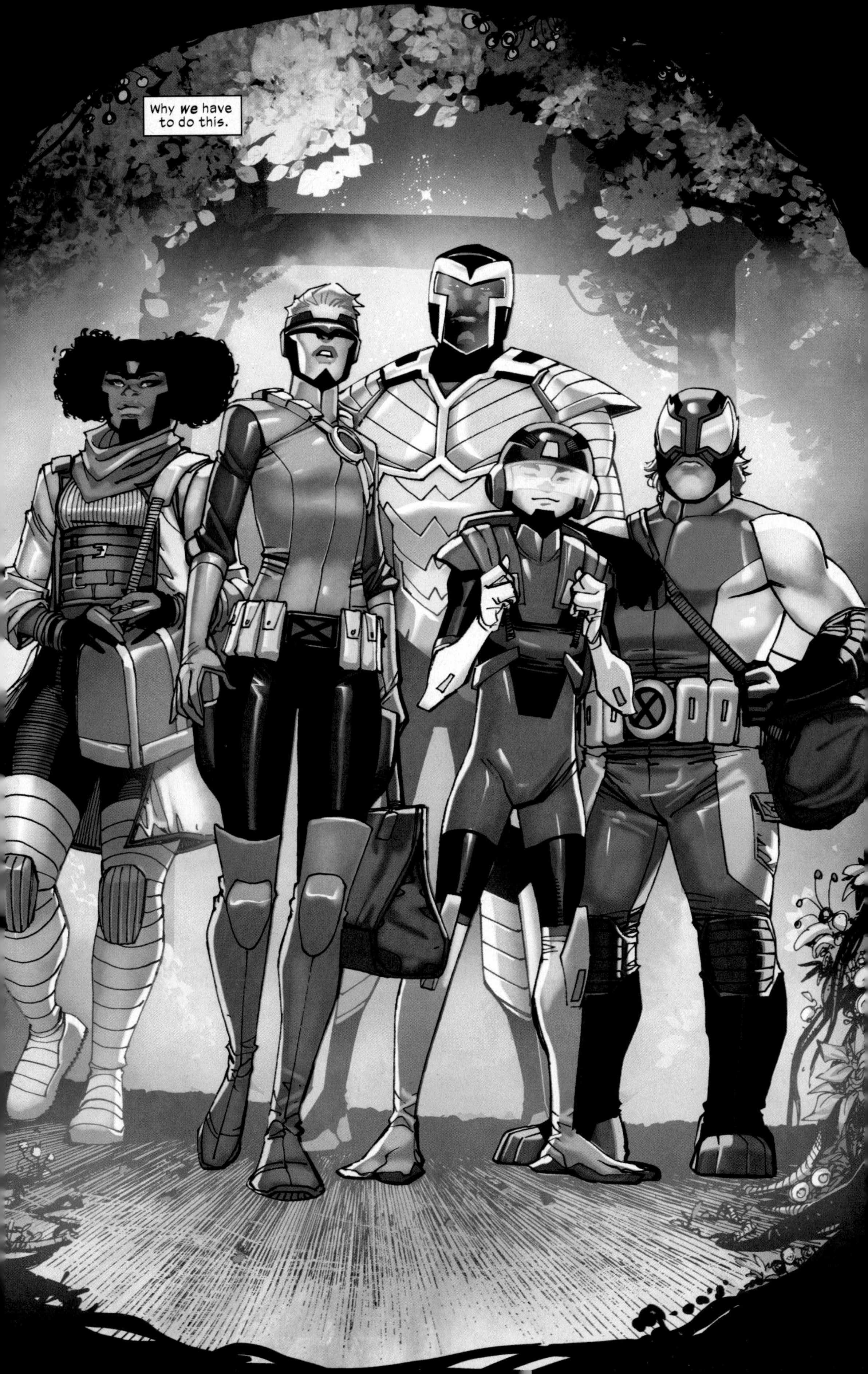
Why we have to do this.

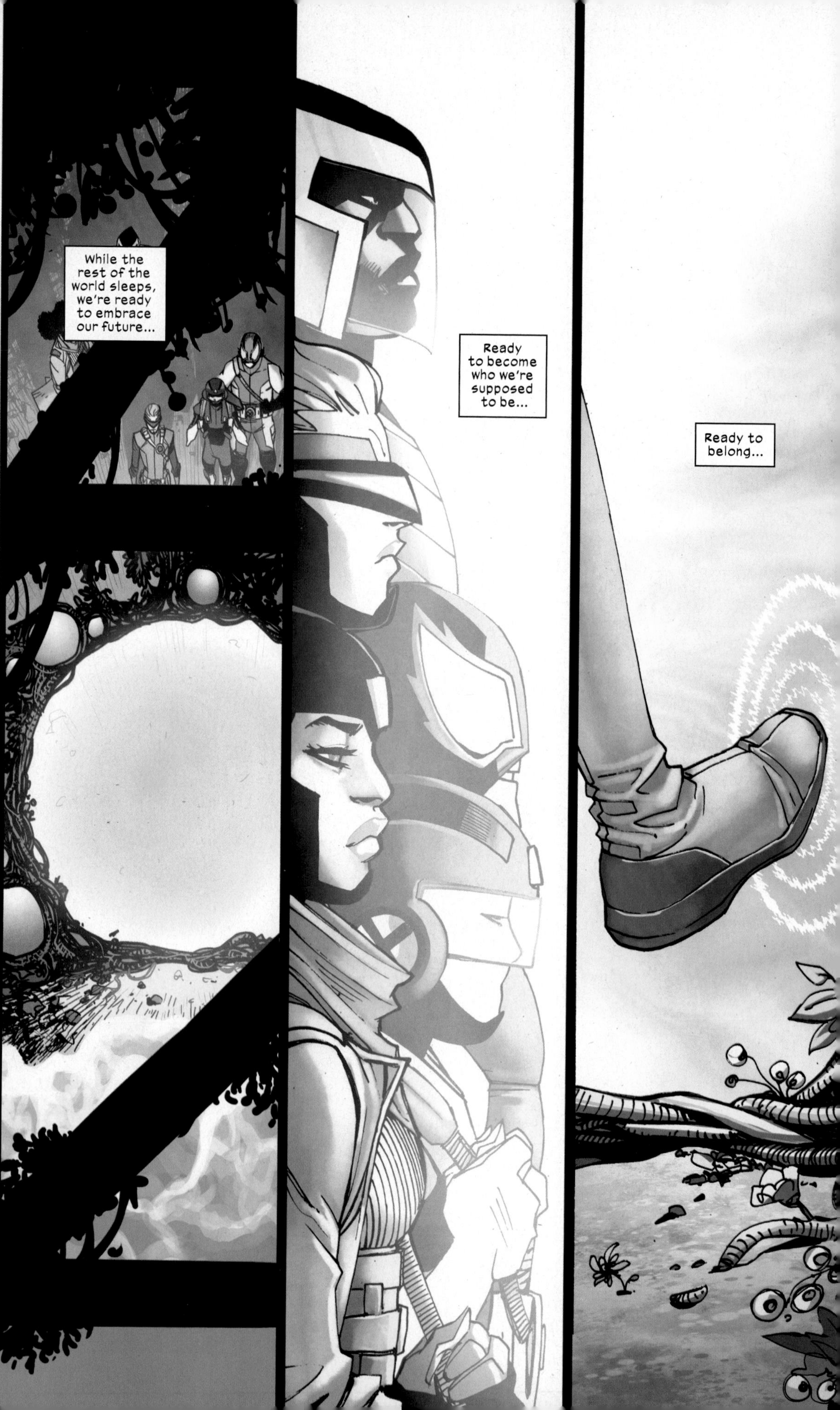
While the rest of the world sleeps, we're ready to embrace our future...
Ready to become who we're supposed to be...
Ready to belong...

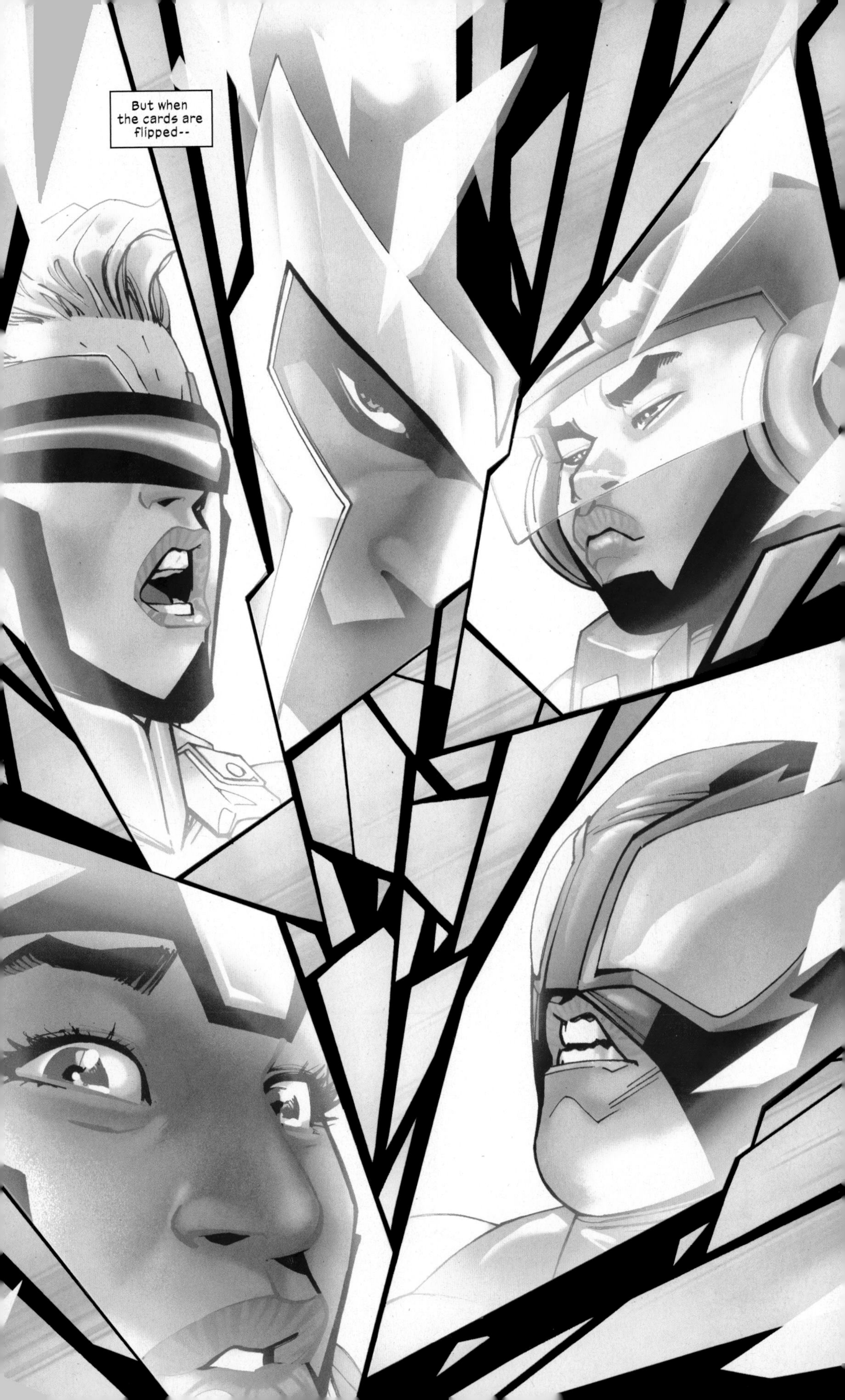
But when the cards are flipped--

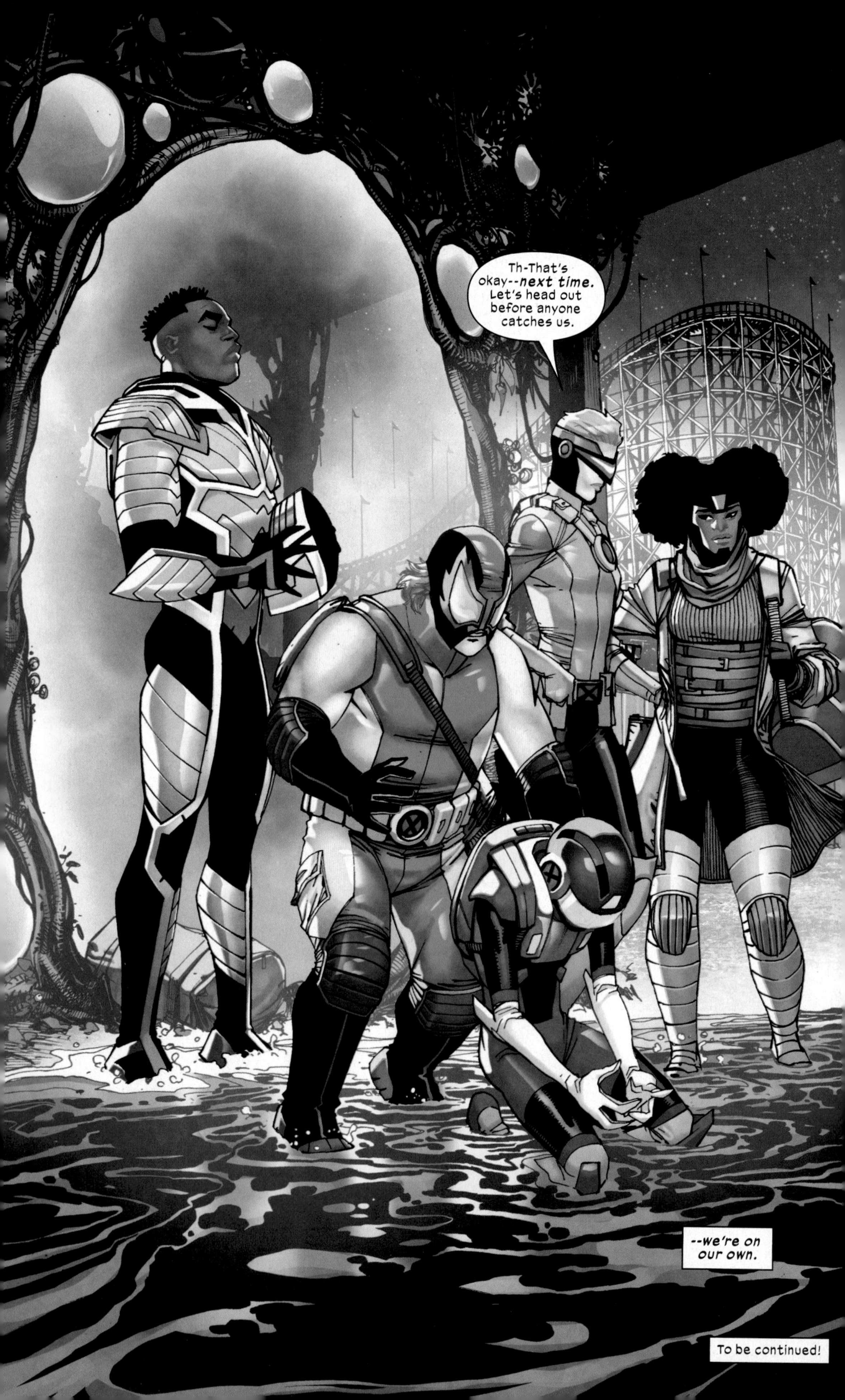
Th-That's okay--*next time.* Let's head out before anyone catches us.
--we're on our own.
To be continued!

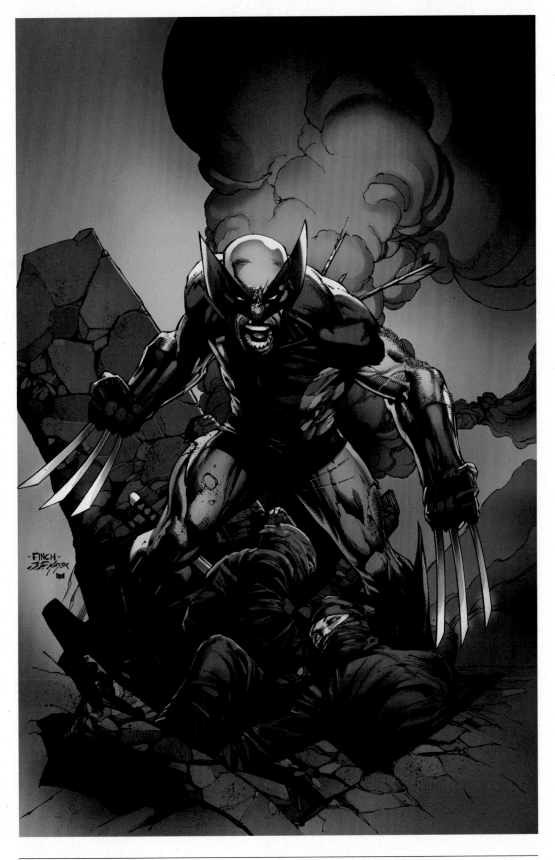

Wolverine #10 Variant

by David Finch, JP Mayer
& Frank D'Armata

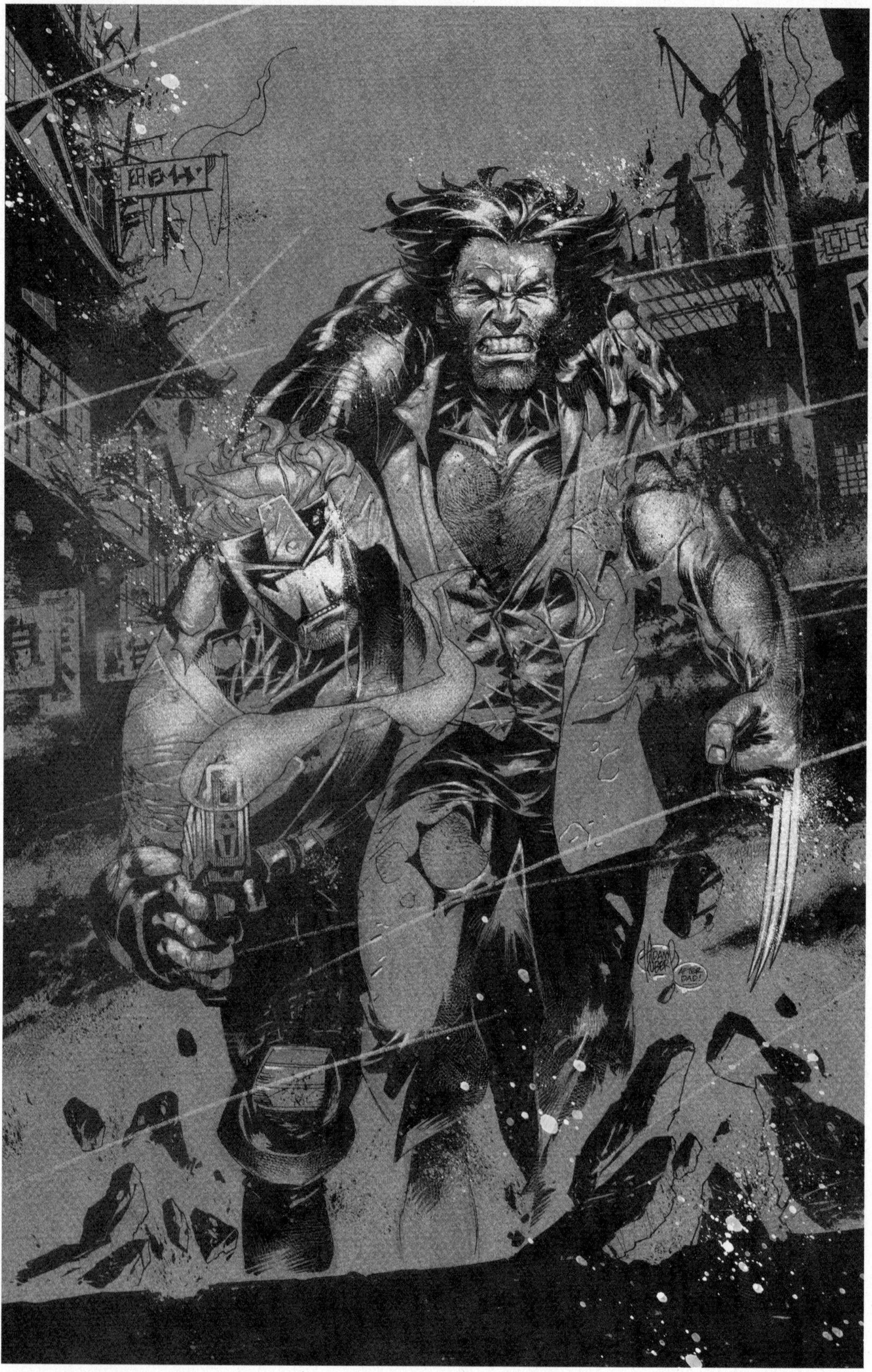

Wolverine #10 Variant by Adam Kubert

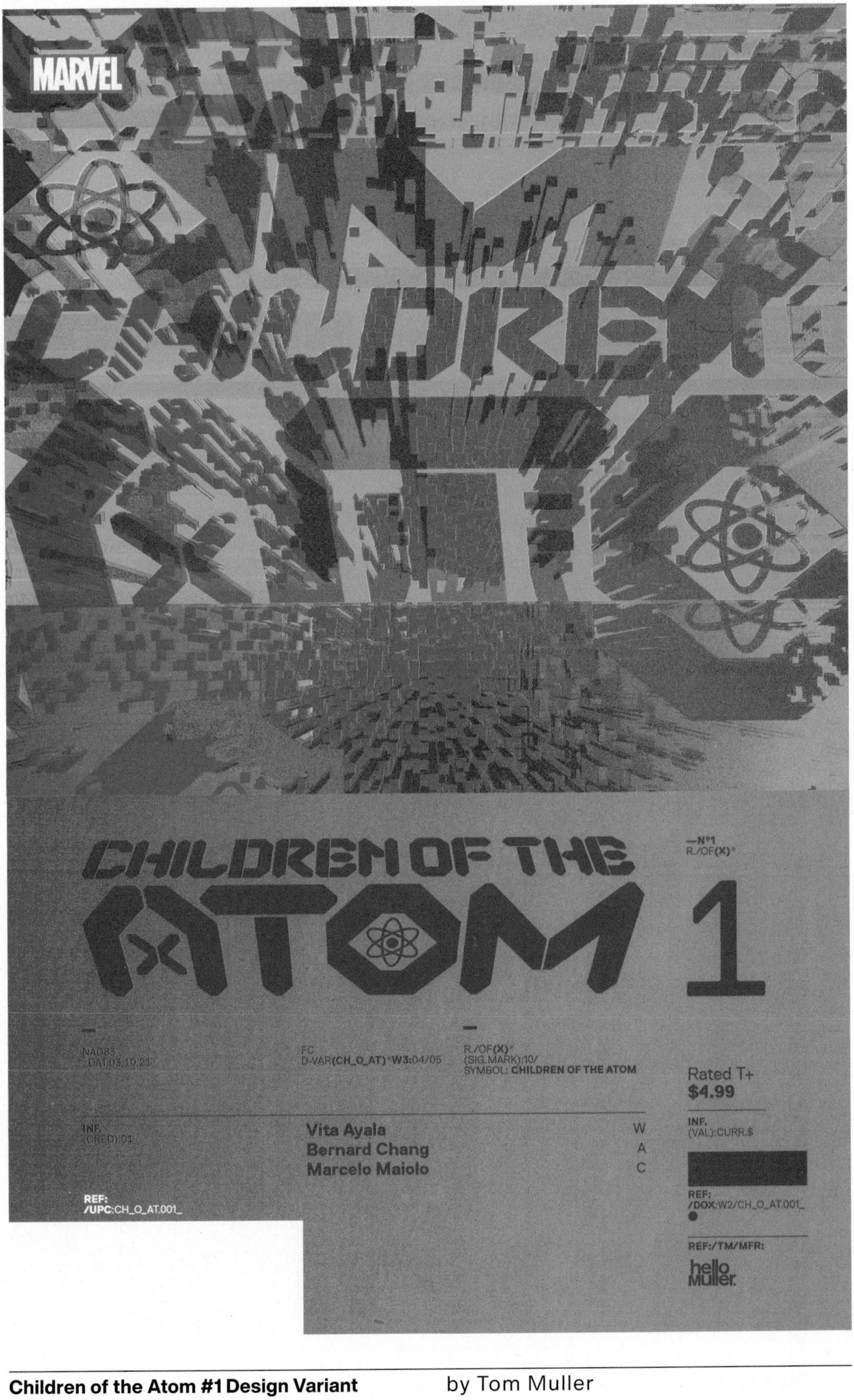
MARVEL
CHILDREN OF THE ATOM
1
—Nº1
R./OF(X)*
NAD83
DAT.03.10.21
FC
D-VAR(CH_O_AT)*W3:04/05
R./OF(X)*
(SIG.MARK):10/
SYMBOL: CHILDREN OF THE ATOM
Rated T+
$4.99
INF.
(CRED):01
Vita Ayala W
Bernard Chang A
Marcelo Maiolo C
INF.
(VAL):CURR.$
REF:
/UPC:CH_O_AT.001_
REF:
/DOX:W2/CH_O_AT.001_
REF:/TM/MFR:
hello Muller.

Children of the Atom #1 Design Variant by Tom Muller

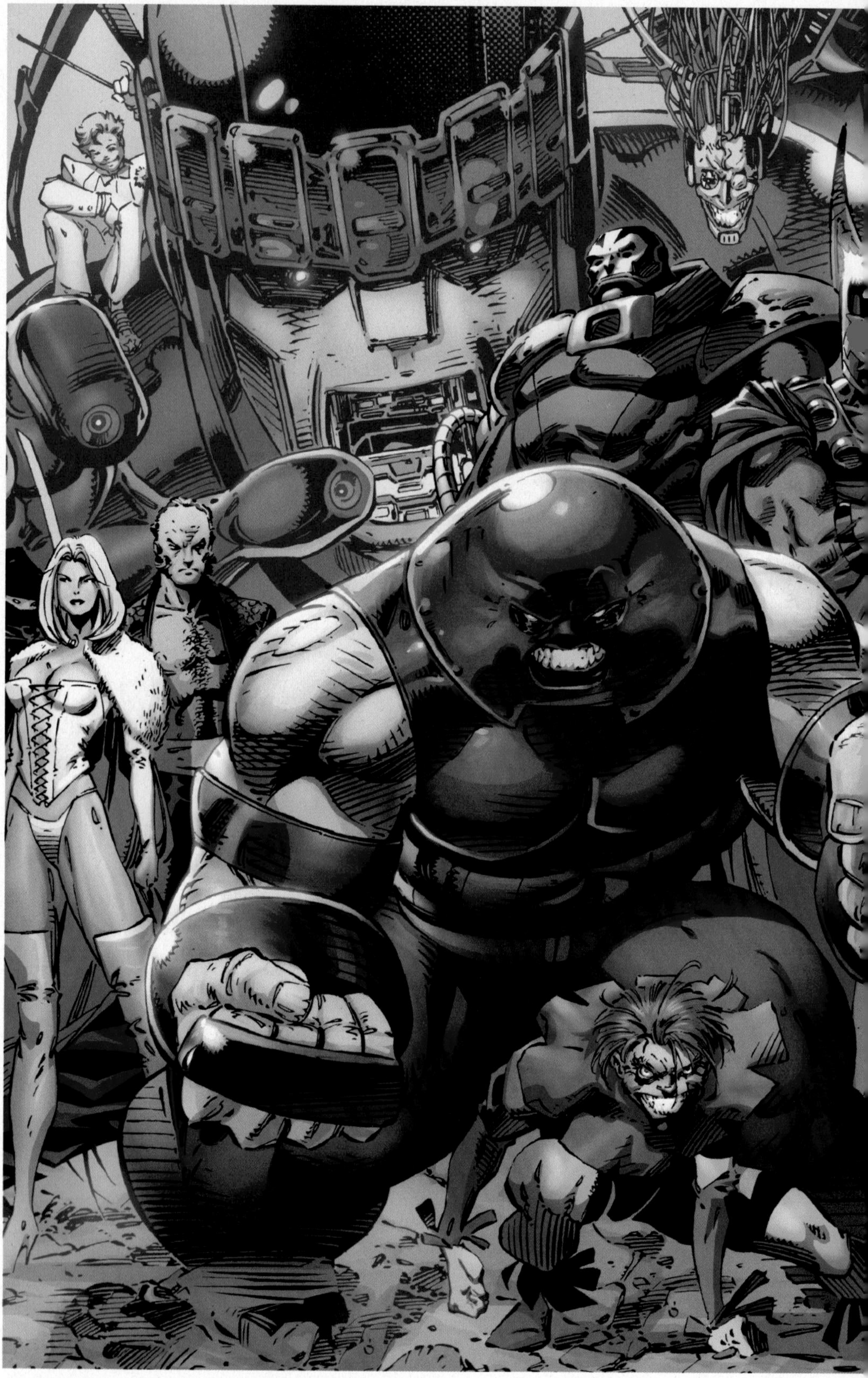

Children of the Atom #1 Hidden Gem Variant

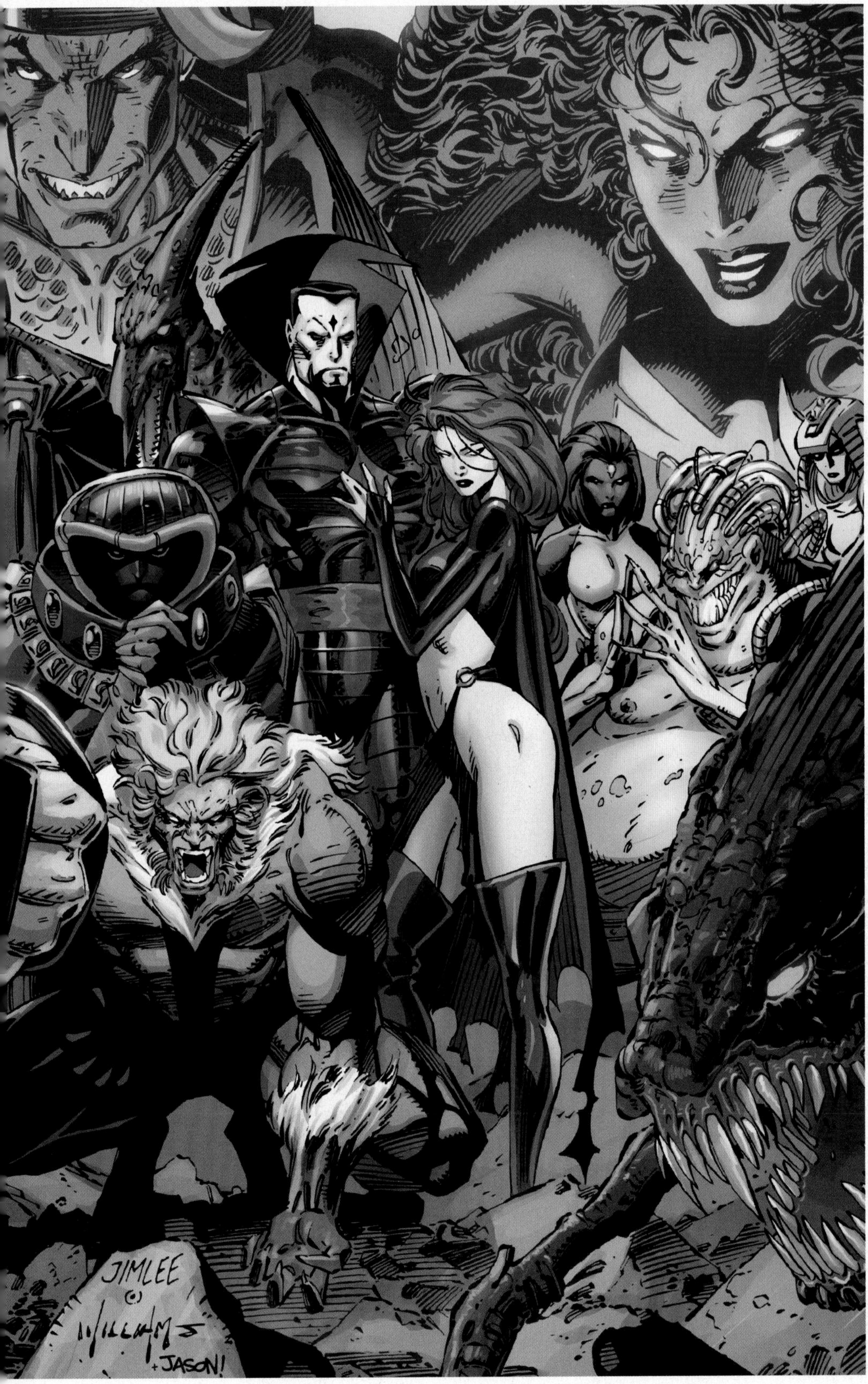
JIMLEE
WILLIAMS
+JASON!

by Jim Lee, Scott Williams
& Jason Keith

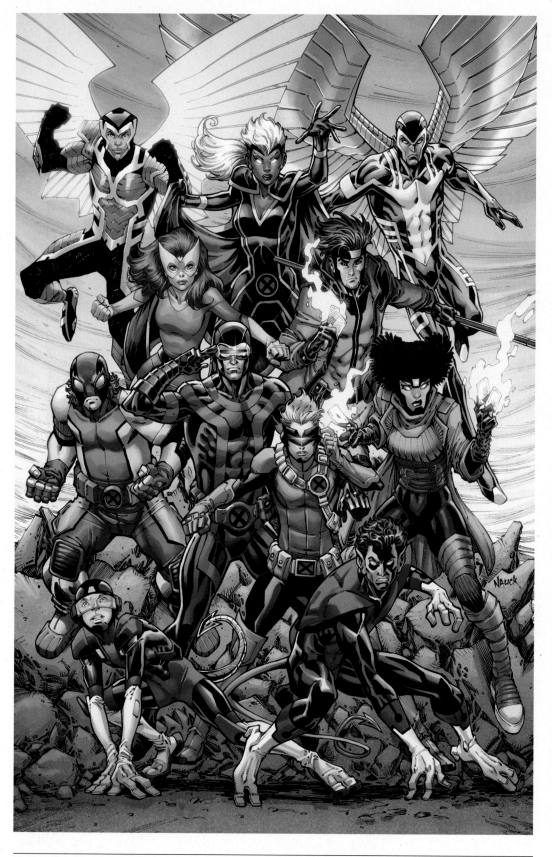

Children of the Atom #1 Variant

by Todd Nauck
& Rachelle Rosenberg

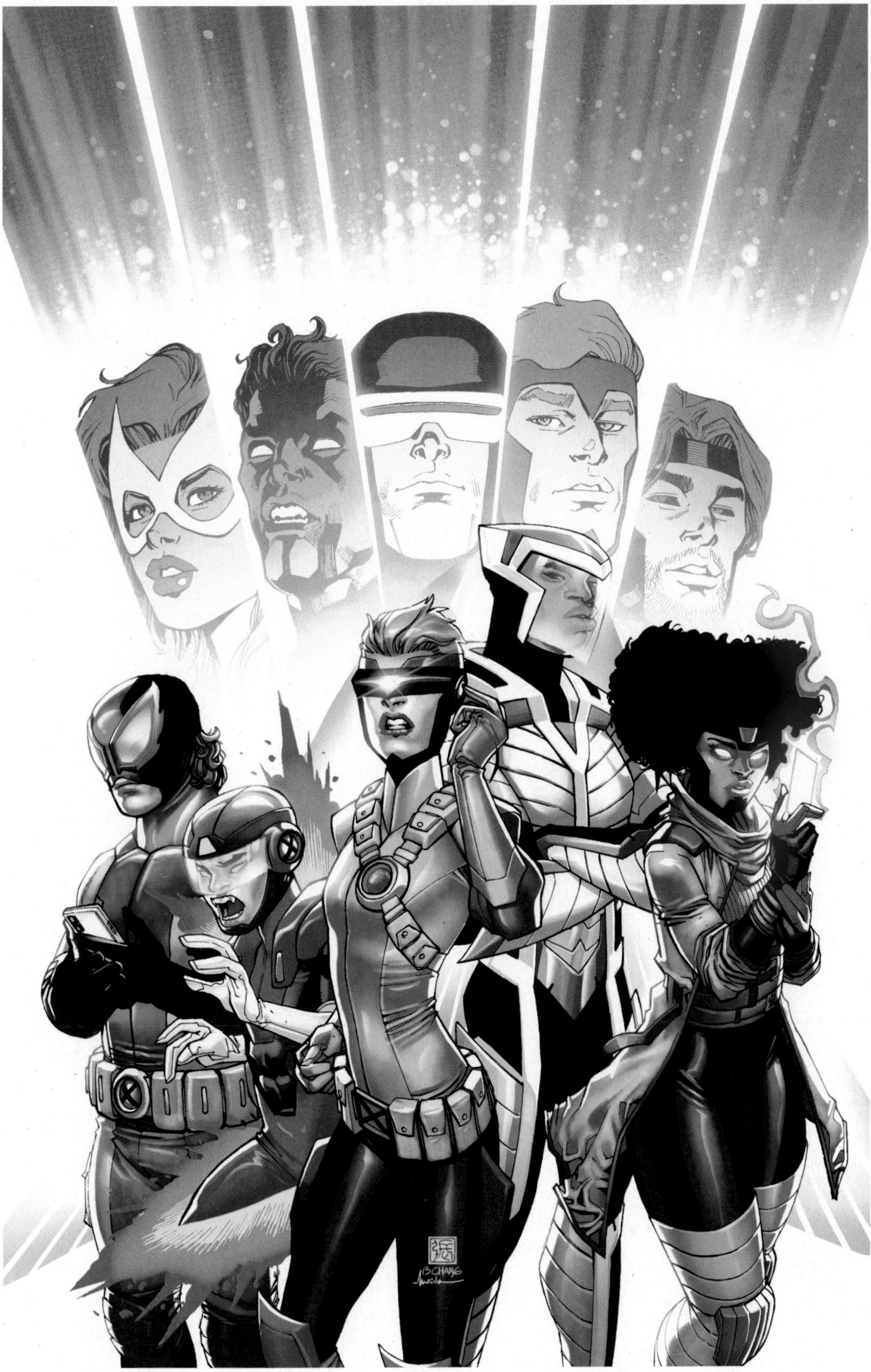

Children of the Atom #1 Variant

by Bernard Chang
& Marcelo Maiolo